New Security Challenges

Series Editor
George Christou
University of Warwick
Coventry, UK

The last decade has demonstrated that threats to security vary greatly in their causes and manifestations and that they invite interest and demand responses from the social sciences, civil society, and a very broad policy community. In the past, the avoidance of war was the primary objective, but with the end of the Cold War the retention of military defence as the centrepiece of international security agenda became untenable. There has been, therefore, a significant shift in emphasis away from traditional approaches to security to a new agenda that talks of the softer side of security, in terms of human security, economic security, and environmental security. The topical New Security Challenges series reflects this pressing political and research agenda.

More information about this series at
http://www.palgrave.com/gp/series/14732

Malte Brosig

The Role of BRICS in Large-Scale Armed Conflict

Building a Multi-Polar World Order

Malte Brosig
Department of International Relations
University of the Witwatersrand
Johannesburg, South Africa

New Security Challenges
ISBN 978-3-030-18536-7   ISBN 978-3-030-18537-4 (eBook)
https://doi.org/10.1007/978-3-030-18537-4

© The Editor(s) (if applicable) and The Author(s), under exclusive licence to Springer Nature Switzerland AG 2019
This work is subject to copyright. All rights are solely and exclusively licensed by the Publisher, whether the whole or part of the material is concerned, specifically the rights of translation, reprinting, reuse of illustrations, recitation, broadcasting, reproduction on microfilms or in any other physical way, and transmission or information storage and retrieval, electronic adaptation, computer software, or by similar or dissimilar methodology now known or hereafter developed.
The use of general descriptive names, registered names, trademarks, service marks, etc. in this publication does not imply, even in the absence of a specific statement, that such names are exempt from the relevant protective laws and regulations and therefore free for general use.
The publisher, the authors and the editors are safe to assume that the advice and information in this book are believed to be true and accurate at the date of publication. Neither the publisher nor the authors or the editors give a warranty, express or implied, with respect to the material contained herein or for any errors or omissions that may have been made. The publisher remains neutral with regard to jurisdictional claims in published maps and institutional affiliations.

Cover illustration: © metamorworks/Shutterstock

This Palgrave Macmillan imprint is published by the registered company Springer Nature Switzerland AG
The registered company address is: Gewerbestrasse 11, 6330 Cham, Switzerland

Preface

Writing about BRICS in large-scale armed conflicts has been a truly exciting and demanding exercise for me and is likely to be for everyone else working on similar issues. Analyzing four conflict case studies (Libya, Syria, Ukraine and South Sudan) and relating them to the group of the five aspiring BRICS countries requires a constant change of perspective and awareness of conflict dynamics as well as global politics. One is easily overwhelmed by details and opinions. It is exciting and relevant to write about this particular topic because the last decade was shaped by both a resurgence of violent conflict and the rise of regional powers such as the BRICS grouping (there is possibly no causal link between these two events). Questions of global order and multi-polarity are passionately debated themes in the discipline of IR as well as geostrategic interests of larger emerging powers. The current debate of multilateralism under strain also fits into this picture.

The rise of BRICS countries by now is no new topic. BRICS can already look back at ten years of history and it continues to evolve and develop. While the topic is not new anymore the debate around this grouping sometimes appears as cumbersome or little mature. This might indeed point to the fact that not only is the inter-state world undergoing a fundamental transition finally leaving the post-Cold War era and entering an era which certainly starts with multi and ends with an ism. But equally academia is involved in globalizing, decentering and redefining its core mission and expanding its research objects. However, both processes have only recently begun and the decentralization in global politics seems to be more advanced than in academia, for now at least.

A prosperous and peaceful world, it is my belief, depends increasingly on our ability to span (transcend) common (limiting) boundaries in minds and borders in real life. Writing this book set me up on a journey around the globe visiting all BRICS countries between 2012 and 2019. My own perspective is very much influenced by my own experience which is the experience of a Westerner educated in Germany, Finland and the UK who has now spent the majority of his academic career in the non-Western world, in South Africa.

The book in the end was written with great sympathy for the pledge of emerging countries calling for a reform of existing global governance structures and curiosity about how these countries would engage the many challenges on their way up the global pecking order. While sympathy with the global South refers more to the author's emotional status, the book is structured following a rather formalistic understanding of research which aims at categorizing and explaining the observed phenomenon from a more neutral perspective. While writing this book I have tried to come as close to the objective of my interest as possible in order to not only better understand BRICS as an external observer but also get insider knowledge. In this regard I thank the National Institute for Humanities and Social Science (NIHSS) in Johannesburg for inviting me to a number of preparatory meetings of the South African delegation to the BRICS Academic Forum and participating in the Forum during the South African Chairship in May 2018. Attending these meetings did a lot in helping me to understand how the grouping works and what the positions, concerns and preferences of individual BRICS countries are.

At the center of the book is the emphasis on knowledge gain in addition to the description of how BRICS respond to large-scale conflicts. Two research questions are guiding the book. How do BRICS countries respond to conflict and how can we explain a particular choice for a certain response type? Both questions are linking up the existing literature on rising and regional powers as well as the literature on BRICS. The chosen timeframe is the last ten years since BRICS came into existence (2009–2018). The empirical chapters start with the outbreak of the Arab Spring (2011) and reach until the end of 2018.

While finishing the manuscript in February 2019 it becomes increasingly apparent that the BRICS grouping is entering not only a numerical second decade of its existence but that this second decade is likely to be significantly different from the first. The book covers mostly the foundational time of BRICS as well as its current phase of consolidation. Initially the visible manifestation of BRICS as reformist forces of meaningful countries was dominating the debate and BRICS became the trademark for multi-polarity, contributing to the debate of relative Western power decline and a changing world order. Research was predominantly interested if BRICS will rise peacefully within given structures of global governance or if they turn out to be revisionist forces abandoning Western-built and still dominated institutions?

With the beginning of the second BRICS decade this question is of lesser interest. The dismantling of multilateral organizations is spearheaded not by rising powers but by established ones. The retreat to national sovereignty as the ultimate yardstick against which successful politics is measured and the quasi-mercantilist economics that underpin the Trump administration turn out to be a much more of a serious challenge than the challenge by the BRICS group. In consequence multi-polarity is not the exclusive trademark of BRICS but seems to be an increasingly attractive objective for others too. This in recent times is going along with increased tensions between larger powers. It is not without irony that the second BRICS decade is likely to be shaped by the group's most sought after concept, multi-polarity, but with unclear prospects for the group's potential to steer a multi-polar world to their advantage. At the moment more polarization is on the horizon with the US being in confrontation with two BRICS members: China and Russia.

However, before speculating about the future pathway of the group it is worth analyzing the traces BRICS has left so far which this book is doing. Beyond formal reform of global governance institutions which BRICS did not affect very much, the book provides ample evidence of the considerable influence BRICS countries have gathered when confronting armed conflicts. Global order is rewritten not only by reforming treaties but also by concrete action in situations of crisis. The book is exactly tracing these responses with the development of a detailed typology and contrasting it with six rather classical foreign policy variables covering a wide spectrum from proximity to conflict, economic and political interests as well as normative reasons for action. Taking all these together the book aims at giving a detailed account and explanation of how BRICS countries respond to the most important conflicts of our time. In this regard the book provides a nuanced account of how rising powers position themselves in important security issues and is guided by an analytical framework which is empirically driven and explanatory in orientation.

Johannesburg, South Africa   Malte Brosig
1 February 2019

Acknowledgments

A book project like this is not possible without the generous support and help from many colleagues, institutions and donors. I am greatly indebted to all my interview partners who I possibly asked too many questions over the years. Special thanks go to Liu Haifang from Peking University who was tremendously helpful in organizing my visit to Beijing in 2017. Thanks also go to Viswanathan from the Observer Research Foundation (ORF) in New Delhi for sharing his invaluable insights on Indian foreign policy with me. Central for writing this book was our working group on BRICS in Peace and Security which was funded by the National Institute for Humanities and Social Science (NIHSS) in Johannesburg. The group consisting of Nirmala Gopal, Siphamandla Zondi, Philani Mthembu and myself gave me the confidence and motivation to start writing this book. I would also like to thank the National Research Foundation (NRF). NRF incentive funding allowed me to organize some of my research trips to BRICS countries which proved to be essential for writing this book. A draft version of the conceptual framework was presented to a workshop on rising powers which took place in April 2018 at the German Institute for Global and Area Studies (GIGA). I thank the organizers Miriam Prys-Hansen, Sandra Destradi and Detlef Nolte for inviting me to the workshop and Derrick Frazier for being the discussant of my paper. Lastly the constructive input by the anonymous reviewers is greatly acknowledged.

CONTENTS

1 Introduction: The BRICS Global Order Between
   Transition and Coexistence   1

2 Theoretical Framework: Modeling BRICS Response to
   Armed Conflict   43

3 Libya: From R2P to Regime Change—The BRICS
   Awakening   61

4 Syria: The World Order Unchallenged or Power Politics
   Above All Else?   93

5 Ukraine: Moving Borders Changing Orders?   125

6 South Sudan: BRICS Active Mediator or Bystander to
   Conflict?   157

7 Conclusion: The BRICS Order in the Making   187

Index   203

ABBREVIATIONS

ACIRC	African Capacity for Immediate Response to Crisis
ACLED	Armed Conflict Location & Event Data Project
ANC	African National Congress
APC	Armored personnel carriers
APSA	African Peace and Security Architecture
ARCSS	Agreement on the Resolution of the Conflict in the Republic of South Sudan
AU	African Union
AUHIP	AU High Level Implementation Panel on Sudan
BASIC	Brazil, South Africa, India, China
BRI	Belt and Road Initiative
CAR	Central African Republic
CNPC	China National Petroleum Company
CPA	Comprehensive Peace Agreement
CPC	Communist Party of China
CRA	Contingent Reserve Arrangement
DIRCO	Department of International Relations and Cooperation (South Africa)
DRC	Democratic Republic of Congo
EU	European Union
FDI	Foreign direct investment
FDLR	Democratic Forces for the Liberation of Rwanda
FFM	Fact-Finding Mission
FIB	Force Intervention Brigade
FOCAC	Forum on China Africa Cooperation
FSA	Free Syrian Army
GCC	Gulf Cooperation Council

GNI	Gross national income
HLRF	High Level Revitalization Forum
IBSA	India, Brazil, South Africa
ICC	International Criminal Court
IGAD	Intergovernmental Authority on Development
IMF	International Monetary Fund
IS	Islamic State
JIM	Joint Investigative Mechanism
JMEC	Joint Monitoring and Evaluation Commission
LAS	League of Arab States
MENA	Middle East and Northern Africa
MINUSTAH	United Nations Stabilization Mission in Haiti
NAM	Non-Aligned Movement
NATO	North Atlantic Treaty Association
NDB	New Development Bank
NIHSS	National Institute for Humanities and Social Science
Norinco	China North Industries Corporation
NPT	Non-Proliferation Treaty
NRF	National Research Foundation
OAS	Organization of American States
OIC	Organization of Islamic Cooperation
ONGC	Oil and Natural Gas Corporation (India)
OPCW	Organization for the Prohibition of Chemical Weapons
OSCE	Organization for Security and Cooperation in Europe
PSC	Peace and Security Council, AU
QCA	Qualitative Comparative Analysis
R2P	Responsibility to Protect
RIC	Russia, India, China
RwP	Responsibility while protecting
SCO	Shanghai Cooperation Organization
SMM	Special Monitoring Mission (OSCE)
SPLA	Sudan People's Liberation Army
SPLM	Sudan's People Liberation Movement
SPLM/IO	Sudan's People Liberation Movement in Opposition
TNC	Transitional National Council
TTP	Tehrik-i-Taliban Pakistan
UCDP	Uppsala Conflict Data Program
UN	United Nations
UNAMID	United Nations Hybrid Operation in Darfur
UNIFIL	United Nations Interim Force in Lebanon
UNMISS	United Nations Mission in South Sudan
UNSMIS	United Nations Supervision Mission in Syria
YPG	People's Protection Units (Kurdish militia)

List of Tables

Table 1.1	Military capabilities 2016	20
Table 3.1	Mapping of response types and motivation: Libya	81
Table 3.2	Trigger variables and countries: Libya	83
Table 4.1	BRICS voting in UN Security Council 2011–2012	103
Table 4.2	Mapping of response types and motivation: Syria	118
Table 4.3	Trigger variables and countries: Syria	119
Table 5.1	Chinese voting on Ukraine	143
Table 5.2	BRICS response types and motivation: Ukraine	150
Table 5.3	Trigger variables and countries: Ukraine	151
Table 6.1	Mapping of response types and motivation: South Sudan	178
Table 6.2	Trigger variables and countries: South Sudan	179
Table 7.1	Mapping BRICS response to armed conflict	190
Table 7.2	Trigger variables and responses	192
Table 7.3	Country, trigger variables and responses	197

LIST OF BOXES

Box 1.1	Ten Years of BRICS Summits	11
Box 1.2	Global Fire Power Rankings 2017	19
Box 3.1	Time Line of Events 2011	62
Box 4.1	Key Events: Syria	94
Box 5.1	Key Events: Ukraine	130
Box 6.1	Key Events: South Sudan	159

CHAPTER 1

Introduction: The BRICS Global Order Between Transition and Coexistence

Since the first formal BRIC(s) summit in 2009 in Yekaterinburg, world affairs have changed substantially and with them BRICS countries emerged as pivotal players on the international scene. While in the first decade of the new millennium we could observe a decline in violent conflict, this trend has been reversed. Since the Arab Spring conflict in the Middle East and Northern Africa (MENA) has intensified, the Ukrainian crisis brought back armed confrontation to Europe and a brutal civil war erupted in South Sudan. Although it is still too early to come to any final conclusions how far the global political, economic and security order has changed and what contribution we can attribute to BRICS, it is now rather a truism than a revelation to categorize BRICS countries as emerging or rising powers. After a decade of the existence of BRICS its countries are now much more established than emerging powers. If the label BRICS stands for anything of importance it is certainly for its status-boosting effect for its members and the normalization if not general acceptance of the discourse on multi-polar global politics. How far multi-polarity reaches and what it entails is still up to debate but there are hardly many scholars who doubt that power is increasingly dispersed around various actors in contrast to its concentration in a few hands.[1] While there is no consensus how exactly the global order changes, there is an implicit consensus that it does change and that BRICS members though not exclusively are key drivers of this change.

© The Author(s) 2019
M. Brosig, *The Role of BRICS in Large-Scale Armed Conflict*, New Security Challenges, https://doi.org/10.1007/978-3-030-18537-4_1

Given their geographical spread across four continents, increasing economic interdependencies, political ambitions and integration in global governance structures, the space in which BRICS interests are not affected is getting smaller and there are very few indicators for a long-term BRICS decline or disappearance. The recent economic slowdown in gross domestic product (GDP) growth and the dominance of domestic political constrains most visible in countries like Brazil and South Africa did not lead to a disintegration of the grouping. On the contrary, BRICS summit meetings are still expanding in terms of thematic working meetings. The establishment of the New Development Bank (NDB) and Contingent Reserve Arrangement (CRA) is a visible sign of converging and even institutionalized common interests.

For a considerable time the debate around BRICS and emerging powers was concentrating on two main questions: Will BRICS be gradually integrated into Western-dominated institutions and align with mainstream discourses or will they form a bloc outside established systems and become an antipode?[2] The realist paradigm framed the debate in terms of either bandwagoning or counter-balancing.[3] A more nuanced picture of BRICS influence is only slowly emerging with scholars developing more sophisticated taxonomies to categorize changes in global order and influence of rising powers, but most studies oscillate between these two positions.[4] However, today we can neither observe a ceding of BRICS criticism toward Western preponderance nor clearly identify a BRICS counter-hegemony. Indeed reform of global governance institutions has been sluggish to non-existent and divisions between BRICS countries remain significant and curtailing the formation of a political alliance which fully uses its newly acquired leverage. De facto BRICS remains a loosely institutionalized grouping of five countries which display significant convergence in their reformist agenda toward global governance institutions but fall short of building an alliance in the traditional sense of forming a political bloc because of diverging preferences.[5] Instead of formulating dyadic assumptions about BRICS following a moderate reform or a revisionist trend,[6] the book is interested in exploring BRICS positioning toward large-scale armed conflict, understanding it as an explorative research question. Exploring BRICS response to armed conflict is important because it constitutes order.

The analysis and evaluation of BRICS in global politics require a short discussion of what BRICS is, its ontology and how it can be studied. There is possibly no single answer to this question and it is often easier to identify what it is not. As such it does not easily fit under the concept of an international organization. BRICS is too loosely organized to call it an organization or institution. Neither does it have a foundational treaty, nor is there a secretariat which oversees policy implementation. Its physical and political existence concentrates very much on annual meetings and declarations reaching from summits of heads of states to numerous issue-specific specialized working groups and fora. For 2018 the official calendar of events listed 117 meetings throughout the year.[7] The recent establishment of the NDB and CRA is one of the most important examples of institutionalization but is rather the exception, only covering a small part of BRICS activities.

Could BRICS be an international regime instead? Regimes are less organized and institutionalized in terms of legalization, stratification and hierarchy. Krasner's classical definition of a regime refers to converging principles, rules, norms and decision-making.[8] Regimes have minimal actorness (in comparison to organizations) but display governing qualities. To some extent this better corresponds to BRICS nature which does formulate policy aspirations at an increasing level but does not endeavor to set up an implementation and supervision machinery which could curtail national sovereignty. However, even this softer form of organization does not fully resemble the BRICS example. Until today BRICS is no regulatory entity which explicitly produces international norms or rules. While its many summit declarations do formulate certain principles for international order and are akin to policy programs, it does not declare them in the form of obligations but rather formulates them as expectations. In any case, the main character of BRICS is not rule or decision-making; in this regard it is no international regime. However, the formulation of common positions in the BRICS format might be translated into action (operational or regulatory) in other international organizations at a later stage. At least BRICS countries have an information advantage when similar issues are discussed at international level following BRICS coordination before. However, it is still unclear if BRICS is systematically and instrumentally used as a strategic tool to influence decision- and rule-making elsewhere.

The remaining terminology and conceptualization of international relation ontologies speaking to the BRICS character are somehow less precise and academically unsatisfying. The literature when referring to BRICS often uses terms like "grouping," "forum," "venue," "association" or "formation." While "grouping" is the most proliferated term it is missing a reliable definition. What we often get instead is a mere description of the activities. The strong emphasis on classical state sovereignty in BRICS documents implies that the term "grouping" refers to actorness, understood as independent decision-making and subsequent action taking, as primarily resting on the constitutive parts of the group which are the member states. In this vein a group exists predominately because it can be compartmentalized and disentangled into its constitutive parts. Members do not delegate powers to the group as in the case of international organizations or regimes. The group activities are not equilibrium outcomes which rational choice institutionalism has conceptualized as principal-agent relationship; they are much more direct expressions of foreign policy priorities. While rational choice institutionalism assumes control over organizations by its members, control is conditioned on equilibrium outcomes which require giving up some priorities to the benefit of the collective gain.[9] This we would not assume to happen in a grouping such as BRICS in which consensus decision finding is the principle.

Much of the criticism against BRICS highlights the internal divisions, asymmetries and even economic and security competition that exist between members of the group which are very practically hampering convergence between these five countries and as a consequence undercut the influence BRICS have in international affairs.[10] However, this criticism while correct in its empirical analysis fails to recognize the basic value of a foreign policy grouping. Indeed as Nikolas Gvosdev finds: "One of the advantages of the BRICS process is that it remains a loose association of states with somewhat disparate interests, so no effort is made to force a common position when the BRICS states cannot agree on one. But these states have also found a way to disagree on some key issues ... without torpedoing the entire enterprise."[11] In other words, the main intention and value of BRICS is not to become an effective governance organization but to gather foreign policy clout in global affairs in situations in which BRICS key preferences are at stake.

With regard to foreign and security issues in contrast to purely technical questions of cooperation one should expect a near-pervasive influence of national strategic interests informing BRICS activities. While this chapter defines the main character of a grouping such as BRICS with regard to the ability to compartmentalize its activities, the grouping at times is more than the addition of its parts. In occasions in which BRICS acts upon commonly shared foreign policy perspectives, individual foreign policy priorities are reinforced and uplifted by the group's collective political weight in global and regional politics. Still the main mechanism of influence is through reinforcing individual positions which only by consensus become BRICS positions.

BRICS hardly creates internal convergence through group activities which are centrally initiated. In the field of security studies this should not surprise as they are traditionally seen as an area of high politics in which countries are especially sovereignty worry. Additionally we should also not forget that BRICS emerged as a result of a collectively shared critique of the existing (external) governance structures in the first place and not because of already internally converging security interests. All together this gives individual foreign policy preferences a fairly large impact on BRICS activities which is wanted and appreciated by its members. In the end, upholding and not pooling of sovereignty and keeping an independent position is a key element of the BRICS normative agenda related to global order questions. At best individual positions are coordinated but BRICS is in most cases no policy-implementing agency.

The prerogative of sovereignty and thus the dominance of individual foreign policy preferences can also be seen in the unwritten rules which constitute BRICS. Group members do not openly criticize each other at BRICS meetings on foreign or security policies. They also do not discuss contentious domestic issues but respect one another's core interests. The result is that BRICS position taking reflects upon individual interests and meetings are a safe environment without opposition to government positions. Contentious issues and existing tensions are rather left out of group statements than effectively mediated, in an act of benevolent neglect.

How to study BRICS in security matters? As BRICS security policies cannot be neatly separated from individual foreign policy because the latter is constitutive of what BRICS can do, the individual foreign policies also need to be regarded as foreign policies of BRICS countries. While this looks like a twisted argument, it might be more a conceptual than an empirical issue. In situations in which an issue is referred to by one of the BRICS formats it can be analyzed under the BRICS label. Naturally declarations by key decision-makers at summit or ministerial level bear relatively more weight than conclusions of technical meetings. In the end, both BRICS group responses and individual state action will be empirically traced in the later chapters of this book.

The main rationale for looking at BRICS as an international grouping as well as exploring individual foreign policies is the increasing political weight these five countries could garner in the last two decades. While much of the literature on rising powers focuses on the economic potential of emerging countries, this book is primarily interested in how BRICS countries are responding to major armed conflicts of our time outside their own borders and therewith become key players within a changing global security order. The emphasis on conflict outside the BRICS group is justified because internal fractions such as the Indian-Chinese border conflict are not discussed at BRICS meetings. The argument is made that while BRICS have been largely ineffective to change formal global governance organizations such as the Bretton Woods institutions, their influence in non-formalized settings of order is recognizable and under-explored in the literature on rising powers as well as on BRICS.

A number of groupings exist from which countries can choose and in which BRICS countries are represented. Here to name are IBSA comprising of India, Brazil and South Africa; the Shanghai Cooperation Organization (SCO) in which India, Russia and China are represented; the Association of Southeast Asian Nations (ASEAN) regional forum on security; the quadrilateral Security Dialogue of Quad in which India and the US are members; the RIC Forum of Russia, India and China; the BASIC consisting of Brazil, South Africa, India and China which emerged at the Copenhagen climate talks in 2009; and last the G20 which all BRICS countries are members of. There is indeed a significant proliferation of acronyms in which emerging powers are represented. However, BRICS stands out of these configurations as a grouping that is representing non-Western powers globally. Most other groups are regionally confined or if cross-regional lack global representation. This gives BRICS a special standing when it comes to global order questions. In this regard as a grouping it is unrivaled while the position of individual BRICS members as regional powers is often contested.

This study understands order not exclusively as a set of formal rules to be found in the UN Charter or regional organization mandates but places emphasis on actual engagement with security-relevant issues. Naturally large-scale violent conflict can be seen as the greatest challenge to the current security order. Therefore the book concentrates on four larger violent conflicts since the emergence of BRICS. These are Libya (2011), Syria (since 2011), South Sudan (since 2013) und the Ukraine (since 2013/14). The analysis will focus on how BRICS and its member countries react rhetorically and sometimes actively (operationally) to these conflicts and thereby build or re-building order through their response. How the world and BRICS countries react to these crises is constitutional to what can be called global security order in which BRICS operates.

The main aim is to explore to which extent the BRICS grouping and individual countries have been successful in crafting and coordinating their interests and exert influence in the context of these major conflicts. Is BRICS used as another tool to leverage individual foreign policy goals and to which extent have these conflicts been used to craft a BRICS position? The study is primarily interested in exploring what prompts BRICS countries to respond to armed conflict and what instruments of engagement are being applied? Empirically the response is traced within different venues. This entails the United Nations (UN) and its organs, regional organizations as well as BRICS meetings and individual responses. The BRICS grouping of course does not operate in an institutional vacuum. To the contrary, the international security architecture is increasingly institutionalized and BRICS constitutes only one part of it but a gradually more relevant one. As mentioned BRICS is not a decision-making and policy implementation-oriented organization. This means that its official statements are often not designed as specific scripts for action but rather lay out the broader context in which action is played out. They are more framework oriented in contrast to detailed and specific.

This introduction discusses both BRICS as a grouping and its individual members. Empirically the main focus is placed on security interests and foreign policies emerging around the four conflict case studies. The chapter starts with a summary and overview of previous BRICS summits and their declarations since the setting up of the grouping in 2009 and until the tenth jubilee summit in Johannesburg in 2018. This is followed by a brief discussion of individual state capabilities and preferences providing an outlook of BRICS as a potential security actor. The main conceptual framework for the book is developed in Chap. 2. Based on the literature on rising powers a taxonomy of ideal response types is developed which describes a nexus of possible responses ranging from cooperative to coercive forms of engagement. While the typology maps the universe of responses (outcome variable), an equally important part of this chapter introduces a number of explanatory conditions. The aim is to map the causal pathways which make states choose between various response types. Six explanatory conditions are introduced. These are: proximity to conflict, availability of power resources in relation to strategic interests, the type of conflict in terms of its effects on global order questions, economic consequences of the conflict on BRICS members, the degree to which extent conflict engagement can resonate with the normative BRICS agenda and lastly responding to conflict in order to act upon global humanitarian norms.

The following section is devoted to the empirical analysis and consists of four case studies. Large-scale armed conflict is selected which emerged since the establishment of BRICS. All these conflicts are taking place outside the borders of BRICS members but to varying degrees affect them. The case studies are the removal of Gaddafi in Libya covering the time from February to October 2011; the Syrian conflict which erupted in 2011 and continues until today; the partition of Sudan (2011) and subsequent civil war in South Sudan (since 2013); and finally the Crimean crisis and civil war in the Eastern Ukraine since late 2013. These four conflicts are among the most important ones of our time and are spreading over three continents and relevant BRICS countries as they raise fundamental questions about the global and regional security order, affect geostrategic interests of BRICS members (to varying degrees) and relate to the reformist agenda BRICS is known for. The final concluding section will evaluate the taxonomy of Chap. 2 and refine the formal modeling. The aim is to present trajectories of conditions for specific response types to be observed. In the end, this serves the purpose of explaining when and how BRICS countries react to armed conflict.

BRICS AND THE GLOBAL SECURITY ORDER: FROM SUMMITRY TO CONCEPT

The historic roots of the BRICS grouping go back several decades. Formations such as the Non-Aligned Movement (NAM) and the Bandung conference provided the ideational grounding on which substantial parts of the BRICS critique toward the Western-dominated global order are built.[12] The Bandung principles of 1955 which were reaffirmed again in 2005 are the basis on which BRICS countries formulate their foreign policy preferences. Among other issues these include a strong emphasis on sovereign equality of all nations, territorial integrity, non-intervention and generally a non-coercive style of international relations and rejection of neo-imperial attitudes.[13] This neo-Westphalian understanding of sovereignty can be understood as a counter-approach toward what BRICS see as problematic Western influence.[14] For example the convenient but selective use of liberal and humanitarian rhetoric to justify military interventions in sovereign states taking place exclusively in non-Western countries. Truly equitable multilateralism is one of the key demands countries from outside the Western core of world politics have formulated for several decades but without much success in actually achieving it. From this perspective the formation of IBSA and later BRICS is "a struggle against discrimination, disrespect, and humiliation."[15] A security architecture which is built on non-inclusive hierarchies within a supposedly multilateral organization of global order finds clear opposition as well as the use of supreme military capabilities in order to foster rather unilateral foreign policy goals.[16] Correcting this historical imbalance of the global order is thus a key and defining feature of groupings like BRICS. Thereby the argument is made that Western dominance as it emerged after the end of Cold War and reaching into the first decade of the new millennium is rather a historic anomaly and will naturally give way to a polycentric order.[17]

As already stated BRICS' influence on reforming global governance institutions remains minimal over the first ten years of its existence. BRICS voting share in the International Monetary Fund (IMF) and World Bank remains marginal (11–14%) and it even appears that the greatest challenge to the liberal world order now emanates from within the West itself (Trump, Brexit, right-wing populism). The lack of institutionalized reform certainly results both from internal disparities (see UN Security Council reform) and from the absence of fundamental reform ambition of the current system. From the BRICS perspective the current order if continuing to resist even adaptational change becomes a risk for the whole system, because it is likely to disintegrate and become dysfunctional.[18] Thus what BRICS calls for is a more equitable distribution of power and representation which is argued to stabilize the system because it also asks emerging countries to take on more responsibilities and provides lost legitimacy for global governance institutions.

Rather than aiming to replace it, BRICS have settled on a neo-Westphalian notion of order which emphasizes the centrality of independent statehood. BRICS is "pursuing a global order where great power is contained so that it is impossible for one state, or group of states, to impose their specific ideology on the rest of the system, or impossible to manipulate the international system to serve their national interests without regard for the common interests of states."[19]

The emphasis on uncompromised sovereignty as the basis for global order is a smart but also pragmatic choice. First, it is based on the widespread acceptance of sovereignty and non-intervention in domestic affairs as it is formulated in the UN Charter and finds practically universal acceptance. This link also makes it difficult for critics to blame BRICS to openly follow a revisionist agenda. Second, it is a pragmatic foreign policy choice. The retreat to uncompromised sovereignty is primarily a tool that serves two purposes. It aims at concealing perceived internal weaknesses by preventing unwanted external interferences in domestic politics. And equally important, it is an instrument to prevent hegemonic domination of the global order by single (often Western) countries or groups.[20] In the end, the BRICS emphasis on multilateralism based on sovereign equality fosters a multi-polar order. However, multi-polarity requires in the first place polarity, thus the concentration of decision-making and power at a center which is exclusively the sovereign state. In order to avoid hegemonic dominance sovereign states have to be placed in a system which guarantees their coexistence.[21] Consequently, coexistence and sovereignty are the preferred choice of conceptual instruments of BRICS countries which widely share an apprehension of Western dominance in global order questions. Global governance in terms of regulatory control of state behavior is not set high on the BRICS agenda. While this model forms a certain contrast to Western models in which countries are pooling sovereignty in international organizations in particular the European Union (EU) and in which non-intervention in cases of severe crisis is seen as problematic (see discourse on responsibility to protect [R2P]), the emphasis on uncompromised sovereignty is no longer the sole trademark of BRICS. The current erosion of multilateralism in the form of partial disintegration in the EU (Brexit), the America-first policy of President Trump and the prominence for bilateral trade partly compromising the WTO system correlates with the BRICS emphasis on state sovereignty. However, it is not clear if this trend actually works in favor of BRICS multi-polar agenda. At the moment global order seems to go through a phase of disruptions because of the growing emphasis on national sovereignty. This is limiting predictability and increasing uncertainty.

BRICS Summitry

Much of the global attention on BRICS focuses on the annual summits (see Box 1.1). While they are the most visible symbol of the BRICS, countless sub-groups and thematic workshops are meeting throughout the year. Most of these meetings are not designed or expected to implement policy strategies but work as a clearing house for mutual coordination and exchange of ideas or simply have symbolic political meaning. Especially in the security field coordination is rather loose and context dependent. BRICS is as such no strategic security alliance but a grouping of countries as defined in the section above. Thus close defense cooperation or

Box 1.1	Ten Years of BRICS Summits		
2009	Yekaterinburg, Russia	2014	Fortaleza, Brazil
2010	Brasilia, Brazil	2015	Ufa, Russia
2011	Sanya, China	2016	Goa, India
2012	Delhi, India	2017	Xiamen, China
2013	Durban, South Africa	2018	Johannesburg, South Africa

collective security aspirations should not be expected. However, if strategic elements can be found in BRICS summit documents, this at least indicates certain aspirations. While the reform of Bretton Woods' institutions figures most prominently in all summit declarations, security issues are forming the second priority area. Throughout all summits recurrent issues remain: The emphasis on a multi-polar order, expressed in a more democratic composition of institutions of global governance, reform of the UN, strict respect for international law and in particular classical sovereign rights of states, peaceful conflict settlement by using means of multilateral diplomacy, condemnation of terrorist activities and the centrality of the UN Security Council in mandating the use of force as a means of last resort.

Most of these issues are recurring topics which are being repeated at each summit declaration. However, over time summit declarations have grown in extent and detail. While during the first meeting in 2009 only 16 paragraphs were adopted and only two or three with regard to security issues (no specific conflicts have been mentioned), the most recent declarations from the 2018 Johannesburg meeting contain 102 paragraphs and make explicit reference to conflicts and even certain armed groups.

BRICS consists of more than summit meetings. Throughout the year different formats are gathering; as mentioned above in 2018, 117 meetings took place. Thereby BRICS also use other fora and organizations to gather, for example at the UN, or G20. With regard to security issues BRICS has brought about a number of groups and fora which meet regularly, for example, the national security advisors' meeting or working groups on cyber security, terrorism and peacekeeping as well as an intelligence forum or the bi-annual meeting of foreign ministers. In contrast to summit meetings, these gatherings at working level do often not produce official documents but merely press statements might be published. How substantial and productive these meetings are is difficult to assess. However, obvious is that BRICS does not operate with a clear definition of terrorism or has detailed how exactly the security-development nexus operates. Statements and declarations often remain aspirational. Many meetings serve as a forum for exchanging views but are not always used for specific policy coordination. This should not be surprising. As such, BRICS is no venue in which conflicts are mediated or solved. Thus the real action of conflict management is taking place outside the group, but with its many statements and declarations BRICS positions itself at least indicating which instruments and processes it deems important, legitimate or inadequate. In the case of terrorism BRICS actually agreed on a specific position. The Goa summit explicitly calls for the adoption of an "international convention for the suppression of acts of chemical and biological terrorism."[22]

The BRICS self-perception to disperse potential opposition against rapidly rising new powers is the argument that: a multi-polar world to which BRICS countries contribute through their economic rise boosts global growth. The principal emphasis on diplomacy to solve security issues is a world which is more stable and peaceful.[23] This rhetoric is aimed at formulating a counter-narrative to the Western-style interventions especially in the MENA region which are characterized by BRICS as missing multilateralism and instead of bringing peace, democracy and prosperity have plunged a whole region into despair. With the intervention in 2011 in Libya, BRICS countries felt outfoxed by the Western-led coalition who they accused of having a premier interest in regime change over interests of protecting civilians. The Sanya summit thus declares "that the use of force should be avoided" and that "the independence, sovereignty, unity and territorial integrity of each nation should be respected."[24] Still the language used does not express fundamental opposition or a counterbalancing strategy against existing structures but rather recalls commonly accepted norms and rules as laid down in the UN Charter.

The following summit in New Delhi was entitled "BRICS Partnership for Global Stability, Security and Prosperity," giving security issues considerably more attention. Since the Delhi summit BRICS declarations explicitly mention violent conflicts and BRICS countries aim at positioning themselves toward them. Implicitly they are assuming the role of order-shaping powers. In 2012 explicit mentioning find Israel/Palestine, Iran, Afghanistan and Syria. In the Syrian case they formulate their aim as "to facilitate a Syrian-led inclusive political process,"[25] which de facto backs up the Assad regime in opposition to Western attempts to remove him from power. Repeatedly BRICS countries condemned acts of terrorism but without going into detail who and where acts of terrorism were committed. Contentious security issues between and within BRICS countries have not been addressed or mentioned.

In 2013 the annual BRICS summit was for the first time on the African continent and thus South Africa took the advantage for bringing in African issues which concentrated mainly on development questions. The leadership role BRICS countries assume for themselves is potentially the strongest when it comes to the developing world. Because of South Africa being the host the number of conflicts to which the summit makes reference expanded further. Iran, Afghanistan, Syria and Palestine remained on the list; conflicts in Mali, the Central African Republic (CAR), the Democratic Republic of Congo (DRC), the Sahel and Gulf of Guinea were added as well as the role of the African Union (AU) to solve these conflicts.[26]

The Fortaleza summit (2014) in Brazil continued the trend of boosting the regional standing of the summit hosting country. While South Africa invited a dozen of African countries to the meeting the BRICS summit in Brazil also aimed at "furthering cooperation between BRICS and South America."[27] For the first time the Fortaleza declaration drew a direct link between security and development. Not only is the developmental path of BRICS countries promoted as a peace and security agenda but global public goods such as international peacekeeping and peace building are mentioned.[28] BRICS self-confidently formulates a participating role in providing these global public goods when stating that: "We will continue our joint efforts in coordinating positions and acting on shared interests on global peace and security issues for the common well-being of humanity."[29] While this statement is certainly very vaguely formulated, it still displays the ambition of coordinating policies and crafting a security agenda and therewith shaping and forming the global security architecture.

Growing convergence seems to be emerging too on issues of military interventions. With the crises in Libya and Syria in mind BRICS countries make it clear that they "condemn unilateral military interventions and economic sanctions in violation of international law" and highlight the "indivisible nature of security, and that no State should strengthen its security at the expense of the security of others."[30] BRICS countries place a strong emphasis on multilateralism and institutional conflict solution within the framework of the UN and its Security Council as well as regional organizations in which BRICS members play an influential role. It is very clear that South Africa wants the AU and African regional organizations to be the prime location where decisions are taken and uses the BRICS format to support this.[31] Indeed, South African influence can be seen repeatedly, for example with the mentioning of the African Capacity for Immediate Response to Crisis (ACIRC) which found entrance into the Fortaleza declaration.[32] The ACIRC is a South African-initiated concept for a military rapid reaction tool for early and quick intervention into Africa's many violent conflicts.

While reference to conflicts in BRICS summits is often declaratory and rather symbolic, in the case of Syria BRICS countries take a more detailed interest, rejecting a "further militarization" and calling for an immediate and "complete ceasefire."[33] Detailed positions have also been taken on the use of chemical weapons in the conflict and repeatedly the importance of respecting Syria's sovereign rights and territorial integrity is mentioned.[34] While it is clear that the BRICS position deviates substantially from those of the US and its supporters, the summit declarations do not openly attack the Western coalition but instead a wording is chosen which connects to commonly accepted international law and the UN Charter.

As the conflict around the Crimean Peninsula and Eastern Ukraine intensified and Russia was hosting the BRICS summit in 2015 for the first time, a large-scale conflict was on the agenda to which a BRICS country is directly involved. While the Ufa declaration calls BRICS a "strategic partnership"[35] the joint statement falls short of formulating common strategic goals with regard to the conflict in the Ukraine. What BRICS agreed on was a general reference to peaceful conflict resolution and the Minsk agreement.[36] Neither did BRICS endorse the Russian annexation of the Crimean peninsula nor can we find a call for the respect of Ukrainian sovereignty or inviolability of its territorial integrity. Of all conflicts mentioned in the Ufa declaration Syria occupies the largest space. Here BRICS "express support for the steps of the Russian Federation aimed at promoting a political settlement in Syria."[37] The emphasis remains on peaceful conflict settlement. A later military involvement of Russia does not find mentioning in either the Ufa or any other (later) declarations. The Ufa declaration now mentions a number of specific terror groups (Boko Haram, Islamic state, Al-Nusra) and condemns their violence. Additionally the Democratic Forces for the Liberation of Rwanda (FDLR) in the DRC is also mentioned following South African military engagement in the Force Intervention Brigade (FIB), a regional peace enforcement operation under the umbrella of the UN peacekeeping mission. In this regard BRICS takes a strategic stance against these groups but does not develop a counter-insurgency strategy in its own right. When terrorist groups are mentioned the fight against them is supported within the framework of the UN but not by unilateral action.

To a large extent the Goa summit declaration from 2016 repeats what previous meetings have agreed on. What is somehow new in this declaration is the explicit reference to peacekeeping.[38] The declaration calls for adherence to established principles of peacekeeping (these are usually neutrality and restraint of the use of force) but also protection of civilians and speaks about strengthening missions. When it comes to peacekeeping missions and questions of external military involvement in conflict, BRICS countries repeatedly highlighted the premier importance of host state consent reinforcing state sovereignty. On the issue of terrorism a joint counter-terrorism working group was established and the summit declaration now mentions explicit instruments on how to engage terrorists.[39]

The BRICS meeting in Xiamen took place in a difficult security environment. China and India encountered a military standoff in the Himalayas and an ever more aggressive North Korea was eager to demonstrate its nuclear and missile capabilities while the summit was meeting. At the security front closer cooperation in the intelligence field was proposed by Brazil.[40] The list of terrorist groups was extended to the Eastern Turkistan Islamic Movement, the Islamic Movement of Uzbekistan, the Haqqani network, Lashkar-e-Taiba, Jaish-e-Mohammed, Tehrik-i-Taliban Pakistan (TTP) and Hizb ut-Tahrir.[41] This takes primarily into account Indian security interests.

No doubt the issue of counter-terrorism is seen by BRICS countries as one of the most important security challenges. However, BRICS has not assumed the role of a problem-solver. No definition of the term "terrorism" has been agreed and thus the list of groups against which action is called upon reflects as much individual geostrategic preferences as objective need to contain dangerous terrorist acts.

In 2018 BRICS countries met in Johannesburg marking ten years after the set-up of the grouping. The Preamble of the summit declaration reflects upon classical elements of a liberal world order by mentioning multilateralism, the rule of law, democracy, international law and the UN Charter as foundation for peace and stability in addition to the traditional BRICS emphasis on sovereign equality and reform of global governance institutions.[42] The stronger than usual emphasis on liberal norms of global order constitutes a contrast to the current debate of its demise.

While in the early phase of BRICS the group was seen by some as challenging the existing order, BRICS now portray themselves as anchor of stability. Indeed, the challenge for multilateralism now also emanates from the West.

The Johannesburg declaration devotes 14 paragraphs to peace and security. In most cases it reaffirms earlier rhetoric of non-intervention and peaceful conflict resolution. The main geographical focus is placed on conflict in the Middle East. BRICS explicitly supports the Iran nuclear deal which was abandoned by the US.[43] "Serious concerns" were issued over a potential arms race in outer space[44] and efforts to denuclearize the Korean peninsula were welcomed.[45] A whole paragraph was devoted to peacekeeping issues.[46] South Africa initiated the setting up of a permanent working group for peacekeeping and the BRICS Academic Forum recommended the establishment of a peace research institute.[47]

In sum, over the years BRICS positions on key security challenges expanded significantly. Reference to violent conflicts in Africa, Asia and Europe is now commonly agreed and demonstrates BRICS willingness to adopt regional and global geostrategic positions. However, there is no joint initiative which could rightly be called strategic and BRICS actorness is only weakly developed. Instead BRICS agrees on rather uncontroversial wording which emphasizes a rules-based order on sovereign equality. Political and violent conflicts which directly affect a BRICS member state are hardly discussed; domestic security issues are seen as not appropriate to discuss. This is true with regard to the Ukraine, the South China Sea or Kashmir. The condemnation of terrorist activities and unilateral military interventions (by the West) remains the area in which convergence of interests is most advanced. While the BRICS summit declarations do not formulate a security strategy, they touch upon many strategic security issues. It remains to be seen if engaging in these security issues without having conceptual clarity at the strategic level is a worthwhile approach. Lastly through the crises in the Ukraine and Syria but also China's rising global military presence the BRICS narrative of a more peaceful and just multi-polar order receives substantial cracks when individual BRICS countries aim at playing great power politics instead of seeking multilateral solutions. While initially the BRICS critique against Western dominance and its negative consequences was well formulated, it increasingly loses track in situations in which individual BRICS countries behave in similar patterns they have criticized before.

BRICS STRATEGIC CAPABILITIES, CONSTRAINTS AND INTEREST

As mentioned BRICS is no alliance, regime or organization but merely a grouping. This should not be discarded as a weakness as such. Bloc building in the traditional sense rather resembles the Cold War era, a time of military confrontation, and somehow contravenes the idea of building a more inclusive multi-polar world order for which BRICS lobbies extensively. The BRICS grouping, while having its shortcomings in the absence of clearly formulated strategies, can also be seen as a modern and better fitting alternative to the heavy bureaucratic global governance machinery (UN) or alliance-building North Atlantic Treaty Association (NATO). Indeed the twenty-first century is characterized better as "a world of numerous overlapping, often issue-specific and quite probably fluid alliances and groupings."[48] BRICS should be seen from this perspective and in context not necessarily opposition to existing other networks and groups of countries. It should be clear from the beginning that a country's interests are not perfectively or exclusively expressed by the BRICS grouping but that BRICS is used flexibly in situations of convergence among its members which are likely issue specific. BRICS should be treated as one grouping or constellation among many others through which countries work. Especially at regional level all BRICS members are integrated into a network of groupings and organizations. The fact that BRICS is not alone does not diminish its relevance. It is a matter of fact that most, if not all, states are members in a multitude of organizations and use them flexibly. In the security field this situation has been explored under the notion of a security regime complex.[49] What makes BRICS stand out from many other regional groupings is the global and cross-continental composition of non-Western countries. This makes it the preferred tool to address global order questions outside Western-driven global governance structures.

However, the geographic spread has disadvantages too. BRICS members are dispersed around four continents and thus do not form a region of their own. While Russia, India and China share common borders, they are also placed in competition to one another and this is true with regard to economic, development, political influence, security matters and demographics. Within BRICS power asymmetries are significant. In terms of population size, GDP and trade relations, China is by far the most advanced country and thus naturally occupies a leading position. However, intra-BRICS trade remains weakly developed and makes up only around

12% of the total trade of BRICS countries and has not changed significantly over the years.[50] Much of the economic rise of BRICS countries is due to their expanding trade relations with established economies and thus power status seeking or maintaining through BRICS is limited. BRICS countries are well integrated into the global economy which created more, but not less, interdependencies. It also remains doubtful if economies which rely mostly on selling commodities to the world market such as Brazil, Russia and South Africa will be able to diversify their economies. More likely is the maintenance of an inner-BRICS relationship in which China and India are significant importers of commodities in exchange for the export of manufactured goods, services and other investments to developed nations.

In the security field BRICS countries form a rather unusual grouping. Their wide geographical spread, the size of their countries and regional dominant but also contested position within their neighborhood complicate, if not prevent, the formulation of specific security strategies or a global agenda. The rather general wording of BRICS summit declarations are an expression of this situation. At a minimum BRICS countries do not challenge the regional position of their partners but allow each member some leverage in their own backyard. This is largely in line with the BRICS preference for a multi-polar world order. While references to sovereignty rights and territorial integrity are commonly endorsed and unilateral interventions rejected by the BRICS countries mentioning examples such as Iraq (2003), Kosovo (1999), Libya (2011) or Syria, support for the concept of narrow sovereignty and non-intervention is not unerring or fundamental. At times it is used as a tool to counter-balance US influence.[51] In other occasions BRICS apply a flexible interpretation of sovereignty to foster their own regional interests. Examples are the Russian intrusion into South Ossetia, Abkhazia and the Ukraine; the Chinese disrespect for its border with India; India's Kashmir conflict; South Africa's intervention in Lesotho without UN Security Council mandate or Brazil's engagement in the Honduran political crisis.

In comparison with their economic prowess, military strength and strategic convergence of BRICS countries is lagging behind. Although India, China and Russia are nuclear powers with command over sizable armies, they have limited capabilities for projecting power globally and do not match up with US military capabilities or NATO as a regional military alliance. Given the supremacy of US military spending and global capabilities to project force, BRICS countries have so far not started an arms race to counter-balance US influence in a significant manner. The US alone in

> **Box 1.2 Global Fire Power Rankings 2017**
>
> | | | | |
> |---|---|---|---|
> | 1. | US | 7. | South Korea |
> | 2. | Russia | 8. | Japan |
> | 3. | China | 9. | Turkey |
> | 4. | India | 10. | Germany |
> | 5. | France | 14. | Brazil |
> | 6. | UK | 33. | South Africa |
>
> Source: 2018 Military Strength Ranking https://www.globalfirepower.com/countries-listing.asp. Accessed 1 Oct. 2018

2016 spent $611bn on defense, while all BRICS countries together reach $368bn.[52] As rising powers BRICS countries still display considerable vulnerabilities concerning their own domestic economic and political systems. Therefore some scholars describe them rather as status quo powers but not as revisionist newcomers.[53] Domestic weaknesses should not be exploited by external (least former colonial) powers and thus the emphasis on classical sovereignty.

When comparing the positions of BRICS with Western countries and the US in terms of military capabilities as ranked by the Global Fire Power index, it becomes clear that China, India and Russia have bypassed all other countries except the US (see Box 1.2). Box 1.2 also makes clear that within the BRICS grouping the military standing is significantly unequal. Russia, China and India by far out-compete the resources Brazil or South Africa can avail. Considering current economic development trends it is most likely that only China and India will continue to push ahead and leave the others behind.

While at the moment BRICS countries do not (yet) out-perform the US and NATO in terms of military capabilities (see also Table 1.1), they have risen in their respective regions to pivotal actors against whose opposition established powers might not want to mobilize their military resources. This does provide the BRICS grouping with a strategic advantage and is not trivial but falls short of acquiring capabilities to play a global dominant role. In other words, BRICS countries are too large to just be followers of others but too small to occupy a fully dominant role. Of course the mere existence of significant military resources does not say much about their potential or effective use. Winning wars and exerting

Table 1.1 Military capabilities 2016

Country	Active personnel	Total aircraft	Combat tanks	Self-propelled artillery	Naval assets	Aircraft carriers	Budget $
US	1,373,650	13,762	5884	1934	415	19	588
Russia	798,527	3794	20,216	5972	352	1	45
China	2,260,000	2955	6457	1710	714	1	162
India	1,363,500	2102	4426	290	295	3	51
France	204,000	1305	406	325	118	4	35
UK	151,175	856	246	89	76	2	46
Japan	248,575	1594	700	202	131	4	44
Turkey	382,850	1018	2445	1013	194	0	8
Germany	180,000	698	543	154	81	0	39
Brazil	334,500	697	469	112	110	0	25
South Africa	78,050	231	195	43	30	0	5

Source: 2017 Military Strength Ranking https://www.globalfirepower.com/countries-listing.asp. Accessed 26 Sep. 2017

influence is not a simple offshoot of counting tanks, aircraft or personnel. But a rising power status does depend on hard military equipment to some extent and we can expect that military spending in China and India will continue following their economic growth rates.

As the BRICS grouping does not formulate a general or specific security strategy which goes beyond the mentioned summit declarations, much of what BRICS countries do in the security realm is deeply rooted in their own foreign and security policies. Thus what BRICS does is to provide a forum or venue for policy coordination and some convergence at best. Therefore the following section surveys individual countries' foreign policy positions and preferences which are making up BRICS positions in the end. Naturally this section cannot and does not aim at providing a comprehensive foreign policy review but only aims at giving a short introduction into key determinants. Countries are presented in alphabetical order.

Brazil

In terms of the size of its economy, number of population and land mass Brazil is a regional champion in South America. The expansion of its economy under the Lula da Silva (2003–2011) presidency catapulted the country into the top ten of the largest economies in the world. For Brazil it is no question that its incorporation into the G20 in 2008 and later BRICS has uplifted its status as a regional and global power. Still there remain doubts if the country has lived up to its newly acquired status as a major power as the presidencies of Dilma Rousseff (2011–2016) and Michel Temer (2016–2018) were marred with domestic political unrest and a considerable economic downturn.[54] Furthermore, its own domestic trajectory and foreign policy legacy seem to hold the country back and created significant tensions between its newly acquired leadership role and traditional foreign policy conceptions.[55] Brazil might best be described as a reluctant hegemon and regional power which is a category also fitting for other emerging powers.[56] In the case of Brazil its hard power capabilities are lagging behind its economic relevance in the region and globally.

The cornerstones of its foreign policy have generally been described as strict adherence to the concept of sovereignty and territorial integrity linked to a clear opposition against interventions and the use of force. This can be seen in article 4 of the country's constitution which provides for basic foreign policy guidelines. The article bases Brazilian foreign policy among others on the principles of non-intervention, equality among the states, defense of peace and peaceful settlement of conflicts.[57] This pro-sovereignty and anti-interventionist position is also reflecting regional norms as they can be found in the Charter of the Organization of American States (OAS), in articles 19–22. Additionally the non-interventionist position and rejection of the use of force are repeated in Brazil's defense doctrines and remains a guiding principle for its foreign policy.[58] The strong emphasis on sovereignty is important for the country for two reasons. First, it aims at reducing foreign and unwanted external influence from its territory. For most of its post-colonial history Brazil was placed at the periphery of global power and thus it feels vulnerable vis-à-vis larger powers. Second, sovereignty is linked to the idea of equality of nations and provides a certain degree of protection against power politics.

Brazil's foreign policy also places a strong emphasis on multilateralism and negotiating diplomatic solutions for conflicts. In this vein it supports global and regional organizations as main tools for conflict resolution. In its direct neighborhood Brazil did not experience significant inter-state wars and thus the country did not need to defend itself with a large-scale military army nor did it feel the need to intervene in neighboring countries to safeguard its own security or other vital interests. This might explain why Brazil can be categorized as a reluctant hegemon and a skeptical intervener.

The rise of Brazil was among other conditions facilitated through high commodity prices in the first decade of the new millennium and also the normative foreign policy of the Lula presidency that furthered a developmental approach which lifted many Brazilians out of poverty. Gradually Brazil formulated (for itself) a leadership role in South-South cooperation and extended diplomatic relations with African countries by opening 38 new embassies on the continent. The 2011 Defense White Paper draws a link between security and development connecting Brazil's social programs with increased domestic security. "Brazil believes there is a causal connection between situations of disfavour and violence."[59] Solving security issues is seen from the perspective of poverty reduction. The reluctant power ambition is also reflected in the idea of leadership without domination as mentioned in the Defense White Paper.[60]

With Brazil's newly acquired role as an emerging power it started carefully to expand its leadership role. This follows the 2005 National Defense Strategy which called to "enlarge the country's projection in the world concert."[61] Subsequently Brazil started to participate and lead the UN Stabilization Mission in Haiti (MINUSTAH), has contributed naval assets to the UN Interim Force in Lebanon (UNIFIL) and shortly played a diplomatic role together with Turkey in the Iranian standoff around its nuclear program. While these initiatives look like rather normal activities for a regional power perfectly acting within multilateral governance structures, they do form an important step forward from a power positioned at the periphery of the global pecking order wary about external influence at home and in its neighborhood toward moving closer to the center of world affairs and making an active contribution to the global security architecture.

These newly started foreign policy initiatives are in line with the country's ambitions to claim a greater global role and become a permanent member of the UN Security Council which has been recognized by BRICS summit declarations. Its continued endorsement for non-intervention and non-military solutions to conflicts is expressed in the abstention on resolution 1973 concerning Libya in 2011 and the promotion of the responsibility while protecting (RwP) as a consequence of the regime change approach applied against Gaddafi and calling for restraint when using force.[62]

Brazil's current status is in doubts again primarily because of the domestic turmoil and economic slump especially at the end of Rousseff's time in office and her forced leave. The changes from the Lula to Rousseff, Temer and since 2019 Bolsonaro presidencies seem to have taken Brazil back in time. Financial resources and visionary ambitions have faded and leave Brazil with a role below its "natural" weight. While the Lula presidency displayed a strong alignment to BRICS, the interest in South-South cooperation and playing a more active foreign policy at a global stage have decreased sharply. Domestic issues are overlaying former foreign policy ambitions. With Bolsonaro becoming president, undoing previous left-wing politics is one priority. Closer links with the US instead of countries from the Global South is another possible scenario.[63] What this means for foreign policy and Brazil's BRICS affiliation needs to be shown in the coming years and is not subject of this study. The 2019 BRICS summit taking place in Brasilia is an important test case for the grouping.

China

Of all BRICS countries China's rise to the top received the greatest attention. It appears to be the only country which in the long term can rival US power economically, politically and militarily. Today China's influence is most visible in its international trade relations. For many countries China is already the largest trading partner. Given the fact that the country's rise is largely dependent on the import of raw materials and export of manufactured goods and increasingly IT technology as well as domestic stability, China is gradually playing a more active role in global affairs. The sheer size of the country, its demographics and economic might make it a global player in any case. The fact that China has not used its already vast power resources in a revisionist manner is usually explained by China profiting from the global capitalist order with its emphasis on capital expansion and free trade which is compatible with China's internal priority of development and modernization requiring a stable international environment.[64]

Indeed China's foreign policy core priorities are rather narrowly focusing on state sovereignty and territorial integrity (one-China policy and fierce rejection of secessionist movements, e.g. Tibet).[65] These priorities require no fundamental reshuffling of the current order but are largely compatible with existing rules and principles of sovereign state rights. Undeniably China and India are also competitors when it comes to security questions. The border standoff between China and India just before the 2017 BRICS summit once more showed how conflictual inner-BRICS relations can be. For this reason China cannot expect much or any support on issues of the South China Sea.

In the triangular relationship between Russia, India and China (RIC) the relationship between China and Russia has developed the most favorable. Security cooperation between the two countries consolidated in recent years. A strategic partnership has emerged. Between 2012 and 2017 16 joint military exercises have been conducted and in 2017 both countries signed a plan for bilateral military cooperation.[66] Additionally the joint veto use in the Security Council in the Syrian conflict visibly demonstrates a joint political agreement.

Despite China's traditional strong emphasis on classical sovereignty, respecting territorial integrity and being skeptical about interventions rather favoring a non-interventionist position, its foreign policy went through a number of transformations. Sovereignty is now not perceived to be total and being in opposition to non-intervention. China's position in debates around the responsibility to protect (R2P) now provides for more flexibility. Interventions are accepted if they are authorized by the UN Security Council, the use of force is applied as last resort and minimally, interventions are non-permanent and only with member state consent.[67] Today China has overcome a strict and orthodox interpretation of non-intervention and continues to reassess its involvement in global security politics.[68] The linkage between R2P and arming of rebels to topple a regime is seen as unacceptable (Libya, Syria). Despite its considerable power China is still worried about secessionist movements on its territory and would hardly support any normative order which legitimizes external (military) support for domestic opposition movements compromising its territorial integrity.

Given China's size and dense economic connections with practically all world regions it inevitably plays an important role for the global security order. To disperse counter-balancing against its growing strength China puts great emphasis on its peaceful rise and responsible execution of its powers.[69] Increasingly China gets involved in maintaining international peace and security far beyond its own borders. It is now the largest troop contributor to UN peacekeeping missions of the P5 and makes the second largest monetary contribution to the peacekeeping budget.[70] While at the beginning of the millennium China hardly deployed any peacekeepers, in April 2019 it had 2497 military personnel serving under the UN.[71] Additionally China participates in the international military operations against Somali pirates and has recently opened a military base in Djibouti.[72]

China's access to global markets and the need for natural resources to keep its economy running make the country a political and security actor.

This is particularly true for relations with Africa. Chinese investment in the Sudanese, South Sudanese oil sector, its arms trade with the region as well as sending peacekeepers and building a military base are illustrative of the complexities in which China operates and displays the extent to which China has become a political, security and economic actor well beyond its own region.[73]

The continuing rise of China with its significant power resources makes it difficult to categorize it as a status quo power. Still China is neither an aggressive revisionist nor is it or can be categorized as a passive peripheral country. Its emphasis has long been on rising within the existing system and claiming greater weight for itself through supporting a reformist agenda by increasing South-South cooperation among which the BRICS grouping features most prominently.

When it comes to China's vision for global governance and macro order questions Shaun Breslin summarizes the country's position quite effectively:

> If there is a normative position underpinning China's official approach to reform of global governance, it is perhaps that there should be no normative basis. For the time being at least, China is less interested in promoting a clearly articulated grand strategy and a new set of universal values than it is in finding pragmatic solutions: primarily solutions to problems that it itself faces, but also at times solutions to problems facing others.[74]

On this basis revising global order governance structures is less about formulating a specific counter-strategy which might find opposition in both the West and the developing world and even BRICS in order to deny China a too dominating role. A more pragmatic approach which relieves China of some of the burdens of global leadership focuses on issue-specific situations and follows a case-by-case logic. Although there might not be a specific Chinese global strategy, the Belt and Road Initiative (BRI),[75] which is an up to $1 trillion heavy infrastructure investment project, is akin to a geostrategic road map for China's rise to become the world's largest economy which undeniably has significant foreign policy meaning. The BRI combines land- and sea-based trade routes and aims at securing Chinese exports of goods and access to natural resources. The scale of this investment and the geographic focus on connecting Asia with Europe, through the Middle East and including Africa, directly link China to all four large-scale armed conflicts explored in this study. With regard to

China's overseas investments it is obvious that only a fraction of it is channeled through BRICS institutions such as the NDB and initiatives like the BRI or the Forum on China Africa Cooperation (FOCAC) are easily outperforming BRICS initiatives. Within the grouping there is a growing disbalance toward China, especially on the economic sphere.

Regarding China's response to armed conflicts, the country has traditionally avoided taking sides. It often abstains in the UN Security Council on controversial political issues. However, its growing investments make it difficult to stay aloof. Conceptually China has emphasized the importance of economic development to stabilize countries and maintain peace.[76] Development has mostly been facilitated through Chinese investment but not developmental aid. Peace through development is propagated and forms a contrast to liberal peace building, emphasizing the role of democratic institutions and political rights. China is also favoring non-coercive means and mediation over punitive measures (sanctions, interventions) trying not to dominate political mediation processes.

As China remains to be a country on the rise a passive bystander role to major armed conflicts might only be temporary and a more assertive foreign policy in the future is quite likely. The change China went through from favoring an orthodox interpretation of sovereignty to the engagement with concepts like R2P and active participation in UN peace missions is already a significant move. Under President Xi Jinping China is assuming an ever more influential role globally and growing self-confidence in foreign policy relations.

India

During the times of the Cold War and in its early years after independence India put a strong emphasis on its political autonomy and the non-aligned movement. It thus comes out of a tradition of not aligning itself to political blocs. Despite this India entertained closer relationships with the Soviet Union than the US during the Cold War and the former remains to be an important supplier of modern weaponry for the country. As a large developing country India's foreign policy expresses solidarity with third world countries and identifies with issues of global distributive justice which earned the country the reputation of being a difficult partner for larger established powers than for small developing countries.[77] The moderate reformist agenda of BRICS resonates with India's South-South developmentalism and partly moralistic approach to global governance reforms.

Its legacy of non-alignment and autonomy-seeking country makes clear that BRICS is not seen as a classical bloc-building institution or strategic alliance.

When it comes to India's security concerns it is significantly more pressured than any other BRICS country. The process through which India re-gained its independence placed the region in great insecurity and finally resulted in a nuclear arms race. Conflicts with Pakistan over Kashmir, the separation of Bangladesh from Pakistan and continued border disputes in the Himalayas with China exert significant pressures on India. Its two main rivals China and Pakistan are both nuclear powers. In order to overcome its political and military weakness and strengthen its autonomy also vis-à-vis unwanted interferences from traditional Western powers, India acquired nuclear weapons outside the Non-Proliferation Treaty (NPT) which it regarded as unfair as it preserves the status quo and one-sidedly favors existing power relations.[78] As India is a rising but vulnerable power and security competition within its direct neighborhood remains tense, the moralistic emphasis on equity and justice in international relations is difficult to maintain. When its own security interests are in jeopardy India acts as a traditional large power, for example opposing Iran's nuclear weapons program and in this case insisting on the rules of the NPT.[79]

The advantages of being a rising power became visible with improving relations with the US. While initially America sanctioned India for its nuclear program it later on changed course and recognized it as a nuclear power. Here India and the US engaged in rather classical counter-balancing against the growing regional influence of China. The Chinese replied by intensifying their economic relations with India's arch enemy Pakistan. India does not take part in any BRI projects. Although Indian-Chinese relations are strained, both countries also manage to pragmatically cooperate on common security threats such as terrorism.[80]

Indian leadership within its region has not only been contested from the outside but apparently the country "displayed a complete lack of initiative, it has failed to develop a clear and consistent 'vision' for its region."[81] This also means that vital security issues are outside India's direct control. This might explain the country's skepticism and opposition when it comes to international interventions. Hardeep Puri's[82] (former Indian ambassador to the UN) book *Perilous Interventions: The Security Council and the Politics of Chaos* is a vivid expression of this position.

While India is the world's largest weapons importer this has not necessarily led to its army becoming more effective. Ian Hall finds that "its military lacks the capacity to punish groups in Pakistan that infiltrate insurgents into Kashmir and terrorists into its cities, and to deter China from aggressive behavior"; furthermore he describes India as "one of the most under-policed societies in the world."[83] Together this displays India's internal and external vulnerabilities quite openly. Security cooperation within BRICS is likely to proceed only if India's vital security interests are not compromised. Given the competition with China the potential for far-reaching cooperation remains limited somehow. However, it is also true that despite regional competition between India and China both countries are managing their relationship within BRICS maturely. Potential bilateral tensions have not incapacitated BRICS or escalated to open or hybrid warfare.

During the post-independence period and Cold War times strategic autonomy and non-alignment were the first choice in Indian foreign policy; such an approach is no longer viable and has been replaced. With multi-polarity gradually emerging and economic growth and development being dependent on the country's integration into global markets, a multi-alignment strategy has been adopted.[84] India's increased engagement in multilateral fora such as IBSA, BRICS, the G20 or SCO is an expression of the multi-alignment approach. In contrast to alliance alignment describes a much looser and flexible cooperation which emerges around common issues and problems with only a light institutional footprint. Such an approach seems to be well suited for India whose regional leadership and national security are contested. Although externally India's security is challenged its growing power base is dependent on its integration into the global economic system. Such a situation requires a careful balancing act which cannot be without contradiction or tensions. The multi-alignment approach is an expression of these pressures and tensions.[85] India is both a rising and constrained power which raises external expectations toward India's role in the world but also limits its real potential to act as a hegemonic power. After all developing concise foreign policy strategies is not the country's first priority but lifting its large population out of poverty and transforming India into a middle-income country is its biggest contemporary project.

On the one hand alignment with the US is sought as a counterbalancing strategy while in other situations US hegemony is opposed. Although India and China are regional competitors, they are partners in regional groupings too. Given these complexities multi-alignment is a flexible approach adequately matching up real foreign policy needs. Being a member of the BRICS grouping fits into this scheme. Multi-alignment can equally be seen as an inhibitor for more convergence among BRICS members as India does not aim at building political or economic blocs, as well as it is a facilitator for cooperation in situations in which intra-BRICS competition is tense but India does not pull out of joint groupings. The 2017 border standoff between India and China just eased before the summit in Xiamen which might be an example of the grouping being able to diffuse tensions or at least prevent an escalation if only for a short while.

When it comes to international conflict resolution outside India's direct periphery, the country is well known for being the largest troop contributor in the history of UN peacekeeping. In April 2019 it deployed 6319 troops, by far the largest number among the BRICS countries.[86] However, despite its growing economic role and active participation in peacekeeping missions, India has not used these "muscles" to acquire a predominant role in international conflict management. These large deployments do not follow rational economic calculations to secure its overseas investments. In this regard these deployments do not follow a geostrategic plan. The country does support multilateral and mediation-based conflict resolution but often takes a passive bystander role. India does hardly bring its own potential leadership role into play if not explicitly asked to do so. Non-interventionist and non-coercive means of foreign policy are preferred instruments. India is a reluctant hegemon.[87] Beyond the general favor for a multi-polar world based on sovereign equality, there is no grand strategic planning of the country's foreign and security policy visible.

Russia

Within the BRICS grouping Russia is somehow the outlier. It is neither a developing country of the South with a post-colonial history nor is it usually characterized as rising power. Instead as a successor of the Soviet Union, Russia for most of the last 25 years experienced an erosion of its power and significant reduction of its sphere of influence. While for the others the BRICS club is seen as a status-enhancing forum for Russia, it serves to consolidate or reclaim lost territory. Russia principally does not need to play catch-up with established powers because it is no new actor in great power games despite its relative decline. Within the BRICS grouping Russia occupies a somehow unique position. It inherited its significant military capabilities from the Soviet Union but continues to face economic difficulties and a population decline while being the geographically largest country within the (any) group. It is both the largest European and Asian country. Economically Russia cannot keep up with Indian- and Chinese-style growth rates and its population of 144 million appears as rather small in comparison to its regional Eastern neighbor. While in the case of Brazil, India and China their economic weight outperforms their military capabilities, it is the opposite in the Russian case. Although Russia committed to a reduction of its nuclear arsenal with the end of the Cold War, it still commands over significant conventional forces. Seen from this perspective it might be less surprising that Russia is the one country which has used its military assets more than any of the other members of the BRICS groupings. Examples range from the Chechen war, the war with Georgia, Ukraine and Syria.

Although Russia seems to be the outlier in a group which strongly emphasizes South-South cooperation and aims at challenging traditional centers of power, there is a fair share of convergence in foreign policy interests. With the end of the Cold War the newly emerging order did not immediately change from bi-polarity to multi-polarity but the US emerged as the sole center of power, a situation all BRICS countries find unacceptable.[88] The uni-polarity of the new order and the perceived and sometimes real disrespect for international law, in particular territorial integrity and sovereignty, made Russia align with the newly emerging powers. For Russia the cases of Kosovo, Iraq, NATO expansion to its borders and Western support for the color revolutions in the Ukraine and elsewhere are seen as direct threat emanating from uni-polarity.[89] Referring to BRIC Putin in 2007 finds that: "There is no reason to doubt that the economic potential of the new centres of global economic growth will inevitably be converted into political influence and will strengthen multipolarity,"[90] hence Russia's interest in establishing BRICS as a counter-balancing grouping.

Russia's direct and most vital security concerns are directed toward the Eurasian region and territory of the former Soviet Union. A particular emphasis is placed on Russian-speakers living outside of Russia. Naturally the Ukraine is regarded as Russia's backyard and cultural heartland which should not fall under US and Western influence. While the Russian economy is no match for either traditional Western powers or its new partners in East Asia, indeed it is now only the size of South Korea, it is of strategic and vital importance as the prime energy supplier for Europe and increasingly for China. Although the control of energy supplies has been used for geopolitics, Russia has never cut supplies for its large customers knowing that its revenue heavily depends on selling its oil and gas. Although the size of the Russian economy is relatively small for the proclaimed great power ambition, it is not hampering Russia from modernizing its armed forces and maintaining a large and capable military power.[91]

Russia does not anymore possess the ability to be a global military actor but strives to be recognized as a great power when often being a regional one. Russia repeatedly demonstrated its willingness to defend its vital interest within its region and close to its borders assertively. Russia's closest competitor within BRICS is certainly China. Chinese economic potency was visibly demonstrated with the BRI which cross-cuts Eurasia, a region which Russia regards as its backyard.

In 2013 Russia adopted an official BRICS strategy.[92] The 18-page document resonates strongly with the BRICS summit declarations mentioned earlier. It displays a strong emphasis on multi-polarity and reform of global governance institutions, adherence to international law and "rejection of power politics and politics infringing on sovereignty of other states."[93] As Russia cannot make the normal and often moralizing claim of crafting South-South cooperation, the document speaks about overcoming East-West and North-South divides. Non-intervention in domestic affairs is referred to as well as territorial integrity. A clear position has been taken toward the UN Security Council and the use of force. Here Russia aims "to prevent the use of the UN, first of all the Security Council, to cover up the course towards removing undesirable regimes and imposing unilateral solutions to conflict situations, including those based on the use of force."[94] Russia does not see BRICS as a coalition for deep-reaching military or political cooperation but as a forum "to coordinate positions on strategic stability, international and regional security, non-proliferation of weapons of mass destruction, settlement of regional conflicts and the maintenance of regional stability."[95] The emphasis is clearly placed on regional security issues and not global ambitions. In this context the question, however, is how much convergence of interests Russia should expect from other BRICS countries when it comes to its own region. The Ukrainian crisis has shown that neither BRICS members condemned Russia for its unlawful annexation of the Crimean peninsula nor did Russia get much support for its approach toward the Ukraine.

The importance of BRICS to Russia should not be underestimated. With the return of Putin as president of the Russian Federation in 2012, the phase of pragmatic cooperation with the West and modernization of the country through closer links with the West under Medvedev came to an end. Since then Russia increasingly highlights its civilizational difference.[96] This and the transition to a multi-polar order in which non-Western powers play a more important role reinforced the perception in Russia that the country can legitimately claim great power status. Coinciding with the establishment of BRICS and despite rather sluggish economic growth Russia has invested heavily in the reform and modernization of its armed forces and continues to do so.[97] It will clearly not match up with the US or Soviet Union times but more agile and better equipped forces provide Russia with a foreign policy instrument it is willing to use should its key security interests be in jeopardy.

At the same time a more nationalistic turn at home functioned as regime-boosting effect for Putin who aimed at immunizing his power against Western liberal critique. Indeed, the BRICS countries have never criticized Russian human rights or democracy issues and neither has Russia criticized any of the BRICS members. Indeed security and economic links with China have intensified in recent years. Russia remains to be a key arms supplier for both India and China.

South Africa

Last in the group comes South Africa which initially did not form part of BRICS but was invited by China a few years later. South Africa was added to the group primarily to provide BRICS with a global reach and connect it to the developing world and African continent. No doubt in the concert of large powers South Africa remains a junior partner. With its population of just 50 million people and a size of the economy equaling that of Sweden and a defense budget of around $5bn, the country would normally not qualify as a globally significant power but it remains the potentially most influential country on the African continent. Limited prospects for economic growth, deep-reaching social and economic inequality, and institutionalized mismanagement and corruption under the Zuma presidency deprive the country of the opportunities and potential usually associated with a rising power. In the case of South Africa it is not the hard power capabilities through which the country can claim its place in the group of rising powers but the identification with the group's political aspirations and reformist agenda.[98] Being part of the BRICS grouping is clearly a status-enhancing opportunity allowing South Africa to punch above its expected diplomatic weight.

Still the inclusion of South Africa into the group is anything but trivial. The country, although closely rivaled by Nigeria, remains the largest and most developed economy on the continent and occupies a leading role in Africa and a dominant one in its direct neighborhood, Southern Africa. Despite South Africa lacking the credentials for being a continental hegemon it can be seen as a pivotal state. Its foreign policy went through substantial changes not only in comparison to the Apartheid regime but also during the Zuma tenure.

Historically the early years after the end of Apartheid were marked by a return of South Africa to the continent and global international politics as the country was banned from many international activities. Clearly Mandela was following a different track than his predecessor government. The politics of military intrusion in neighboring countries to suppress liberation movements abroad and at home had to be replaced. South Africa's domestic experience with reconciliation, mediation and liberation also inspired its foreign policy. Numerous examples exist in which South Africa used quiet diplomacy and mediation to solve violent conflict. Here to mention are the DRC, Darfur, Ivory Coast and Zimbabwe.[99]

With the presidency of Thabo Mbeki (1999–2008) the country's foreign policy sharpened in profile. Mbeki is best known for his African renaissance concept which anchors South Africa in the continent and promotes a political, economic and social emancipation from the existing peripheral position of the continent.[100] In this context South Africa has formulated a leadership position on the continent which goes beyond being a peacemaker and chief mediator. The country also sees itself as "a champion of Africa's interests abroad"[101] and places "Africa at the centre of South African foreign policy."[102] Within the BRICS grouping South Africa occupies the position as a gateway to Africa and in 2013 during the BRICS summit in Durban it invited a large African delegation to the meeting which was repeated in 2018 at the Johannesburg summit.

When it comes to the issue of global governance reform and security policies we can observe both a substantial degree of convergence and deviations from other BRICS countries. The 2011 Foreign Policy White Paper called "Building a Better World: The Diplomacy of Ubuntu" lays out the strategic thinking of the country. In the section on multilateralism it formulates dissatisfaction with the current system of global order which has changed little since the end of the Second World War and is deemed unfit for the twenty-first century. Unilateral action is clearly rejected. The White

Paper also identifies an "over-emphasis of the developed world on issues of peace and security" and calls for a closer alignment with the developmental agenda of Africa and the global South.[103]

The relationship with the UN resembles those of other BRICS countries in the sense that the primacy of the UN Security Council is recognized but a reform of the organization is demanded to provide for greater equity. A fairly detailed reform program was adopted in 2005 by the African Union, the Ezulwini Consensus, in which the continent claims seven seats to the Security Council, two permanent ones with veto power and five non-permanent.[104] On the question of interventions the South African and African position deviates from those of BRICS to some degree. On the African continent military interventions to end conflicts or out of national power interests are no singular event but occur frequently. While formally the use of force must be sanctioned by the UN Security Council AU member states found that a greater role must be played by regional organizations. Consequently the Ezulwini Consensus claims that in "certain situations, such approval could be granted 'after the fact' in circumstances requiring urgent action."[105] The authority of the Security Council is not seen as total and this view deviates from those of Brazil, Russia India and China who have formulated a more orthodox understanding of the role of the Council.

Regarding sovereignty South Africa takes a differentiated position. The Foreign Policy White Paper reiterates the importance of sovereignty as all other BRICS countries do but also says that "[t]he historical concepts of sovereignty and non-interference in domestic affairs are coming under legal scrutiny in the search for suitable responses for intervention."[106] Indeed interventions are a tool of South African foreign policy as can be seen in its engagement in Lesotho 1998 (without UN Security Council mandate), in Burundi initiating the first AU peacekeeping mission, the support for the FIB in the DRC, the military mission to the CAR or the initiation of a rapid intervention instrument at the level of the AU, the ACIRC. The latter even found entry into several BRICS summit documents. In terms of practicing interventions into armed conflicts South Africa might be the most actively involved country within the BRICS group.

In 2011 when the Security Council authorized resolution 1973 regarding the implementation of a no-fly zone over Libya and all BRICS countries served on the Council, only South Africa voted in favor of the resolution but later joined the BRICS voices in condemning the overstretching of the mandate and supporting the Brazilian position on the responsibility while protecting.[107] With the South African economy largely stagnating and tax revenue declining, the leeway for playing an active military role in armed conflict seems to shrink. In fact, South Africa's contribution to UN peacekeeping has halved in recent years, declining from roughly 2000 to around 1000 troops. At the same time other African countries, like Ethiopia, have taken over the top spot in the UN by deploying more than 8000 troops.[108] At the moment there is a leveled decline of South African military capability and a prolonged stagnation of its economy. In combination with the many corruption cases and state capture incidents the Zuma administration left South Africa considerably weakened.[109] Zuma was finally forced out of office and followed by his deputy Cyril Ramaphosa, who became president in February 2018. In his first year in office foreign policy priorities have shifted moderately. A more pragmatic approach attracting foreign direct investment (FDI) emphasizing the importance of economic diplomacy to overcome domestic weaknesses is getting stronger in contrast to a more ideologized approach of his predecessor.[110]

Conclusion

This first chapter provided an overview of the state of development and character of BRICS as a foreign policy grouping primarily focusing on security aspects. Thereby the group component and individual foreign policy positions are interconnected and cannot be neatly separated from one another. At the group level, BRICS countries display a fair degree of cohesion which they regularly express in summit declarations. Accordingly a rules-based order built on sovereign equality is at the center of BRICS rhetoric which is favoring a multi-polar world order and rejects unilateral interventionism. Regarding security aspects, BRICS does not form a strategic alliance. Only the fight against terrorism seems to be equally relevant for nearly all group members. Domestic security issues are generally not discussed. Due to the absence of clearly formulated strategic goals the response to large-scale armed conflict is only partially determined by fundamental group positions as expressed at summit meetings. Equally, if not more, important are individual foreign policy positions and trajectories which this chapter is introducing. While the common foreign policy thread within the group is their dissatisfaction with the current structure of the global order and their position as regionally powerful states, they do vary significantly with regard to their ability to project power. China, Russia and to some degree India (all three nuclear powers) have considerably more military power resources available than Brazil or South Africa. There are many more dividing lines between BRICS members reading their geopolitical interests, government systems or size of economies. While these differences do not as such incapacitate the group, they are likely to have a profound impact on the choice of response to armed conflict. Thus the BRICS group and individual country responses are both intimately connected with one another and separate fields. This will become visible in the later empirical Chaps. 3, 4, 5 and 6. The next chapter reviews the literature on regional powers providing a typology for response types as well as introducing six causal conditions explaining the choice for particular responses.

Notes

1. Acharya, Amitav (2017) "After Liberal Hegemony: The Advent of a Multiplex World Order" *Ethics & International Affairs* 31(3) 271–285.
2. Prys-Hansen, Miriam and Nolte, Detlef (2016) "BRICS und IBSA: Die Clubs der aufsteigenden Mächte verlieren an Glanz" GIGA Focus 5, October 2016, p. 6.
3. Hurrell, Andrew (2006) "Hegemony, liberalism and global order: what space for would-be great powers?" *International Affairs* 82(1), p. 6.
4. For a bargaining approach see: Narlikar, Amrita (2013) "Introduction Negotiating the rise of new powers", *International Affairs* 89(3), 561–576. A broader taxonomy is delivered by Destradi, Sandra (2010) "Regional powers and their strategies: empire, hegemony, and leadership" Review of International Studies 36, 903–930 or Prys, Miriam (2010) "Hegemony, domination, detachment: differences in regional powerhood." *International Studies Review* 12:479–504.
5. Regarding convergence a number of studies have explored BRICS voting within the UN; among them are: Ferdinand, Peter (2014) "Rising powers at the UN: an analysis of the voting behaviour of brics in the General Assembly", *Third World Quarterly*, 35(3), 376–391. Montenegro, Renan and Mesquita, Rafael (2017) "Leaders or Loners? How Do the BRICS Countries and their Regions Vote in the UN General Assembly" *Brazilian Political Science Review* 11 (2) 1–32.
6. Lipton, Merle (2017) "Are the BRICS reformers, revolutionaries, or counter-revolutionaries?" *South African Journal of International Affairs*, 24(1), 41–59.
7. Events for South Africa's 2018 BRICS Chairship, http://www.brics2018.org.za/sites/default/files/Documents/Calendar.pdf accessed 3 May 2018.

8. Krasner, Stephen (1983) *International Regimes*. Ithaca, London: Cornell University Press, p. 2.
9. Shepsle, Kenneth (2006) "Rational Choice Institutionalism" in Rhodes, R.A.W. et al. (eds) The Oxford Handbook of Political Institutions. Oxford: Oxford University Press, 23–38.
10. Pant, Harsh (2013) "The BRICS Fallacy", The Washington Quarterly, 36(3), 91–105.
11. Gvosdev, Nikolas (2012) "The Realist Prism: What the US can learn from the BRICS." *World Politics Review*, June 22. Accessed 7 May 2018 https://www.worldpoliticsreview.com/articles/12087/the-realist-prism-what-the-u-s-can-learn-from-the-brics
12. Pham, Quynh and Shilliam, Robbie (eds) *Meanings of Bandung, Postcolonial Orders and Decolonial Visions*. London, New York: Rowman & Littlefield.
13. Vieira, Marco (2012) Rising States and Distributive Justice: Reforming International Order in the Twenty-First Century, Global Society, 26(3), p. 323.
14. Thakur, Ramesh (2014) "How representative are BRICS?", *Third World Quarterly* 35(10), p. 1814.
15. Nel, Philip (2010) "Redistribution and recognition: what emerging regional powers want" *Review of International Studies* 36, p. 963.
16. Ibid., p. 968.
17. Hurrell, Andrew (2018) "Beyond the BRICS: Power, Pluralism, and the Future of Global Order" Ethics and International Affairs 32 (1), p. 93. See also Stuenkel, Oliver (2015) *Post-Western World How Emerging Powers are Remaking Global Order*. Cambridge and Malden: Polity.
18. Viswanathan, H.H.S (2015) "Building a Fair World Order" in Tolaraya, Gregory (ed) *VII BRICS Academic Forum*. National Committee on BRICS Research, Moscow, pp. 23–24.
19. De Coning, Cedric, Mandrup, Thomas, Odgaard, Liselotte (eds) (2015) *The BRICS and Coexistence: An Alternative Vision of World Order*. London and New York: Routledge, Taylor & Francis, p. 3.
20. De Coning (2015) "BRICS and coexistence" in De Coning, Cedric, Mandrup, Thomas, Odgaard, Liselotte (eds) (2015) The BRICS and Coexistence: An Alternative Vision of World Order. London and New York: Routledge, Taylor & Francis, p. 47.
21. De Coning, Cedric, Mandrup, Thomas and Odgaard, Liselotte (2018), p. 18.
22. BRICS Goa Declaration 2012, para. 58.
23. BRICS Sanya Declaration 2011, para. 5–6.
24. Ibid., para. 9.
25. BRICS Delhi Declaration 2012, para. 21.

26. BRICS eThekwini Declaration 2013, para. 24–31.
27. BRICS Fortaleza Declaration, 2014, para. 3.
28. Ibid., para. 26.
29. Ibid., para. 27.
30. Ibid., para. 27.
31. Ibid., para. 30.
32. Ibid., para 36.
33. Ibid., para 37.
34. Ibid., para 37.
35. BRICS Ufa Declaration 2015, para. 1.
36. Ibid., para 43.
37. Ibid., para. 36.
38. BRICS Goa Declaration 2016, para. 13.
39. Ibid., para. 59.
40. BRICS Xiamen Declaration 2017, para. 36.
41. Ibid., para. 48.
42. BRICS Johannesburg Declaration 2018, para. 5–7.
43. Ibid., para. 47.
44. Ibid., para. 49.
45. Ibid., para. 48.
46. Ibid., para. 52.
47. BRICS Academic Forum, Envisioning Inclusive Development Through a Socially Responsive Economy 28–31 May 2018, Johannesburg, Recommendations to the 10th BRICS Leaders' Summit, Johannesburg, 2018, para. 19.
48. Breslin, Shaun (2013) "China and the global order: signalling threat or friendship?" *International Affairs* 89(3), p. 628.
49. Brosig, Malte (2015) *Cooperative Peacekeeping in Africa Exploring Regime Complexity*. London, New York: Routledge. See also Klingebiel, Stephan (2016) "Global Problem-Solving Approaches: The Crucial Role of China and the Group of Rising Powers" Rising Powers Quarterly 1(1) 33–41. Patrick, Stewart (2014) "The Unruled World: The Case for Good Enough Global Governance" Foreign Affairs January/February 2014.
50. Singh, Kalpana (2016) "Intra-Brics Trade intensities: An Analytical study" *Journal Of Humanities And Social Science* 21(6), p. 107.
51. Troitskiy, Mikhail (2015) "BRICS Approaches to Security Multilateralism" *ASPJ Africa & Francophonie*, p. 77.
52. Tian, Nan, Fleurant, Aude Wezeman, Pieter and Wezeman, Siemon (2017) Trends in World Military Expenditure, 2016. SIPRI Fact Sheet April 2017. Accessed 26 Sep. 2017 https://www.sipri.org/sites/default/files/Trends-world-military-expenditure-2016.pdf
53. Kahler, Miles (2013) "Rising powers and global governance: Negotiating change in a resilient status quo", *International Affairs* 89(3), 711–729.

54. Kenkel, Kai Michael (2016) "Die Talfahrt einer aufstrebenden Macht: Brasiliens Krise und globale Präsenz" GIGA Focus | Lateinamerika | Nummer 2 | Juli 2016.
55. Degaut, Macros (2017) "Brazil's Military Modernization: Is a New Strategic Culture Emerging?" *Rising Powers Quarterly*, 2 (1), 271–297.
56. Destradi, Sandra (2017) "Reluctance in international politics: A conceptualization" *European Journal of International Relations*, 23(2), 315–340.
57. The Constitution of Brazil. Accessed 25 Sep. 2017. http://www.v-brazil.com/government/laws/titleI.html
58. Kenkel, Kai Michael (2012) "Brazil and R2P: Does Taking Responsibility Mean Using Force?" Global Responsibility to Protect 4, p. 14.
59. Former Defense Minister Jobim cited from Degaut, Macros (2017) "Brazil's Military Modernization: Is a New Strategic Culture Emerging?" *Rising Powers Quarterly*, 2 (1), p. 275.
60. Ibid., p. 276.
61. Ibid., p. 291.
62. Kenkel 2012, p. 28.
63. Stuenkel, Oliver (2019) "Bolsonaro's 5 Key Foreign Policy Challenges in 2019" Americas Quarterly, 16 January 2019. https://www.americasquarterly.org/content/bolsonaros-5-key-foreign-policy-challenges-2019 accessed 22 Jan. 2019.
64. Cheng, Joseph (2015) "China's Approach to BRICS," *Journal of Contemporary China*, 24:92, p. 358.
65. Breslin, p. 623.
66. Sinkkonen, Elina (2018) "China-Russia Security Cooperation Geopolitical Signalling with Limits" FIIA Briefing Paper 231, p. 7.
67. Liu, Tiewa and Zhang. Haibin (2014) "Debates in China about the responsibility to protect as a developing international norm: a general assessment," *Conflict, Security & Development*, 14:4, 403–427.
68. Hodzi, Obert (2019) *The End of China's Non-Intervention Policy in Africa*. Cham: Palgrave Macmillan.
69. White Paper: China's Peaceful Development Road (2011) State Council Information Office of China.
70. UN DPKO website http://www.un.org/en/peacekeeping/ accessed 27 Sep. 2017.
71. In August 2017 it even deployed 2654 troops. https://peacekeeping.un.org/en/troop-and-police-contributors accessed 27 May 2019.
72. Reuters: China formally opens first overseas military base in Djibouti. 1 Aug. 2017. https://www.reuters.com/article/us-china-djibouti/china-formally-opens-first-overseas-military-base-in-djibouti-idUSKBN1A-H3E3 Accessed 27 Sep. 2017.
73. Patey, Luke (2014). *The New Kings of Crude. China, India, and the Global Struggle for Oil in Sudan and South Sudan*. London: C. Hurst & Co.

74. Breslin, p. 633.
75. World Bank, "Belt and Road Initiative" Brief 29 March 2018. https://www.worldbank.org/en/topic/regional-integration/brief/belt-and-road-initiative accessed 1 Oct. 2018.
76. Xuejun, Wang (2018) "Developmental Peace: Understanding China's Africa Policy in Peace and Security" in Alden, Chris et al. (eds) *China and Africa Building Peace and Security Cooperation on the Continent*. Cham: Palgrave Macmillan, 67–82.
77. Narlika, Amrita (2013) "India rising: responsible to whom?" International Affairs 89(3) p. 605.
78. Mohan, Raja (2010) "Rising India: Partner in Shaping the Global Common?" *The Washington Quarterly* 33(3), p. 137.
79. Ibid., pp. 141–142.
80. Dasguptal, S 2016, "India, China agree on terrorism issue amid Azhar controversy", *The Times of India*. Accessed 28 May 2018, from http://timesofindia.indiatimes.com/india/India-China-agree-on-terrorism-issue-amid-Azhar-controversy/articleshow/54550860.cms
81. Destradi, Sandra (2017) "India's Reluctant Approach to R2P: Lessons from Perilous Interventions" *Global Responsibility to Protect* 9(2) p. 233.
82. Puri, Hardeep (2016) Perilous Interventions: The Security Council and the Politics of Chaos. Uttar Pradesh, London, Toronto, Scarborough, Sydney, New York: Harper Collins Publishers.
83. Hall, Ian (2015) "Is a 'Modi doctrine' emerging in Indian foreign policy?" *Australian Journal of International Affairs* 69(3) p. 250.
84. Hall, Ian (2016) "Multialignment and Indian Foreign Policy under Narendra Modi", *The Round Table*, 105(3) 271–286.
85. Sridharan, Eswaran (2015) "Rising or Constrained Power?" in Malone, David et al. (eds) The Oxford Handbook of Indian Foreign Policy. New Delhi: Oxford University Press, 699–712.
86. UN, DPKO: https://peacekeeping.un.org/en/troop-and-police-contributors accessed 1 Oct. 2018.
87. Destradi, Sandra (2017) "Reluctance in international politics: A conceptualization" European Journal of International Relations 23(2), p. 329.
88. Nikonov, Vyacheslav (2013) "BRICS: analysing the security dimension." BRICS Information Centre. Accessed 29 Sep. 2017 http://www.brics.utoronto.ca/newsdesk/durban/nikonov.html
89. Eitelhuber, Nobert (2009) "The Russian Bear: Russian Strategic Culture and What it Implies for the West" *The Quarterly Journal*, 9(1)10–12.
90. Putin's Prepared Remarks at 43rd Munich Conference on Security Policy. 12 February 2007. Accessed 29 Sep. 2017 http://www.washingtonpost.com/wp-dyn/content/article/2007/02/12/AR2007021200555.html
91. Rosefielde (2017) The Kremlin Strikes Back, Russia and the West after Crimea's Annexation. Cambridge: Cambridge University Press, 129–165.

92. Concept of participation of the Russian Federation in BRICS, Moscow 2013.
93. Ibid., para. 8b.
94. Ibid., para. 14a.
95. Ibid., Para. 16a.
96. Tsygankov, Andrei (2016) *Russia's Foreign Policy Change and Continuity in National Identity*. Lanham, Boulder, New York, London: Rowman & Littlefield, 4th edition, 233–260.
97. Klein, Margarete (2018) "Russlands Militärpolitik im postsowjetischen Raum, Ziele, Instrumente und Perspektiven" SWP Studie 19, September 2018, p. 13.
98. Alden, Chris and Schoeman, Maxi (2013) "South Africa in the company of giants: the search for leadership in a transforming global order," *International Affairs* 89(1), p. 115.
99. Curtis, Devon (2018) "South Africa's Peacemaking Efforts in Africa: Ideas, Interests and Influence" in Adebajo, Adekeye and Virk, Kudrat (eds) *Foreign Policy in Post-Apartheid South Africa*. London, New York: I.B. Tauris & Co. Ltd., 69–92.
100. Thabo Mbeki, The African Renaissance, South Africa and the World. United Nations University 9 April 1998. Accessed 2 Oct. 2017 http://archive.unu.edu/unupress/mbeki.html
101. Maite Nkoana-Mashabane, foreign minister, cited from Alden and Schoeman (2013), p. 116.
102. Building a Better World: The Diplomacy of Ubuntu White Paper on South Africa's Foreign Policy. Pretoria 13 May 2011.
103. Ibid., p. 24.
104. The Common African Position on the Proposed Reform of the United Nations. Executive Council 7th Extraordinary Session 7–8 March 2005, Addis Ababa, Ethiopia. P. 9.
105. Ibid., p. 6.
106. White Paper on South Africa's Foreign Policy, pp. 15–16.
107. Brosig, Malte and Zähringer, Natalie (2015) "Norm Evolution a Matter of Conformity and Contestedness: South Africa and the Responsibility to Protect" Global Responsibility to Protect 7(3) 352–378.
108. UN, DPKO: https://peacekeeping.un.org/en/troop-and-police-contributors accessed 1 Oct. 2018.
109. BBC News, "Zuma corruption claims: South Africa state capture inquiry opens" 20 August 2018. https://www.bbc.com/news/world-africa-45245121 accessed 22 January 2019.
110. SA News "Heads of Mission urged to lead investment drive" 23 Oct. 2018. https://www.sanews.gov.za/south-africa/heads-mission-urged-lead-investment-drive accessed 22 Jan 2019.

CHAPTER 2

Theoretical Framework: Modeling BRICS Response to Armed Conflict

BRICS countries over the years have acquired and maintained considerable military capacities. While they are still some distance away from matching their resources with traditional powers like the US, their capacities have grown to an extent which often makes them indispensable powers when it comes to conflict resolution. In order to have an influence on global order questions it might not be necessary to out-match capabilities of the current hegemon but it may suffice to have capabilities which rival or block the hegemonic competitor. If the twenty-first century is characterized by the observation that "power is becoming easier to disrupt and harder to consolidate,"[1] then the role of BRICS is almost naturally defined by shaping global order through blocking hegemonic power. Indeed BRICS countries might not always have the capacities to dominate solutions in armed conflicts but it is increasingly difficult to ignore or operate against the will of these countries. They have become pivotal powers.

In order to evaluate the influence BRICS countries exert in the global concert of nations it is not enough to refer to their economic weight or military equipment. More important is to explore how and when emerging powers get involved in armed conflict and what role they play. Research on BRICS and its security ambitions is still in its infancy and is dominated by grand conceptualizations which often address the issue of cooperation versus conflict.[2] Authors arguing from a realist perspective highlight the conflictive character of new powers rising while those from a liberal institutionalist perspective highlight how much the existing global governance

© The Author(s) 2019
M. Brosig, *The Role of BRICS in Large-Scale Armed Conflict*, New Security Challenges, https://doi.org/10.1007/978-3-030-18537-4_2

structures have facilitated the growth of new powers and thus assume that they are interested more in maintaining the status quo than radically changing it.[3]

In the end, a binary framing of the debate appears as too simplistic. BRICS countries are neither only spoilers and revisionist powers nor willful followers of the West. A more nuanced picture needs to be drawn to map the response of BRICS countries comprehensively in order to understand and evaluate their role in global politics and how they shape order. Given the diversity within the BRICS grouping and the diversity of foreign policy challenges these countries are facing, we should assume that they respond with a rich *repertoire* of instruments which is multi- but not mono-directional.

In this book global order questions are addressed by exploring the response of BRICS countries to large-scale armed conflict since the group was set up. The emphasis is not on reforming or transforming existing global governance institutions but rests on the actual playing out of international politics in specifically selected case studies. For the global security order violent conflicts constitute hard test cases. Around conflicts which are situations of stress, uncertainty and change through brute force global order is challenged, shaped or maintained. From this perspective the conceptual aim of this book is not to build an all-encompassing theory of rising powers and global order but to conceptualize rising powers and global order by exploring and explaining their response to large-scale armed conflict. This is primarily done by using a typological approach in which ideal type responses are formulated and contrasted with a number of causal conditions which are assumed to steer the involvement of BRICS countries in a variety of conflicts. Global order, it is argued, emerges from the interaction and involvement of these countries in violent conflicts. Such an approach takes account of multidimensional aspects of BRICS countries and their foreign policies which are not static but dynamically change from one issue area to another.

In the end, this study shows how far the influence of BRICS countries has grown when we focus on actual politics in cases of violent conflict. While reform attempts in global governance institutions are sluggish and BRICS seems not to be capable of transforming the UN, World Bank (WB) or the International Monetary Fund (IMF) substantially to its favor, the emphasis on institutional impact is not the only or most important instrument to evaluate influence on global order. The global security order also manifests itself through non-institutionalized interaction. In the field of great power politics and armed conflict the response to these conflicts constitutes global and regional order. The empirical sections will show that BRICS countries have grown to pivotal actors in the global security architecture, a fact that still finds too little attention in the literature. Emerging powers have already arrived at the center of global order and are actively shaping it.

A Typological Approach to Rising Powers

The advantage of a typological approach is that it is able to integrate a diversity of factors and variables in a systematic manner while still making causal conclusions. It avoids over-simplification and takes account of complex relationships without revoking the chances of exploring causal relationship which can lead to building better theories. In the words of George and Bennett typological theories consist of the "development of contingent generalizations about combinations or configurations of variables that constitute theoretical types."[4] The emphasis of a typological approach rests mainly on the exploration of configurations or sets of conditions for a particular outcome. In our case the question is, how do BRICS countries respond to armed conflict and which conditions impact on the selection of a specific response type?

Logically we can assume that the repertoire of responses is diverse and countries are responding differently in different situations. Based on the literature on rising powers we can develop a number of ideal type general responses and add a number of more specific sub-types which are forming the dependent variable. This will be done in the paragraphs below. For modeling BRICS response and role in armed conflict a range of causal conditions can be assumed to impact on the choice of response types. Very likely the number of independent variables is extensive and changing between actors and cases. In opposition to traditional methods of comparison (Mill) the aim is not to isolate a single master condition but to empirically verify a combination of conditions that lead to a particular response. In this regard a typological approach highlights the importance of configurations of causal conditions and takes account of the phenomenon of equifinality. The research design of the study is thus more case- than variable-oriented. In order to avoid the problem of over-determination (generalization) from only a few cases and countries the study explores four major conflicts tracing the involvement of the five BRICS countries in them. This provides for a solid set of cases and variables to explore.

How Do BRICS Countries Respond to Armed Conflict?

Because BRICS is no organization and has little agency of itself the operationalization of the dependent variable, response type, takes inspiration from the literature on emerging and regional powers.[5] Interest in research on emerging and regional powers equally increased with the formation of BRICS if not already before it.[6] The establishment of the BRICS grouping is certainly an offspring of the growing economic and political weight of rising powers in the world and thus the literature is interested in very similar questions which circle around how these countries are going to change the existing global order.[7] Very often the emphasis was placed on economics.[8] Few studies have explored the security multilateralism of BRICS and developed a typology of responses.[9] In general research did not presume the existence of a blueprint for behavior and thus scholarship often referred to different types of responses. Unfortunately the literatures on rising powers and on BRICS hardly cross-reference each other. While research on rising powers has developed a number of conceptual frameworks for analysis, research on BRICS is predominantly empirically oriented. Therefore this study aims at connecting these two streams of research by transferring some conceptual ideas from the rising powers literature to the analysis of BRICS and their role in global order questions.

The rising and regional powers literature often operates with three/four baseline assumptions. According to Pedersen regional great powers can be categorized by exerting power as unilateral hegemon, cooperative hegemon, through empire and in concert.[10] Destradi distinguishes between leadership, hegemony and empire.[11] Prys compares and characterizes regional powers as regional detached powers, hegemons or dominators.[12] Wigell develops a typology for regional powers and their geo-economic interests in which he distinguishes between four types: neo-imperialism, neo-mercantilism, hegemony and liberal institutionalism.[13] Frazier and Stewart-Ingersoll explore regional powers within security complexes and characterize their behavior as consisting of three main types: regional leadership, regional custodian and regional protector.[14]

While differences exist in detail between these various typologies most authors have in common that they describe a nexus between coercion understood as unilateralism, domination, political power on the one side and cooperative behavior in the form of leadership and multilateralism on the other. Often a hybrid category is placed somewhere in the middle which combines the use of classical power resources with cooperative elements. Regional powers, it is assumed, do not display a single type of response but vary according to different context.[15] What is missing in the literature is often a deeper-reaching analysis of what conditions are leading to what type of responses. It is in this area to which the study wants to make a conceptual contribution.

The typologies which have been developed in the literature usually take a macro approach. They are developed to explore the general standing of regional powers mostly within their regional neighborhood and sometimes within the context of global order. While the latter certainly also consists of the former the focus of this study transcends the traditional focus of regional power influence in either their home region or at the global stage. The BRICS perspective ideally links the two spheres and additionally provides for a cross-regional perspective given the wide geographical distribution of the BRICS countries. Furthermore, this study applies to four specific cases of large-scale armed conflict. This warrants specifying and adapting existing typologies by additional sub-types. The following paragraphs are based on the literature mentioned above and adapt to the specific case studies explored in this study.

At the macro level a distinction is made between cooperative, hegemonic and neo-imperialist behavior as ideal type possible responses to large-scale armed conflict (see Fig. 2.1). Each response type is accompanied by two sub-types which can be seen as a soft and hard version of it. Attached to each response (sub)-type are instruments and means through

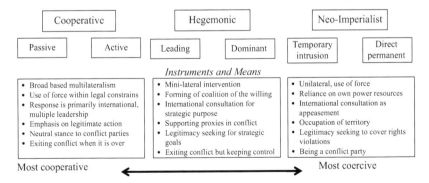

Fig. 2.1   Ideal response types and instruments

which engagement in armed conflict is further operationalized. Accordingly cooperative behavior is characterized by either a passive acceptance of international multilateral solution finding or a more active building of an international response to a crisis using established means of global governance. The hegemonic response can be divided between hegemony which is leading in concert and hegemony which aims at domineering but using mini-lateral followership to reach its goals. Lastly neo-imperialistic behavior can be characterized by either direct and permanent intervention or temporary but intrusive engagement.

A wide range of instruments and means exist through which regional powers exert their influence. In the cooperative response type we would assume that whatever action is chosen it is integrated into a multilateral framework which extends beyond narrow coalition partners of the respective home region. Action is taken within the confines of international law. With regard to interventions and the use of force it needs to be authorized through the UN Security Council and be compatible with the UN Charter in addition to procedures and obligations stemming from regional organizations. A strong emphasis is placed on legitimate action and multilateral action which ideally aims at bringing violent conflict to an end through appropriate means which usually excludes becoming a warring party in the conflict pursuing individual goals. This cooperative response can be taken either through passively following a multilateral approach already started by others or by actively shaping this process, for example by providing crucial resources for conflict mediation or containment such as supporting the UN in peacekeeping missions. Providing such global public goods needed for conflict solution can be seen as acting out of a sense of responsibility and global citizenship and is a case of collective burden-sharing.

The hegemonic response type partly changes the perspective from multilateralism and non-partisan engagement in armed conflict to engagement which is based on a coalition of the willing who act under the leadership or dominance of a regional power. While action is principally multilateral and legal, strategic considerations play an important role. Coalition building and seeking international legitimacy are means to reach certain strategic ends. Engagement in armed conflict may or may not be about wanting to see a particular party winning or losing but the hegemon is getting involved to exert influence in the long run.

Finally the neo-imperialist perspective is the most coercive response type. Here a distinction can be made between temporary intrusion and permanent and direct domination. Neo-imperialist action is characterized by unilateral action which requires the use of individual power resources. The neo-imperial power may not actively seek international legitimacy but uses consultations (multilateral instruments) as a means to appease the international community in order to disperse concerns about its expansionist approach. Neo-imperialism might also imply a territorial dimension and the permanent occupation of territory. The neo-imperialist power is a warring party in the conflict either directly through sending its own troops or by controlling and arming proxy forces in line with its strategic interests.

These are ideal type responses which occupy a nexus between cooperative and coercive behavior. Very likely regional powers as well as BRICS as a grouping will display a large variety of responses adapted to the context in which they are operating but not necessarily only a single type. The typology also only displays ideal responses which in practice may be more difficult to isolate neatly from one another. The ideal type responses and their means and instruments for action basically describe possible foreign policy options from which states can select their most preferred one. Whether states actually follow a certain rationality and reasoning of action remains to be seen and will be explored in the empirical chapters of this book. The extreme forms of response as characterized by being either fully multilateral or fully neo-imperial might indeed be rare exceptions. As BRICS countries display significant power resources the likelihood of these countries to use them can be assumed to be relatively high, while at the same time none of the BRICS countries is large and dominant enough to be able to enforce unilateral solutions.

More likely are middle-ground positions in which countries aim at equally exploiting the advantages that come with cooperative multilateralism (international legitimacy, pooling of power) and neo-imperialism (uncompromised influence) by avoiding their potential disadvantages of having only limited influence on events and being portrayed as an international outcast (rogue state). A middle hegemonic position of minilateralism and strategic use of legitimacy might be the preferred method of rising powers such as BRICS.

One of the key research goals of this study is not only to explore how BRICS countries respond to large-scale conflict but also explaining the choice for a specific response. The next section presents a number of variables which help explaining what response type countries choose and why they move between choices.

Variables and Response Types

Most of the literature on emerging powers and BRICS aims at exploring the effect rising countries have on questions of global and regional order. There is no shortage of typologies as mentioned above. The consequences of power shifts are increasingly well documented and the literature on rising powers has started revisiting and updating its conceptual frameworks, of which most of them have been developed almost a decade ago.[16] What is less researched, however, are often the underlying causes of responses mapped out in the various typologies. The literature often remains rather general and at the macro level of analysis. Therefore, this section presents a number of causal conditions which are assumed to impact on the choice of response type. A total of six variables are introduced. The variables proposed are a combination of various traditional foreign policy analysis (FPA) conditions and partially also the peace and conflict literature.[17] They are based on a variety of mainstream international relations (IR) theories. The spectrum ranges from more realist and rational choice arguments of material power capabilities and economic interests placed in the context of strategic and rational decision-making to constructivist arguments around norms and legitimacy in international relations. Empirically it needs to be shown which combination of conditions can be linked to a particular response type. The six variables presented are primarily a collection of conditions which are logically assumed to have an impact. No prior statement is made about a hierarchy of effects. The following chapters need to show if how, when and why these conditions are influencing the response to armed conflict. Rather unlikely seems to be the assumption that there will be a single master variable explaining outcomes. More likely is that response types can be traced back to their own set of combination of conditions. What combination of conditions leads to what particular response type is an empirical question.

First, BRICS countries are mostly regional powers with the exception of China which has global influence. This means the influence of individual BRICS countries is somehow limited to their home region or at least can be expected to be the greatest within their region in opposition to having global or cross-regional impact. For the involvement in armed conflict this means that geography matters. Far away conflicts outside the home region can be assumed to provide a much smaller incentive to get involved than conflicts in the vicinity. Proximity to conflict can thus be a trigger variable providing for a baseline motivation for engagement. The closer the conflict, the more likely we can expect a response.

Geography and conflict have been a focus of parts of the peace and conflict literature. The spatial dimension of conflict has traditionally been explored as being linked to border disputes or issues of conflict contagion.[18] Later research has further developed the geospatial ontology by highlighting that spatiality is also a social dimension and that proximity cannot exclusively be counted in kilometers from a certain place.[19] Cultural spaces or international trade relations extend far beyond the narrow parameters of national borders or the spatial confines of violent conflict.[20] For example the extensive trade relations China has developed with most of the rest of the world connect the country almost inevitably with conflict zones far away from its borders and might have a considerable effect on its economy and thus become a question of strategic interests too. In this context the rise of BRICS countries was primarily facilitated through an acceleration of economic globalization and an intensifying of global trade. None of the five members was growing its economy solely on the basis of a strong domestic market.

For BRICS countries proximity to conflict is thus a dimension which should be defined in terms of its interconnection to conflict-affected areas. This can take different forms such as direct military effects (attack of its border by armed groups), disruption of international trade, loss of property and investment in conflict-affected areas, physical threat to foreign nationals or conflict contagion to the wider region. Given that many violent conflicts are intra-state but also have a regional dimension and usually affect questions of international order and power, the likelihood is quite high that one or more BRICS countries are affected by armed conflict in one way or the other. The declarations of the annual BRICS summits have thus considerably expanded over time and now make regular reference to almost all (major) conflicts of our time. In the end, one can assume that the closer BRICS countries are positioned to a conflict in terms of their interconnectivity, the more likely it is for BRICS countries to take a position and engage.

Second, a realist and rational choice-oriented approach highlights the importance of power capabilities. A classical understanding of power defines it as control over resources. While indeed many definitions exist and the term remains contested this section refers to its classical realist understanding.[21] The emphasis of power as a resource following the realist perspective might be warranted as we are operating in the realm of power politics and strategic interest. If BRICS countries are engaged in armed conflict and take a deliberate choice to do so, we would assume that consideration has been given to available individual power capabilities which are set in relation to strategic goals.[22] In principle only available resources can be used and the use of them is conditioned on the strategic goals the country wants to achieve. As we are dealing with armed conflict, military but also political power resources do play a central role.

Following the operationalization of the dependent variable one can think of a number of instruments reaching from direct military encounter, to arming proxy actors, implementing an arms embargo (or preventing one) or using economic sanctions or political pressure. In principle one can assume that the larger the individual power basis is, the more inclined the countries are to use their resources in order to achieve their goals. Naturally the use of resources is not simply reducible to individual capabilities and achieving strategic goals but would also correspond to the use of resources by other actors involved. As discussed in Chap. 1 BRICS countries are on average more powerful in the economic sphere and are not currently matching up with the military power of larger Western countries. This can compromise goal attainment by use of military capabilities. From this perspective one would assume that BRICS countries are rather reluctant to use their military might, given that their prospects for goal attainment are uncertain. However, in situations in which resources are easily available and prospects for success are good one should assume that their use is significantly more likely.

Third, the type of conflict might influence the response from BRICS countries. Engagement in violent conflict, assuming countries aim at reaching certain foreign policy goals which usually require some influence on the ground, needs to match the degree of the conflict. Localized domestic unrest hardly justifies a military intervention and the use of diplomatic and economic tools might be sufficient to have a stake and reach one's goal. In large-scale conflicts more assertive action might be needed to make a difference which might include military assets such as sending peacekeepers, arming groups or intervening directly. As this study only explores BRICS engagement in large-scale violent conflict, instances of lower-level violence are not examined. The question with regard to BRICS and its agenda is to which extent is large-scale violent conflict addressing and changing the political order? Is it confined to the country in conflict and thus merely of domestic relevance or does it address questions of regional importance in which a BRICS member plays a pivotal role? And lastly is the conflict altering the global order?

In principle one would assume that BRICS countries as a group are drawn into conflict if it can alter the global order in opposition to conflicts which might be intense but are mostly localized. The motivation for BRICS engagement in armed conflict affecting global order might be twofold. It can be seen as providing the opportunity to influence changes in global order in favor of BRICS priorities or engagement in violent conflict is seen as preventing changes in global order running against their core interests. If conflicts are used to fundamentally alter basic principles of external intervention, constructing legal and moral authority this should be high on the BRICS agenda and provide first-class incentives for BRICS engagement.

From a regional position the perspective looks somehow different. If conflict merely touches upon regional order, this might not affect all BRICS countries equally and thus has an asymmetric effect. In such situations one might expect that the group interest is somehow limited but countries are generally supportive to each other or at least do not undermine their peer's policy in the respective home region. The issue becomes more complicated if regional leadership is unclear or contested, which is the case in Asia with India and China. In all other cases BRICS members do not overlap with one another in their particular region.

Fourth, given the size of BRICS economies and the untamed globalization which brings growing international interdependencies, economic interests undeniably play an important foreign policy role. A rather simple baseline assumption is that the economic significance of the conflict conditions the response from BRICS countries. Hardly is it realistic to assume that BRICS countries take a keen interest in conflicts to which there are only peripheral linkages. While situations in which vital economic interests are at stake are better suited for external responses. However, what constitutes vital or peripheral economic interests certainly varies between countries. For a strong manufacturing and export-oriented nation such as China access to natural resources, free trade and securing its foreign investments are key priorities. In the case of export-oriented countries which rely on selling natural resources to global markets such as Brazil, Russia and South Africa, their economic well-being often simply depends on high commodity prices which is typically linked to strong global growth. As regional hegemons they are also often heavily invested in their home region.

Most likely different conflicts will display different sets of economic priorities for BRICS countries. While in the case of Libya and South Sudan access to natural resources is of higher relevance to China and India,[23] it is of no economic priority for Brazil, Russia and South Africa. In the case of Ukraine it of course has the strongest links to Russia while being of no importance to the rest of BRICS. In the case of economic interests it might well be that it is not possible to clearly identify a common BRICS position as there is great diversity between countries and conflicts. However, at the individual level economic interests may well provide direct and strong incentives to strongly respond to armed conflict. Whether strong economic incentives are leading to more coercive behavior to protect key interests or cooperative behavior to safe investments needs to be explored empirically.

Fifth, beyond capability and interest-oriented arguments which are mostly based on material and rational choice decisions there is also a social dimension.[24] As regards BRICS group involvement in armed conflict one can assume that those conflicts which allow countries to act upon their normative (BRICS) agenda provide for better access points than conflicts which do not resonate with this agenda. The argument made here is one which has been well articulated in the compliance research, especially within the field of norm adoption in Europe.[25] Within the concept of misfit states are assumed to be more likely to comply if their domestically held norms are in match with international norms. In cases in which a significant mis-match is obvious states will adopt and apply these policies much more reluctantly. The underlying logic is one of domestic cost-benefit calculations. Policies are likely to diffuse more easily when domestic adjustment costs are low; the opposite applies if they are high.[26]

For the case of BRICS countries the question is if engagement in armed conflict resonates with the normative BRICS agenda which emphasizes the importance of a neo-Westphalian order built on uncompromised sovereign equality. An equal emphasis has been placed on the primacy of the UN Security Council for dealing with violent conflict, compliance with the UN Charter as well as the non-use of force and apprehension against coercive means of foreign policy. While these are rather broad goals different conflicts might vary considerably in the degree to which they can be linked up to these goals. Thus one can assume that the greater the normative match between conflict characteristics and the BRICS agenda, the more likely it is that BRICS countries relate to a conflict jointly.

Sixth, following a more constructivist understanding of international relations emphasizing the constitutive role of norms, identities, political culture and legitimacy there may also be a deeper-reaching social dimension of how and when BRICS countries relate to violent conflict.[27] In other words BRICS response might not exclusively be a consequence of geostrategic or economic interests, but it may also result from acting upon global social norms which call upon the international community to solve violent conflicts multilaterally through instruments of, for example, conflict mediation or peacekeeping and within existing multilateral structures. In this context the motivation for engaging in armed conflict might not be narrow self-interest but acting in line with global humanitarian norms, aiming to contain further bloodshed and creating conditions for lasting peace. This perspective might indeed be of relevance for emerging powers, as their growing influence suggests a greater role of these countries when it comes to providing global public goods and representing the international community normatively. A country like China has for a long time invested in its image as a peacefully rising power. Engagement in armed conflict as a peacemaker thus provides opportunities for large powers to present and act upon global norms.

Conclusion

In sum, six conditions are explored which are expected to impact on the selected choice of response type to violent conflict. These are: proximity to conflict understood as effects of conflict on BRICS countries, availability of power resources in relation to strategic interests, the type of conflict in terms of its effects on global order questions, economic consequences of the conflict on BRICS members, the extent to which conflict engagement can resonate with the normative BRICS agenda and lastly responding to conflict in order to act upon global humanitarian norms. The empirical analysis needs to show which combination of conditions is leading to what particular response type. Furthermore, response types and variables are formulated in a manner which allows a two-level analysis. We can explore both the reaction of individual BRICS member states and the response of BRICS as a grouping. Because BRICS is as such no independent actor, its essence is very much the sum of its members; a strong emphasis is placed on individual country behavior and how this converges (or not) into a collective response which is expressed within the BRICS framework. In the end, the two spheres cannot always be separated neatly.

While the sections above have operationalized the outcome as well as formulated causal variables, a key question remains. What is the mechanism through which the independent variables work and influence the choice of response type? The literature refers to the space in-between the causal and outcome variable usually as the causal mechanism.[28] This study conceptualizes the causal mechanism through the availability of opportunity structures which guide the way from causes to effects. The issue of opportunity structure has usually been discussed within the literature on protest movements referring to exogenous conditions inhibiting or facilitating movements to develop.[29] In the context of this study the focus on opportunity structures simply refers to those six conditions introduced above in combination with a rational choice approach highlighting costs and benefits of presumed action.[30] The lighter the costs but higher the benefits, the more likely the countries are willing to respond to armed conflict. If costs are higher and benefits are uncertain the less likely engagement becomes. With regard to response types a baseline assumption is that the more favorable the opportunity structure is, the more likely engagement in armed conflict becomes as well as more coercive. The degree of intrusion thus depends on favorable opportunities in terms of cost-benefit calculations.

To use a specific example: A BRICS member state feels compelled to respond to armed conflict if it is close to it, commands over military capabilities which can be made available fairly easily corresponding to the attainment of certain strategic interests and if the conflict affects the country's economic development there are good reasons to assume that the reaction is fairly strong. If one or more of these conditions are weaker the response will mostly likely adjust and change to less coercive or intrusive instruments. Less intrusive responses might also be a consequence of a more normative approach. If the key motivation for responding to armed conflict is to be aligned to the normative BRICS agenda or is based on humanitarian grounds to be perceived as a good global citizen, hegemonic or neo-imperialist behavior is counter-productive. Furthermore, the country can be expected to use the BRICS grouping as a venue to multilateralize its action if fellow members are either sharing the same or a similar opportunity structure or if the conflict addresses global order questions and resonates with the BRICS agenda.

These are baseline logical assumptions which need to be validated in detail empirically. A number of questions can be raised already now. Do all conditions need to display a positive opportunity structure in order to respond in a neo-imperial coercive manner or is there a single master variable? If a combination of conditions leads to a particular response type (cooperative, hegemonic, neo-imperial) in a particular conflict does it transcend and the same combination can be found in the other case studies?

Are some variables more relevant than others in triggering a certain response? How will individual countries and the BRICS group respond if the cost-benefit calculation is inconclusive or deviates significantly among themselves? What happens if the opportunity structures provide for opposing incentives between causal conditions? These questions can only be answered after a cross-case empirical analysis and will be addressed in the concluding chapter which also engages in hypotheses building on the basis of the empirical analysis, following an inductive approach to research design.

Notes

1. Naím, Moisés cited in Stuenkel (2016) *Post Western World How Emerging Powers Are Remaking Global Order.* Malden, MA: Polity, p. 27.
2. See for example: Breslin, Shaun (2013) "China and the global order: signalling threat or friendship?" International Affairs 89(3), 615–634 or Kastner, Scott L. and Saunders, Philip C. (2012) "Is China a Status Quo or Revisionist State? Leadership Travel as an Empirical Indicator of Foreign Policy Priorities" *International Studies Quarterly* 56(1), 163–177.
3. Kahler, Miles (2013) "Rising powers and global governance: Negotiating change in a resilient status quo", International Affairs 89(3), 711–729.
4. George, Alexander and Bennett, Andrew (2005) *Case Studies and Theory Development in the Social Sciences.* Cambridge, Massachusetts, London: MIT Press, p. 233.
5. Hart, Andrew and Jones, Bruce (2010) "How Do Rising Powers Rise?", Survival, 52(6), 63–88. Nolte, Detlef (2010) "How to compare regional powers: analytical concepts and research topics" Review of International Studies 36, 881–901.
6. Hurrell, Andrew (2006) "Hegemony, liberalism and global order: what space for would-be great powers?" International Affairs 82(1), 1–19.
7. Kahler, Miles (2013) "Rising powers and global governance: Negotiating change in a resilient status quo", International Affairs 89(3), 711–729.
8. Narlikar, Amrita (2013) "Introduction Negotiating the rise of new powers", International Affairs 89(3), 561–576. Wigell, Mikael (2016) "Conceptualizing regional powers' geoeconomic strategies: neo-imperialism, neo-mercantilism, hegemony, and liberal institutionalism" *Asia Europe Journal* 14, 135–151. Stephen, Matthews (2014) "Rising powers, global capitalism and liberal global governance: A historical materialist account of the BRICs challenge" European Journal of International Relations 20(4) 912–938.
9. The exception is Troitskiy, Mikhail (2015) "BRICS Approaches to Security Multilateralism" ASPJ Africa & Francophonie 76–88 who is maybe the

only one who has categorized BRICS responses toward the West. He distinguishes between four response types which are asymmetric, legal constrains, matching strategies and cooperation.
10. Pedersen, Thomas (2002). "Cooperative hegemony: power, ideas and institutions in regional integration", *Review of International Studies* 28, 682.
11. Destradi, Sandra (2010) "Regional powers and their strategies: empire, hegemony, and leadership" *Review of International Studies* 36, 903–930.
12. Prys, Miriam (2010) "Hegemony, domination, detachment: differences in regional powerhood", *International Studies Review* 12, 479–504.
13. Wigell, Mikael (2016) "Conceptualizing regional powers' geoeconomic strategies: neo-imperialism, neo-mercantilism, hegemony, and liberal institutionalism" *Asia Europe Journal* 14, 135–151.
14. Frazier, Derrick V. and Robert Stewart-Ingersoll (2010) "Regional Powers and Security: A Framework for Understanding Order within Regional Security Complexes" *European Journal of International Relations* 16(4): 731–753.
15. Destradi, p. 929.
16. Nolte, Detlef (2018) "Regional powers revisited: Status and leadership roles" paper presented at the Regional Powers Revisited conference at GIGA Hamburg 26–27 April 2018.
17. Carlsnaes, Walter (2013) "Foreign Policy." In Walter Carlsnaes, Thomas Risse, and Beth A. Simmons, eds., *Handbook of International Relations*. 2nd ed. London: Sage, 298–325.
18. Diehl, Paul (1991) "Geography and war: A review and assessment of the empirical literature" *International Interaction* 17(1) 11–27.
19. Starr, Harvey (2005) "Territory, Proximity, and Spatiality: The Geography of International Conflict" *International Studies Review* 7, 387–406.
20. Robst, John, Polachek, Solomon and Chang, Yuan-Ching (2007) "Geographic Proximity, Trade, and International Conflict/Cooperation" *Conflict Management and Peace Science* 24(1) 1–24.
21. Mattern, Janice (2008) "The Concept of Power and the (Un)discipline of International Relations" in Reus-Smit, Christian and Snidal, Duncan (eds) *The Oxford Handbook of International Relations*. http://www.oxfordhandbooks.com/view/10.1093/oxfordhb/9780199219322.001.0001/oxfordhb-9780199219322-e-40 accessed 14 Nov. 2017.
22. Frazier, Derrick V. and Robert Stewart-Ingersoll (2010).
23. Patey, Luke (2014). The New Kings of Crude. China, India, and the Global Struggle for Oil in Sudan and South Sudan. London: C. Hurst & Co.
24. Vendulka Kubalkova (ed.) (2001) *Foreign Policy in a Constructed World*. Armonk, NY: M.E. Sharpe.

25. Treib, Oliver (2014) "Implementing and complying with EU governance outputs", *Living Reviews in European Governance*, 9(1): http://www.livingreviews.org/lreg-2014-1 accessed 16 Nov. 2017.
26. Börzel, Tanja (2000) "Why There Is No 'Southern Problem': On Environmental Leaders and Laggards in the European Union", *Journal of European Public Policy* 7(1): 141–162. Risse, Thomas, Cowles, Maria, Caporaso (2001) "Europeanization and Domestic Change: Introduction" in Risse, Thomas et al. (eds) Transforming Europe Europeanization and Domestic Change. New York: Cornell University Press.
27. Finnemore, Martha (1996) "Norms, culture, and world politics: Insights from sociology's institutionalism," International Organization, 50 (2): 325–347. Finnemore, Martha and Sikkink, Kathryn (1998), "International Norm Dynamics and Political Change" International Organization 52(4), 887–917.
28. Falleti, Tulia and Lynch, Julia (2009) "Context and Causal Mechanisms in Political Analysis," *Comparative Political Studies* 42, 91,143–1166. Bennett, Andrew (2013) "The mother of all isms: Causal mechanisms and structured pluralism in International Relations theory" *European Journal of International Relations* 19(3) 459–481.
29. Meyer, David and Minkoff, Debra (2004) "Conceptualizing Political Opportunity" *Social Forces* 82 (4) 1457–1492.
30. Snidal, Duncan (2013) "Rational Choice and International Relations" in Carlsnaes, Walter, Risse Thomas and Simmons, Beth (eds) *Handbook of International Relations*. Sage Publishing, 85–111.

CHAPTER 3

Libya: From R2P to Regime Change—The BRICS Awakening

Of all violent conflicts explored in this study the Libyan crisis is likely to be the most researched and most passionately debated one.[1] This has much to do with the complex environment in which the crisis took place. Humanitarian reasons for intervention are in as much credible as grand politics was played out mostly, but not exclusively, by Western powers. What makes the Libyan case particularly intricate is the first-time application of the concept of the responsibility to protect (R2P) by using force to stop violence against civilians through ousting a charismatic but brutal African leader, Muammar Gaddafi.[2] This sparked considerable academic and policy debate. Issues of military intervention as well as norm evolution have been discussed in the literature extensively. In contrast, this chapter is closely tracing and exploring the response of BRICS countries to the crisis.

The Libyan crisis is an important one because it was the first major international crisis since the establishment of BRICS. By coincidence in 2011 and 2012 all BRICS countries were members of the Security Council, giving the group of emerging powers potential leverage on the diplomatic scene. It is thus an important but early test case for BRICS and opportunity to demonstrate how a more multi-polar world would manage violent conflict.

It is no secret that the BRICS received the events in Libya with much bitterness as they felt once more outfoxed by a Western-led coalition which uses humanitarian language to poorly disguise their neo-imperial politics and regime change. However, at the center of this and the following chapters are not the Western engagement and its open or concealed strategic goals but the BRICS countries and their response to the crisis. Even though BRICS did not acquire a clear leadership role in this crisis, its reaction to it is anything but marginal and has far-reaching consequences for later conflicts and in particular the war in Syria. In this regard the Libyan crisis constitutes a formative phase for BRICS with regard to international security politics. It has fundamentally formed convictions about military interventions, R2P and reinforced the feeling among BRICS that their pledge for a multi-polar world is needed more than ever.

The empirical chapters first provide a short overview of the main events happening during the conflict before tracing the individual positions and responses of each country within the BRICS grouping. Later sections

---

Box 3.1   Time Line of Events 2011

15 February	Protest begins in Eastern Libya in the city of Benghazi
22 February	League of Arab States condemns use of force against civilians
26 February	UN Security Council adopts Resolution 1970, refers Gaddafi to the ICC
27 February	Formation of the Transitional National Council (TNC) in Benghazi
5 March	TNC declares itself as sole representative of Libya and calls upon international community to protect the population
7 March	The Gulf Cooperation Council calls for a no-fly zone, followed by the Organization of Islamic Cooperation on 8 and LAS on 12 March
10 March	France is the first country to recognize the TNC, while the AU rejects any kind of foreign intervention in Libya
17 March	UN Security Council adopts Resolution 1973
19 March	Coalition forces begin bombing government positions
22 March	BRICS blames West for overstepping mandate and demand immediate ceasefire
25 March	AU adopts road map for Libya
11 April	AU High Level Panel travels to Libya
14 April	BRICS summit, Sanya
15 April	The US, the UK and France announce bombings would continue until Gaddafi is removed
30 May	South African President Jacob Zuma meets Gaddafi in Tripoli
21 June	The chairman of the TNC, Mahmoud Jibril, visits Beijing
27 June	ICC issues arrest warrant for Gaddafi
22 August	Rebel forces capture Tripoli
16 September	UN officially recognizes TNC
20 October	Gaddafi gets killed

explore the collective response of BRICS and apply the conceptual framework with its differentiation between various response types and the six variables which are assumed to steer the choice of response to the conflict.

The Libyan Conflict Unfolding

Events in Libya and the international reaction to it developed rather rapidly. From the outbreak of public protest against Gaddafi in mid-February 2011 to military intervention by 19 March only 32 days passed; five months later Tripoli fell to the rebels and by 20 October Gaddafi was murdered (see Box 3.1). Within the first 30 days of the crisis the UN Security Council adopted two resolutions. This rapid speed of events certainly privileged those actors with clear strategic goals and better coordination. The phase for multilateral interest formation was rather short. Thus established powers within the Security Council like the P3 had a certain advantage over the BRICS group which was placed for the first time into a situation in which rapid and far-reaching decisions had to be made. From the unraveling of events both in Libya and in New York BRICS countries appeared as somehow outpaced by the P3 and throughout the crisis struggled to formulate an alternative to the Western-led and Arab-supported intervention.

The roots of the Arab Spring are many. Maybe the most important ones are long-term autocratic regimes which left people with little opportunity to express their grievances. Rulers like Ben Ali, Hosni Mubarak and Muammar Gaddafi have been in power for decades leading their countries into political inertia, leaving little prospect for political reforms. Unlike autocratic leaders in Morocco or Jordan who can claim political legitimacy from their status as religious leaders, leadership in Tunisia, Egypt, Libya and Syria was mostly secured through building a police state and using means of suppression for dissenting voices. Missing economic opportunities for the rapidly growing and young population while ruling elites accumulated enormous wealth gradually nurtured revolutionary resistance. As the internal pressure from these structural conditions was mounting, it is difficult to predict when dissatisfaction and anger have built up to an extent leading to a mass popular movement which is courageous enough to demand the ousting of its leadership. Consequently, very few predicted the outbreak of the Arab Spring which spread across countries within days. Thus the international community including BRICS countries was mostly unprepared to respond. It was also not clear how Arab countries would react and if the security apparatus would be strong enough to cope with mass protest or how long protests would last, form a worthwhile civilian opposition or if the regime used force would turn into armed resistance. These questions were at the table but no one knew the answer to it in early 2011.

Events in the four countries which experienced the most intense public upheavals—Tunisia, Egypt, Syria and Libya—took different paths. The least violent and most positive development could be observed in Tunisia. In a surprise move Ben Ali left the country and in the following years democratic elections were held and the country avoided a violent revolution. In Egypt Mubarak left office after protests intensified and the regime used force against protesters. However, the military was still in power allowing an experimental phase of democratic elections which the Muslim Brotherhood won. In a counter-coup the military claimed back power and the old regime reestablished itself. In Syria the regime early on responded to public protest with utmost violence, leading into a long-lasting civil war which internationalized quickly, produced millions of refugees and claimed hundred thousands of lives. With the support of Iran and Russia Assad managed to stay in power despite weakening considerably over the years.

In Libya protests emanated from the Eastern part of the country. The center of resistance was the city of Benghazi. Soon after the outbreak of protests on 15 February the regime lost control over the second largest town of the country. Gaddafi left no doubts about his intention to stay in power. As a self-declared revolutionary leader he could hardly accept a revolutionary movement against himself. However, protests showed no sign of abating and the regime was determined to suppress the growing movement early on. The League of Arab States (LAS), which is rather known for upholding sovereignty rights and regime survival,[3] was the first international organization which suspended Libya's membership and condemned the violence on the ground (22 February). Early on Arab organizations placed significant distance between themselves and Gaddafi. In a speech broadcast on TV Gaddafi made it clear that he was not to resign and threatened protesters to use force against them.

> Muammar Gaddafi is the leader of the revolution, I am not a president to step down. ... This is my country. Muammar is not a president to leave his post.
>
> I have not yet ordered the use of force, not yet ordered one bullet to be fired ... when I do, everything will burn.[4]

In a press statement on the same day the UN Security Council also condemned the violence.[5] Inflammatory speeches by Gaddafi continued in the following weeks leaving little doubts about the intentions of him using force to stay in power.

Within the next few days the Security Council took action. There was no support for Gaddafi from the 15 members of the Council, and not even from the three African members at that time: Gabon, Nigeria and South Africa. No one wanted to appear as defending him.[6] On 25 February Libya was excluded from its membership in the UN Human Rights Council. The same day the Libyan delegation to the UN defected from Gaddafi after addressing the Security Council which was deliberating on Libya. The permanent representative Abdel Rahman Shalgham painted a gloomy picture of Gaddafi leaving little doubt about his willingness to stay in power whatever the costs.[7] The UN Secretary-General found that "the actions taken by the regime in Libya are clear-cut violations of all norms governing international behaviour, and serious transgressions of international human rights and humanitarian law."[8]

The next day after 12 hours of discussion the Security Council adopted resolution 1970. The resolution was initiated by the UK and was adopted by consensus and co-sponsored by 11 countries. Brazil, India, Russia and China were not among them.[9] Resolution 1970 demanded an immediate stop of the violence, implemented sanctions on the regime (asset freeze, arms embargo, travel bans) and referred the case to the International Criminal Court (ICC). The language used in the resolution was framed within the concept of R2P when "Recalling the Libyan authorities' responsibility to protect its population."[10]

The resolution had no effect on the ground. In Benghazi a Transitional National Council (TNC) was founded on 27 February which soon claimed sole representation for Libya. The Gulf Cooperation Council (GCC) on 7 March called for the implementation of a no-fly zone. It was followed by the Organization of Islamic Cooperation (OIC) and the LAS a few days later. On 10 March France was the first country fully recognizing the TNC. The momentum against Gaddafi within Libya and outside was further increasing. However, it was also clear that Gaddafi would not be able to be prosecuted by the ICC as long as he stayed in power. The ICC referral and the sanctions were no immediate remedy to stop the violence and protect civilians, although this was hoped for by some Security Council members. Indeed only in June did the ICC issue an arrest warrant against Gaddafi and his close associates.[11]

It was clear that further action needs to be taken. Intensive negotiations started in the Security Council which led to the adoption of resolution 1973. The resolution makes reference to the African Union (AU)'s political mediation mission, establishes a no-fly zone in order to protect civilians and allows the use of "all necessary measures ... to protect civilians ... under threat of attack" but excluding "a foreign occupation force."[12] The resolution was adopted by narrowly reaching the necessary majority of nine affirmative votes with five countries abstaining. These were Brazil, China, Germany, India and Russia. From the BRICS grouping only South Africa voted in favor.

Skepticism toward the West who was leading the UN's response to the crisis was growing. The use of force and the issue of military intervention have been met with reluctance. At the same time BRICS countries accepted the urgent need to take action and thus they abstained in order not to be seen as siding with an increasingly isolated Libya and outcast Gaddafi. A vetoing of China or Russia of the resolution would have also called into question their image as responsible great powers as they voted in favor of resolution 1970, the removal of Gaddafi by international jurisdiction, however unlikely it was during the passing of the resolution.

In the end, a deep rift between BRICS countries and the Western-led coalition emerged soon after the passing of resolution 1973. France, the UK and the US moved quickly and started an air campaign against Gaddafi's force within the next 48 hours. The speed and rigor with which a military solution was sought irritated BRICS countries. While Putin branded the campaign as "medieval crusade,"[13] Zuma opposed "any foreign military intervention ... whatever its form."[14] Although South Africa voted in favor of the resolution it felt betrayed by its implementation which left little to no space for political mediation which the country supported strongly through the sending of the AU High-Level Ad-Hoc Panel on Libya, of which President Zuma was a member. Despite the bombing campaign the AU pushed forward its roadmap for Libya which aimed at negotiating a ceasefire and political negotiations in order to seek a peaceful solution to the conflict.[15] In the end, mediation failed as the rebels boycotted talks and Gaddafi's forces lost ground soon.

Meanwhile the US, the UK and France made it very clear that the air campaign would continue until Gaddafi was removed from power.[16] The hardly covered arming of the rebels increased alienation of BRICS countries from the West.[17] At its annual summit in Sanya, China, the BRICS used diplomatic language to express their position. Accordingly, "the use of force should be avoided," the territorial integrity respected and the conflict in Libya should be solved "through peaceful means."[18] However, beneath this diplomatically worded declaration which avoids openly criticizing the Western coalition is the conviction that humanitarian reasons for intervention have been unduly used to follow a regime change approach.

As peace negotiations failed and Gaddafi's forces were on the retreat the TNC could gain more international recognition. On 22 August rebels took the capital Tripoli, a very important symbolic and strategic victory. Gaddafi retreated to Sirte, his birth town, but had practically lost power over the country. At the UN the TNC was officially recognized as sole representative of Libya on 16 September. All BRICS countries apart from South Africa supported the TNC in the General Assembly.[19] Gaddafi was finally captured in late October and quickly executed on 20. A short period of calm was followed by political and military disintegration and factionalism. Today the country is split between different militias and two centers of power: one internationally recognized government in Tripoli and the other in Eastern Libya around the oil fields and controlled by General Haftar. De facto a civil war continues in the country.

Based on the developed typology and discussion of input variables what is the most likely response to the crisis? We would assume that BRICS primarily respond through multilateral institutions to the crisis if the conflict is geographically distant, BRICS countries do not have the military capacities to dominate conflict solution by themselves and economic links to the crisis are not substantial. A more diplomatic response in opposition to hegemonic response should be expected if the conflict is only peripherally linked to the BRICS normative agenda. A going along with the mainstream liberal discourse at organizations such as the UN can be expected if no key interests get compromised but countries are willing to demonstrate global citizenship by facilitating multilateral legitimate action (norm based). The following analysis first goes through individual responses before exploring the overall reaction to the Libyan case.

Individual BRICS Positions

Brazil

Of the BRICS countries only South Africa and Brazil are members of the ICC. When resolution 1970 was adopted Brazil was holding the monthly rotating presidency of the Security Council. Following the statements of its permanent representative Mrs Maria Luiza Viotti, Brazil views the implementation of sanctions and the referral of "the situation" in Libya to the Prosecutor of the ICC[20] as a means to "halt violence" and "protect civilians."[21] Brazil portrayed itself as a "long-standing supporter of the integrity and universality of the Rome Statute."[22] As Libya is no member of the ICC prosecution by the Court requires Security Council referral. In this context Brazil has been the most progressive country within the BRICS even formulating a universal application of criminal justice which it aims to apply to the Libyan crisis. This falls very much into the traditional Brazilian line of solving conflict through peaceful and rather non-interventionist means. We can expect that targeted sanctions and criminal prosecution (although only after some time) would be seen as instruments of choice in order to exert pressure on Gaddafi and stop the violence. Before the adoption of resolution 1970 Council members discussed the conditions of the ICC referral. Brazil, India, China and South Africa initially opposed immediate referral to the Court but opted for threatening prosecution if violence continued.[23] In the end, the majority decided otherwise and Brazil did not want to abandon the unanimity with which the resolution was adopted and was also following the initiative taken by regional organizations such as the LAS, OIC and GCC.

Still Brazil decided not to co-sponsor the resolution which 11 of the 15 Council members did. The reason for this decision does not rest in principled concerns over the role of the ICC but has more to do with paragraph six of resolution 1970. In this paragraph referral to the ICC is limited excluding all nationalities which have not ratified the Rome Statute except Libyans. Viotti expresses "strong reservations" against this exceptionalism in a move to defend the Court's integrity. Brazil was the only country in the Security Council which issued these concerns. India's, Russia's and China's opposition toward the ICC are well known and thus Brazil agreed to the resolution while rejecting paragraph six.

Brazil is generally among the skeptical nations when it comes to the use of force to solve conflicts which is a deeply rooted position in its foreign policy. It therefore did not vote in favor of resolution 1973 but abstained. However, the concerns and reservations issued this time are much more fundamental. Viotti made it clear that Brazil does not believe that the use of force will improve the situation of civilians under threat or result in an immediate end of the violence. She also issued concerns that the wording of the resolution goes "far beyond" the intention of just establishing a no-fly zone and that an intervention can cause more harm than good.[24] Brazil's favored approach was to allow a diplomatic solution instead of seeking a military one. In this regard Viotti supported the AU mediation approach. In order to avoid to be seen as aligning too closely to Gaddafi Brazil decided to abstain but still mentioning the need to protect civilians.[25] Thus abstention did not mean opposition to the resolution as such.

As the North Atlantic Treaty Association (NATO) military campaign against Gaddafi started soon after resolution 1973 was adopted and ended only with his removal from power, Brazil was practically confined to issuing its concerns diplomatically without having much or any influence on events unfolding on the ground. However, Brazil reemerged as norm entrepreneur later in 2011 with coining a new notion of the responsibility while protecting (RwP).[26] The Brazilian-initiated debate around RwP aims at highlighting Brazilian concerns over the use of R2P language and its implementation in Libya, respectively the lack of oversight of the implementation and mandate overstretching.[27] Short reference was made to the term by Dilma Rousseff's speech to the General Assembly in September when she reiterated that the use of force can only be an instrument of last resort.[28] Associated to RwP are also the following principles: do no harm, proportional use of force, legitimate authority and accountability. However, these principles are not new and can be found in the seminal report of the International Commission on the Intervention and State Sovereignty (ICISS) which in a 108-page document introduced the term "responsibility to protect" and presents clear guidance when military force can be used.[29] In this regard the Brazilian initiative did not provide much normative innovation.

Still it is perceived as a rare instance in which an emerging power acquires the role of norm shaper. With Brazil leaving the Security Council by the end of 2011 it has also vacated the position of a norm entrepreneur. The concept of RwP was not well received in Western circles and even among BRICS Brazil did not get much followership. The concept did not find entrance into BRICS or IBSA (India, Brazil and South Africa) summit declarations of that time. Despite this the debate around RwP remains to be linked to the Libyan crisis and was a somehow vague, but still articulate, response to the Western-led intervention. The RwP debate is also a rare situation in which a BRICS member makes a conceptual contribution to a central debate in international affairs. While Brazil is certainly the least directly affected country within the BRICS grouping by the conflict it was making a conceptual contribution to questions of global order maybe because of Brazil's missing direct linkages and lack of material effect in the crisis.

Brazil's response to the crisis best fits into the category of active cooperation. In general Brazil was only acting within the multilateral framework of the UN and initiating the RwP debate. It supported resolution 1970 and abstained from voting on resolution 1973. Although Brazil criticized the regime change approach which later dominated the intervention, it did not actively try to form an opposition group. Regarding the six conditions discussed in the previous chapter, it is clear that the crisis in Libya did not pose any significant security threat for the country and economic links to Libya were also minimally developed. The Libyan case, however, matches well with the BRICS normative agenda and BRICS ideals on global order which emphasize non-intervention and peaceful settlement of conflict. In this regard Brazil was agreeing to use the ICC but skeptical about the military intervention that followed.

India

The Indian response to the Libyan crisis is similar to those of Brazil. Although for both countries there are no direct effects of the crisis to their country's security, in the case of India some 16,000–18,000 Indian nationals were living in Libya and the first priority was given to evacuating them. Indian nationals were mostly working in the oil, gas and construction industry and were soon affected by the outbreak of violence. As regards to India's position on R2P it had formally consented to the 2005 world summit document which was devoting two paragraphs to the concept but this did not stop the then permanent representative to the UN, Nirupam Sen, to continue to denounce the concept.[30] A change in orientation and move away from a dogmatic understanding of sovereignty could be found with the appointment of Hardeep Singh Puri to the UN. Like Brazil India prefers preventive diplomacy and conflict mediation over military intervention to address humanitarian needs and contain violent conflict.

Regarding the adoption of resolution 1970, the Indian position on the ICC deviates from that of Brazil to some extent. Ambassador Singh in a statement after the passing of the resolution made it clear that India was not full heartily agreeing to the referral of the Libyan situation to the Court, highlighting that a third of the Security Council members are not members of the ICC. India agreed to an immediate referral only because the defected Libyan representative was calling for it and it received support from regional organizations. Singh concluded that "We have therefore gone along with the consensus in the Council."[31] India did not express much independent leadership in shaping the content of the resolution. The concern around the immediate referral to the ICC was not only determined by Indian skepticism about the Court as such but also because of fears that Gaddafi might scale up violence after the resolution was adopted and this would have negative consequences for Indian nationals in Libya.[32] For this reason Singh wished for a more "calibrated" approach which gives Gaddafi a chance to comply with the Security Council resolution instead of referring it straight to the ICC.[33] In this context India also mentioned article 16 of the Rome Statute which allows the Security Council to suspend investigations. However, these concerns did not find entry into the resolution but were issued only by the permanent representative to the UN.

Before, during and after the adoption of resolution 1973 India raised a number of substantial concerns which were akin to those of Brazil. However, India articulated its reservations using slightly stronger language. A main concern over the implementation of a no-fly zone and use of all necessary measures was that there is no "clarity about details of enforcement measures, including who will participate and with what assets, and how these measures will exactly be carried out." Singh continued warning that "we have to ensure that the measures will mitigate and not exacerbate an already difficult situation for the people of Libya."[34]

Despite these concerns which were shared among BRICS and other nations India did not occupy or seek a leadership position in the Council. Instead what the country seemed to have worried about once its nationals were evacuated was not to be isolated.[35] Gaddafi's attempt to influence India's decision by offering special oil contracts backfired.[36] Appearing as being bribed by an increasingly isolated regime would have damaged India's reputation and would have isolated it in the Council, a situation India has given priority to avoid, especially as it was elected to the Council after 19 years of being absent from it. Furthermore, openly rejecting resolution 1973 would have meant straining relations with the Arab world and Western powers: both are important cornerstones in India's wider security architecture.[37] Most of India's oil imports originate from the Gulf region and India sought alignment with the US to counterbalance Chinese influence in Asia. Concerns over India's position in the concert of large powers and its own ambitions for a permanent seat might have also played a role when the country went along with the majority in the Council.[38]

In this context abstaining from the vote was a viable option. It takes account of India's concerns over the use of force but does not consent to military intervention. It also does not antagonize Western and Arab partners and avoids siding with the Gaddafi regime. Lastly it avoids diplomatic isolation as Russia, China, Brazil and Germany abstained too. The issue of mandate overstretch and lacking oversight was identified by India as main concern. In May 2011 during a Security Council debate on the protection of civilians Singh said the following:

> I cannot but ask the question: *Quis custodiet ipsos custodies?* Who watches the guardians? There is a considerable sense of unease about the manner in which the humanitarian imperative of protecting civilians has been interpreted for actual action on the ground.[39]

India's opposition to NATO bombings did not change until the end of the campaign. Its decision to abstain from voting is in hindsight seen as the right decision. The Libyan case reinforced skepticism against external interventions. At the 2011 UN General Assembly India's Prime Minister Manmohan Singh said that "[s]ocieties cannot be reordered from outside through military force."[40]

In sum, India's response to the crisis can be categorized as passive cooperative. India's response like Brazil's remains within the framework of the UN but the country although formulating its apprehension against the military intervention and regime change did not start an initiative on its own. India was most affected by the crisis through Indian workers being trapped in a conflict zone. This did not suffice to become more active. The relative distance from the conflict and the reliance on oil imports and US support for India in addition to its traditional position on non-intervention resulted in India's passive cooperative response.

China

China's stakes in the Libyan conflict were much higher than those of other BRICS countries. Although Libya is geographically far away from China and revolutionary contagion was rather unlikely as well as China's oil supply was not substantially threatened by the war, its growing economic links to the African continent make it increasingly difficult to follow a traditional approach of adhering to a strict non-interventionist approach.[41] This could be seen in the Libyan crisis.

Chinese foreign policy priorities can be summarized around four issues: the prerogative of sovereignty in international relations, guarding Chinese economic interests, building a positive image as rising and responsible power and engaging in counter-balancing when its vital interests are affected.[42] In the case of Libya these four priorities have been difficult to reconcile. Traditionally China is hardly known for actively supporting popular uprisings against an internationally recognized government; quite to the opposite the expected response of China to the uprising would have been to rule out any intervention, propping up the regime in order to secure its economic investment and counter-balance Western preponderance when possible. The Chinese response to the Libyan crisis somehow deviates from the expected trajectory.

Chinese investments in Libya during 2011 were estimated around $18bn, with most investments taking place in the construction and oil sector.[43] While only 3% of China's oil imports originated from Libya, China was Libya's third largest buyer of crude oil. With Western powers soon turning against Gaddafi China was a critical player which could, if it wanted, keep Gaddafi alive economically speaking, for example, by preventing or ignoring an international oil embargo. At the diplomatic front Gaddafi actively lobbied BRICS countries hoping to prevent the adoption or at least softening of the wording of resolution 1973. Only days before the resolution was adopted Gaddafi offered to replace Western investment (most Italian and French) in the country with those from BRICS countries, announcing a major strategic shift toward BRICS.[44] BRICS countries including China did not respond to this offer and there is very likely no link between the abstention from voting to short-term and uncertain economic benefits. While the Chinese investment in Libya was significant it was not large enough and competing with other issues to keep Gaddafi in power at all costs. Like India, China would not have wanted to be accused of being on Gaddafi's payroll and damage its carefully crafted image as a responsible power.

Gaddafi comparing his response to protesters with that of China's during the 1989 Tiananmen protests in order to remind Beijing of its own preference of sovereignty was counter-productive as China rather tried to tilt memories of this event than use it as an argument for non-intervention.[45] It also stood against China's image as a responsible rising power. In the end, China's immediate concern was to evacuate its 35,000 nationals which captured some attention at home. Furthermore, diplomatic relations between China and Libya were poorly developed before 2011, if not strained. Gaddafi, despite publicly committing to the one-China policy, continued to maintain relations with Taiwan and even accused China of neo-colonial ambitions in Africa. Thus there might have been little to no incentives for China to aggressively defend Gaddafi's crumbling regime when the crisis broke out.[46]

In the Security Council China only reluctantly uses its veto power. Since taking its seat in 1971 until the Libyan crisis it used the veto only six times. This follows a tradition of staying aloof from many issues, not taking up conflicts actively and keeping a low profile while concentrating on domestic growth. The initial response to the crisis seems to fall into this pattern too. Of all countries being at the Security Council the Chinese permanent representative Li Baodong provided one of the shortest comments. In only two paragraphs following the adoption of resolution 1970 he hardly expressed any Chinese interests or concerns over the resolution but only mentioned the importance of finding a peaceful solution and explaining Chinese approval by reference to Arab and African interests.[47] Given Chinese economic investment and security of its nationals being in danger, China appeared as strangely detached from events. Instead of formulating its own interests straightforwardly it was keeping a low profile and going along with regional organizations.[48] Still what was important to China in resolution 1970 was not the call for ICC prosecution or the sanction regime but article 2 b which urged the government to "[e]nsure the safety of all foreign nationals and their assets and facilitate, the departure of those wishing to leave the country."

Resolution 1973 was adopted under Chinese presidency of the Security Council. This time the Chinese response was more explicit. Li Baodong expressed that "China has serious difficulty with parts of the resolution."[49] During the drafting process China and other countries asked for more details on how the resolution was expected to be implemented with regard to the phrase "all necessary means" but with little effect. Given China's economic stakes and traditional skepticism around military interventions one would have expected China to use its veto right. It decided to abstain. In the response statement Li Baodong provided after the resolution was adopted it became clear that China did not want to be seen as siding against the expressed will of regional partners and fellow developing countries. As the call for a no-fly zone originated from Arab organizations and the AU pushed for political mediation, both of which were referred to in the resolution and a military occupation was ruled out, China abstained.

With the air campaign starting Chinese comments left little doubts about their anger. The Foreign Ministry declared, "We've seen reports that the use of armed force is causing civilian casualties, and we oppose the wanton use of armed force leading to more civilian casualties."[50] Calls for an immediate ceasefire to protect civilians instead of bombing Gaddafi troops were widely shared among BRICS countries.

Despite China's opposition to the implementation of the resolution 1973 the country did not turn to Gaddafi to support him. In a rather pragmatic and non-dogmatic move Chinese officials soon started meeting with rebels. As it became clear that Gaddafi would not have a future in Libya, China built up its contacts with the TNC. From June onward meetings took place in Qatar and Benghazi, culminating in a trip of TNC leader Mahmoud Jibril to Beijing, where he was received by the foreign minister.[51] Formally the TNC was not recognized by China until mid-September. This fairly early move to establish and not conceal contacts with the TNC can be explained by the uncertainty around Gaddafi's future. If China was to maintain or rebuild a good relationship with Libya Gaddafi was a man of the past. In the General Assembly later in 2011 in which Brazil, India, Russia and South Africa made critical statements about the intervention in Libya China almost appeared disengaged. Its foreign minister simply said, "On Libya, China respected the choice of Libyans and recognized the National Transitional Council as the governing authority."[52] Verhoeven assumes that Chinese economic long-term interests played a more significant role than dogmatic non-interventionism when arguing that "Beijing grasped fully well that regime change was a likely outcome—and one preferable for Chinese economic interests rather than a protracted civil war—and decided not to use the veto."[53]

China's response to the crisis very closely resembles those of India and can be categorized as passive cooperative. China did not start any specific initiative on its own despite criticism of regime change and mandate overstretch. This is somehow surprising as the country is the most heavily invested in Libya of all BRICS countries and it was having a sizable number of its nationals in the country too. Like India, China relies on oil imports from Gulf countries and decided not to take up opposition against the Western course of action. China focused primarily on evacuating its nationals from Libya using its naval forces but otherwise was taking a rather pragmatic position. Given the continuing civil war in Libya its multibillion-dollar investment in the country is still insecure. China would have some moderate military and economic means to intervene in the conflict but decided not to do so following its long-standing position of non-intervention into domestic affairs.

Russia

Within the BRICS grouping only Russia and China enjoy the privilege of veto power in the Security Council. However, it is not only the veto power which distinguishes Russia from the rest of the group. As successor of the Soviet Union Russia is no emerging power and thus is no newcomer to great power politics. Although the self-consciousness of a great power which naturally expects to get involved in shaping world affairs has taken a hard hit in the post-Cold War era, Russia today aims at occupying an increasingly pro-active leadership position claiming back some of its lost influence of the past. Of the BRICS grouping Russia is located the closest to Libya although there are no direct security issues emanating from the war in Libya. There is however a history of strategic partnership between the two countries. In the late 1970s Gaddafi became an ally of the Soviet Union which helped him to build several missile bases. Over the years up to 11,000 Soviet soldiers stayed in Libya.[54] In 2008 Russia canceled several billions of dollars of debt to the Soviet Union in exchange for weapon sales and a contract for a railway line. The package deal was estimated to be worth $5–10bn.[55] While it is clear the post-Cold War Russia would not be able to play a dominant or leading role in all places the Soviet Union once considered its sphere of influence, Libya was not far outside the Russian ambit. Russia's return to Libya in 2016 with the support of Khalifa Haftar, a leader of the internationally not recognized government in Eastern Libya, vividly demonstrates Russia's willingness to play an active geostrategic role. A $2bn weapons deal was agreed with Haftar which consolidated his position in a fragmented political battle over the control of Libya.[56] While the future of political leadership over Libya is still contested the support for Haftar gives Russia some leverage over any potential future solution in the country.

However, with the beginning of conflict Russian influence was far less clear-cut and its interest vague. Draft resolutions on Libya were initiated by Western countries and BRICS including Russia did not form and present a viable initiative countering Western influence. In hindsight we can say that events in Libya, Syria and the Ukraine contributed significantly to the resurgence of Russian influence in the world. Initially the prospects for Russian power expansion were not self-evident.

Although Russia agreed to resolution 1970 its interpretation of the resolution and expectations differed from those of the West as well as from those of other BRICS members. The very experienced Russian permanent representative to the UN Vitaly Churkin who led the Russian delegation between 2006 and 2017 referred to the need of "all parties," not only Gaddafi, to refrain from the use of force. Furthermore, Russia interpreted the use of sanctions as a means to interfere into domestic affairs.[57] While India and Brazil viewed that the referral to the ICC and sanctioning policy is part of a solution to the conflict, Russia displayed greater reservations early on.

Churkin's reservations against resolution 1973 to which Russia abstained resemble those of China and India and have been formulated straightforwardly:

> In essence, a whole range of questions raised by Russia and other members of the Council remained unanswered. Those questions were concrete and legitimate and touched on how the no-fly zone would be enforced, what the rules of engagement would be and what limits on the use of force there would be. ... Provisions were introduced into the text that could potentially open the door to large-scale military intervention. ... However, we remain convinced that the quickest way to ensure robust security for the civilian population and the long-term stabilization of the situation in Libya is an immediate ceasefire ... destabilizing developments must be avoided.[58]

As in the case of other BRICS countries the implementation of resolution 1973 found opposition in Russia. Then Prime Minister Putin called the humanitarian reasons for intervention a pretext and denounced the resolution as "defective and flawed. It allows everything. ... It resembles medieval calls for crusades."[59] Taking Churkin's and Putin's comments and reservations in mind it is surprising that if Russia foresees the application of the resolution correctly and disagrees to it why did it not veto it?

Indeed Churkin's and Putin's views were not the only or dominant opinions during that time. Under President Medvedev the Libyan case still falls within a time in which Russia has not taken a course actively opposing Western leadership. This should change with Putin retaking the presidency. In conflicts like Syria and the Ukraine Russia plays a much more active role, shaping events and not just being a bystander to events. The Libyan experience has surely contributed to this shift in foreign policy. However, in 2011 there was no fully coherent position on Libya. Konstantin Kosachev, leading the Russian International Affairs Committee of the Duma, supported the military ousting of Gaddafi. Mikhail Margelov, presidential envoy to Libya, sympathized with the TNC and Gaddafi's referral to the ICC. President Medvedev openly disagreed with Putin over using the term "medieval crusades."[60]

Despite initial lack of clearly articulate interests, criticism and strong rejection of military intervention in Libya prevailed. Foreign Minister Sergey Lavrov found that "attempts to go beyond the Security Council mandate are unacceptable, since they undermine its authority and compound the suffering of innocent civilians."[61] The experience from the Libyan crisis has directly and sustainably influenced Russian foreign policy. The Concept of the Foreign Policy of the Russian Federation adopted in February 2013 in paragraph 31b finds:

> It is unacceptable that military interventions and other forms of interference from without which undermine the foundations of international law based on the principle of sovereign equality of states, be carried out on the pretext of implementing the concept of "responsibility to protect."[62]

Like India and China Russia played only a passive cooperative role during the war. It shared the critique of its fellow BRICS members against the intervention but did not use its veto in the Security Council nor did it provide military support for Gaddafi. Significant economic links to Libya did not exist and the strategic value of the country is also less compelling than Russia's involvement in later conflicts in Syria or the Ukraine.

South Africa

Of the five BRICS countries the position and response of South Africa deviate to some extent from those of the others. Indeed one gets the impression that South Africa's position was not coordinated with the BRICS. This in the end may not surprise us as most countries when elected to join the Security Council tend to privilege their own concerns over aligning to regional organizations or other groupings. South Africa also joined the BRICS group only a few months before the Libyan crisis and so far for all BRICS countries the Libyan case constituted a first hard test case. Within BRICS South Africa is the only African member and thus the crisis in Libya fell within the continental foreign policy aspirations of the country.[63] Political relations with Gaddafi had been long-standing and deep-reaching. His support for the African National Congress (ANC) during the time of Apartheid had not been forgotten. Gaddafi together with Thabo Mbeki and Olusegun Obasanjo had been critical in building the newly founded AU to which South Africa pays considerable attention as the prime organization which is mandated to address African issues and formulate a regional Africa-led response to conflicts on the continent.

In terms of geographical distance or closeness to Libya South Africa has only a remote position. It is roughly 6700 km away from Tripoli which is more than twice the distance from Moscow (3200 km); even New Delhi (6000 km) is, geographically speaking, closer to Libya than South Africa is. Indeed the influence of South Africa and the AU on North African affairs has never been very articulate and the geographical remoteness of South Africa has contributed to this.

Before the Security Council adopted resolution 1970, the AU Peace and Security Council (PSC) on 23 February issued a communiqué condemning the violence against peaceful protesters but did not formulate a strategy of its own to mediate in the crisis.[64] Thus the initiative was taken over by the Security Council who adopted resolution 1970 three days later. South Africa was fully content with that decision. Its permanent representative Baso Sangqu found:

> This unanimous resolution sends a clear and unambiguous message to the Libyan authorities to end the carnage against their people. Further, it complements the decision of the African Union Peace and Security Council. ... We are confident that the measures contained in this resolution will contribute to the long-term objective of bringing peace and stability to this sisterly nation.[65]

In the AU's PSC on 10 March,[66] in which South Africa together with Nigeria which also served in 2011, another communiqué was adopted. This communiqué adopted a somehow different language than resolution 1970. The AU formulated its concerns in a more distanced manner, recognizing "the legitimacy of the aspirations of the Libyan people for democracy" and condemning "the indiscriminate use of force and lethal weapons, whoever it comes from."[67] The latter formulation includes the TNC and Gaddafi. Furthermore, the AU announced "its rejection of any foreign military intervention, whatever its form."[68] In order to seek a mediation solution the establishment of an Ad-hoc High Level Panel on Libya was agreed in which five heads of state would be represented, among them Jacob Zuma.

However, in the coming days the AU's fundamental opposition to any kind of intervention had little chances to find endorsement. Arab organizations had started calling for a no-fly zone and the US made it clear if a no-fly zone was to be established it would need to actively destroy and engage Libyan forces; in other words it would be a military intervention by air. South Africa found itself pushed in a corner. Its influence within the UN Security Council was fairly limited and the debate concentrated on the implementation of a no-fly zone which would contradict the AU's position. Although Baso Sangqu asked the Security Council to wait until the AU panel would have visited Libya by 17 March, deliberations were not postponed.[69] However, in resolution 1973 a foreign occupation was ruled out and the AU's mediation efforts had been mentioned. This combination of conditions allowed it to vote in favor of the resolution. A phone call by Presidents Obama and Sarkozy to Zuma just before the Council voting might also have influenced the country's decision.

The South African vote was indeed decisive to get the resolution through. A simple abstention would have failed it also because Nigeria was expected to vote with the South Africans.[70] While South Africa voted in favor of the resolution it was soon disappointed about its implementation, with the direct targeting and removal of Gaddafi from power and the sidelining of the AU mediation mission. This was certainly not what South Africa intended. The country came under considerable pressure to explain its position. A spokesperson of the delegation to the UN explained that South Africa was voting for the resolution in order to stop violence on the ground. The resolution was meant to "pose a threat to Gaddafi by demanding a ceasefire," which the AU mission would be negotiating. The spokesperson continued: "We can't bear responsibility for what is happening now. We knew people had different ideas and ulterior motives, but we had to vote in favour, otherwise we would have been accused once again [of neglecting human rights considerations] and it would be said that we are siding with [Gaddafi]."[71] With the air strikes in full swing and the coalition determined to remove Gaddafi the AU's plans for a political roadmap which were developed soon after the adoption of resolution 1973 had little to no prospects to materialize. This increased alienation with Western powers involved in military action in Libya in the end brought South Africa closer to BRICS opposing the intervention. In his address to the General Assembly Zuma summarized his misgivings clearly by calling on the UN to maintain its principle of impartiality, referred to great power abuse of the UN, highlighting the central role of regional organizations in peace mediation and that "military actions were preferred over peaceful means."[72]

South Africa was taking an active cooperative position during the conflict. It is the only BRICS country which worked through the regional bodies such as the AU to get directly involved in the conflict. Its preferred and only instrument was conflict mediation. This indicates that South Africa was giving the conflict high priority, despite the fairly large distance between the two countries and no direct security implications for South Africa. However, as political mediation was the only instrument available and no other power resources (economic or military), South Africa had to watch events unfolding from the outside with little to no impact on the fate of the country.

Conclusion: BRICS and the Libyan Crisis

When evaluating the BRICS response to the crisis through the typology developed in the last chapter (Fig. 2.1), it is largely clear that the dominant response type falls within the category of active/passive cooperation (Table 3.1). BRICS countries responded fairly coherently with no divisions among them. Positioning to the crisis occurred mainly through membership and decision-making within the Security Council. Broad-based multilateralism was the preferred choice of response. The passing of Security Council resolutions and calling for their adherence was the dominant form of reaction to the crisis. Although BRICS nations turned out to be vocal critics of the Libyan intervention, the critique voiced was not directed against multilateral action under UN mandate as such but was

Table 3.1 Mapping of response types and motivation: Libya

Country	Russia	China	South Africa	Brazil	India
Response type	Cooperative (passive)	Cooperative (passive)	Cooperative (active)	Cooperative (active)	Cooperative (passive)
Main motivation	Opposing military intervention and regime change	Evacuating Chinese nationals, pragmatic politics, opposing military intervention and regime change	Multilateral conflict mediation, opposing military intervention and regime change	Favoring criminal justice, opposing military intervention and regime change	Evacuating Indian nationals, opposing military intervention and regime change

opposing the one-sided and arbitrary interpretation of resolution 1973 which turned a no-fly zone into an instrument to remove Gaddafi. BRICS countries operated well within the multilateral confines of the UN. No attempt of hegemonic mini-lateralism or neo-imperialist behavior can be identified. BRICS did not become warring parties in the civil war that followed until Gaddafi's death.

The Libyan case certainly increased skepticism against the concept of R2P. Using force against a recognized government by referring to the term R2P by a predominantly Western-oriented coalition of the willing raises opposition among BRICS countries, despite any humanitarian issues involved.[73] To which extent the accusation of power politics against the West holds ethical meaning is a matter of debate.[74] Equally one could claim that BRICS argumentation is mostly self-referential, also worrying about their own power status more which was not adequately considered in the Libyan situation than humanitarian concerns. Could civilians be protected with Gaddafi remaining in power? Indeed BRICS role during the crisis was rather one of a critical bystander but not of an active leader and this despite the serious discomfort diplomats issued repeatedly.

It also remains puzzling why BRICS countries, if having substantial misgivings against the military intervention that followed resolution 1973, did not veto it. The argument that they were misled is only partially convincing. Two weeks before the adoption of the resolution US Secretary of Defense Gates was giving a public statement on how the US would implement the no-fly zone with attacking and destroying Libya's air force. International news agency Reuters on 2 March 2011 reported: "The United States is moving several amphibious assault ships to the Mediterranean as the United States and other nations seek to force a defiant Gaddafi to end his 41-year rule."[75] Even if wrongly anticipating how events unraveled later on both messages could have alerted BRICS countries of the political and military intentions of the Western coalition before the adoption of a resolution which allows the use of "all necessary measures." However, actively arming rebels was in fact hardly covered by the resolution and indeed humanitarian considerations for intervention were not the only ones relevant for intervening forces. What the Libyan case reveals is also poor BRICS coordination. The group while being at the Security Council missed an opportunity to formulate its core interests clearly, coordinate individual positions quickly as well as finding and creating support for its position.

Table 3.2 Trigger variables and countries: Libya

	Russia	China	South Africa	Brazil	India
Proximity	+	−	− − −	− − −	−
Capability interests	−	+	−	− − −	− −
Type of conflict	+ +	+ +	+ +	+ +	+ +
Economics	+	+ +	− − −	− − −	+ +
BRICS agenda	+ + +	+ + +	+ + +	+ + +	+ + +
Humanitarian norms	− −	− −	+	+ +	+

+ and − indicate various degrees of importance or lack thereof of the trigger variables

What conditions can explain the cooperative passive response type BRICS countries displayed? Table 3.2 provides an overview of the six input conditions introduced in the previous chapter. In the case of cooperative behavior within multilateralism and international law which is non-coercive one would assume that BRICS countries are not directly affected by the conflict (proximity to crisis), have little strategic interest and limited capabilities to influence events, and the conflict has limited economic consequences. Furthermore, a cooperative mode might be explained by the advantage to garner global legitimacy by acting collectively upon humanitarian values in a crisis situation. For the response of BRICS as a group is expected to rely on the ability of the crisis to resonate with the BRICS reformist agenda and the type of conflict (local to global order sensitive). Does the response of BRICS countries and BRICS as a group fit into the expected patterns?

On average we can observe that indeed the BRICS individual response correlates with the expectations. No country was directly affected by the crisis regarding its own security and Libya did not top the list of foreign policy priorities for any of the BRICS countries. However, in the case of India and China evacuation of their own nationals was a priority. This influenced the position of India which argued for a more calibrated approach regarding international criminal prosecution of Gaddafi, fearing reprisals against the Indian population. BRICS countries also lacked material capabilities to take a leading role in the implementation of the no-fly zone. As such there was no substantial opposition against a no-fly zone among BRICS countries. It is rather the implementation which created opposition. If BRICS countries had the military capabilities to actively participate in the monitoring of Libyan airspace the campaign very likely would have looked differently. In the end, only NATO displayed the necessary institutional structure to manage the intervention. A lack of institutional capacity was also visible on the African side. While the AU developed an African Peace and Security Architecture (APSA) which is built on sub-regional support, the Northern African component is the most poorly developed element.[76] In the end, the Western-led initiative had taken over because strategic priorities have been clear, military capabilities were available, swift action was preferred and no other policy option could rival the intervention effectively.

Regarding economic priorities of BRICS countries, the group is divided. While Brazil and South Africa practically have no stakes in the country Russia, India and China were risking investments of several billion dollars. Given the size of these three countries economic interests were likely not substantial enough to get involved in the crisis through more meaningful ways but the loss of investment is not trivial. China which was the country which lost the most economically applied a pragmatic approach and, despite opposing military intervention as a means to remove Gaddafi, met with the TNC leadership early on. Later Russia decided to directly support a rebel faction in 2016, now engaging in active geostrategic politics.

The passive cooperative response to the crisis might result not only from missing capabilities and clearly formulated strategic interests toward a remote and locally confined conflict but also from garnering legitimacy through supporting multilateral humanitarian action. Practically all BRICS countries avoided to be associated with Gaddafi as his regime was falling into disgrace in international media coverage and at the UN as well as at regional Arab organizations. India after a long absence from the Council wanted to show its responsibility as a world leading country. During South Africa's previous term in the Council the country was criticized for supporting human rights violating regimes in Myanmar, Iran and Zimbabwe.[77] China and Russia would have lost credibility by condemning acts of violence and protecting the Gaddafi regime. The dominant discourse of the time defined legitimate action with stopping violence which was associated with Gaddafi's forces. The problem of those who disliked the removal of Gaddafi was that keeping him in power was largely incompatible with legitimate action which was framed in terms of R2P. Initially BRICS countries linked up their response to the crisis to dominant discourses of human protection and prosecution of war crimes by the ICC.

To which extent was the conflict in Libya resonating or undermining the BRICS normative agenda? Although the conflict in Libya was mostly confined to the country's borders and only years later indirectly spilled over into neighboring Mali, the issue of international military intervention is certainly of the highest concern for BRICS countries. While they had limited material capabilities and interest in actively getting involved militarily, the linking of humanitarian rhetoric with regime change was uniformly seen as unacceptable. The international response clearly violated the BRICS understanding of uncompromised sovereignty and host state agreement to intervention.

At individual country level BRICS high-ranking state officials voiced their concerns over events in Libya many times; official BRICS documents display a rather diplomatic language. At the 2011 summit which was taking place a few weeks after the adoption of resolution 1973 BRICS countries referred to Libya by stating that: "We share the principle that the use of force should be avoided. We maintain that the independence, sovereignty, unity and territorial integrity of each nation should be respected."[78] In a statement in November 2011 they found that "it was inadmissible to impose solutions on the MENA states through outside intervention in the internal political processes."[79] What shines through these formulations is a certain reluctance to use the BRICS label to form an opposition group against the West. The response remains cooperative in principle despite harsh criticism from single countries. Indeed during the 2011 general debate at the UN in which some BRICS countries did voice their concerns over Libya, no country referred to BRICS and Libya. Only the Russian foreign minister did but stating that "BRICS does not aim at confrontation with anyone."[80]

This response poses a certain contrast to the expected effect of normative match to the BRICS agenda and conflict types which have the potential to substantially alter the existing world order. With regard to Libya one would have expected that countries more actively gather around the BRICS core trademark which is one of reforming global governance institutions in order to build a more equal order based on sovereign equality. Instead BRICS countries decided not to take up open confrontation through the BRICS Forum or at the UN by voting against resolutions 1970 and 1973.

What is interesting when exploring the relative influence of the six input conditions is that the Libyan case strongly links up to the BRICS agenda and the type of conflict, an international intervention resulting in regime change, indicates a stronger reaction of BRICS than actually occurred. What speaks in favor of a more cooperative but passive response is the relative distance to the conflict and partly lacking capabilities to intervene in the conflict. Economically we can see a difference between the IBSA countries which hold no significant economic links to Libya contrasting Chinese and Russian links to the country. Humanitarian concerns played a role in as far as BRICS countries at no point justified the use of force against civilians despite their criticism against regime change and calling for respect of Libya's sovereignty.

In spite of the generally rather passive position BRICS have taken during the conflict, this does not mean that the Libyan events left no traces on BRICS. To the opposite, it reinforced the belief that the grouping is much needed in order to overcome the pervasive imbalance in favor of the West and to prevent a second Libya. In the end, the Libyan crisis was a case in which BRICS had on average moderate economic interest, limited material capabilities to influence the international response to the crisis but were confronted with a dis-favorable outcome. This experience left traces. In the Syrian crisis we can observe a significant hardening of positions when it comes to the use of force and intervention. In a sense the Libyan experience was sharpening BRICS worries about military intervention and constitutes a foundational experience of the group. It certainly helped and reinforced the BRICS agenda.

Notes

1. The literature especially on Libya is vast. The most informative contributions might be the following: Hehir, A. (2013) The permanence of inconsistency: Libya, the Security Council, and the Responsibility to Protect. *International Security.* 38(1), 137–159. Neethling, Theo (2012) "Reflections on norm dynamics: South African foreign policy and the no-fly zone over Libya", *South African Journal of International Affairs*, 19(1), 25–42. O'Brien, Emily and Sinclair, Andrew (2011) "The Libyan War: A Diplomatic History", (New York: New York University, Center on International Cooperation). Williams, Paul D. and Bellamy, Alex J. (2012) Principles, politics and prudence: Libya and the new politics of humanitarian war. *Global Governance*, 18(3), 273–297.
2. Bellamy, Alexander J. (2014) "From Tripoli to Damascus: lesson learning and the implementation of the responsibility to protect," *International Politics*, 51(1), 23–44. Stuenkel, Olivier (2014) "The BRICS and the Future of R2P Was Syria or Libya the Exception?" *Global Journal of the Responsibility to Protect*, 6, 3–28. Thakur, Ramesh (2013) "R2P after Libya and Syria: Engaging Emerging Powers," *The Washington Quarterly*, 36(2), 61–76. Zifcak, Spencer (2012) "The Responsibility to Protect after Libya

and Syria" *Melbourne Journal of International Law* 13, 1–35. Tocci, Nathalie (2016) "On Power and Norms: Libya, Syria and the Responsibility to Protect" *Global Responsibility to Protect*, 8, 51–75.
3. Barnett, Michael and Solingen, Etel (2007) Designed to Fail or Failure of Design: The Origins and Legacy of the Arab League" in Acharya, Amitav and Johnston Alastair (eds) Crafting Cooperation Regional International Institutions in comparative Perspective. Cambridge: Cambridge University Press, pp. 180–220.
4. Al-Jazeera "Defiant Gaddafi vows to fight on" http://www.aljazeera.com/news/africa/2011/02/201122216458913596.html 23 Feb. 2011. Accessed 24 Nov. 2017
5. United Nations Security Council, 'Security Council Press Statement on Libya, SC/10180-AFR2120, 22 February 2011. http://www.un.org/News/Press/docs/2011/sc10180.doc.htm Accessed 24 Nov. 2017.
6. Puri, Hardeep (2016) Perilous Interventions: The Security Council and the Politics of Chaos. Uttar Pradesh, London, Toronto, Scarborough, Sydney, New York: Harper Collins Publishers, p. 62.
7. Ibid., pp. 64–65.
8. UN Security Council 6491st meeting, 26 February 2011.
9. Hardeep, p. 72.
10. UN Security Council, Resolution 1970, 26 Feb. 2011, preamble.
11. ICC, Warrant of Arrest for Muammar Mohammed Abu Minyar Gaddafi, 27 June 2011. https://www.icc-cpi.int/pages/record.aspx?uri=1099321 Accessed 24 Nov. 2017.
12. UN Security Council, Resolution 1973, 17 March. 2011, para. 4.
13. The Moscow Times, Putin Rips 'Medieval Crusade' in Libya https://themoscowtimes.com/news/putin-rips-medieval-crusade-in-libya-5751 March 22, 2011. Accessed 27 Nov. 2017.
14. Zuma, Jakob (2011): Keynote address by His Excellency President Jacob Zuma at the Commemoration of the National Human Rights Day, Athlone Stadium, Cape Town, 21 March 2011.
15. AU High-Level ad hoc Committee on Libya, Nouakchott, Mauritania 19 March 2011. http://www.dirco.gov.za/docs/2011/au0322.pdf Accessed 27 Nov. 2017.
16. Obama, Barack, Cameron, David and Sarkozy, Nicolas (2011): "Libya's pathway to peace," The New York Times, 14 April 2011. http://www.nytimes.com/2011/04/15/opinion/15iht-edlibya15.html Accessed 27 Nov. 2017.
17. Jolly, David and Fahim, Kareem "France Says It Gave Arms to the Rebels in Libya" the New York Times 29 June 2011. http://www.nytimes.com/2011/06/30/world/europe/30france.html Accessed 27 Nov. 2017.

18. BRICS Annual Summit, Sanya Declaration, para. 9–10.
19. UN, General Assembly "After Much Wrangling, General Assembly Seats National Transitional Council of Libya as Country's Representative for Sixty-Sixth Session" New York 16 Sep. 2011. https://www.un.org/press/en/2011/ga11137.doc.htm Accessed 27 Nov. 2017.
20. UN Security Council resolution 1970, para. 4.
21. UN Security Council 6491st meeting, 26 February 2011.
22. Ibid.
23. Hardeep, p. 71.
24. UN Security Council, 6498th meeting, 17 March 2011. p. 6.
25. Ibid.
26. Stuenkel, Oliver (2013) "Brazil as a norm entrepreneur: the Responsibility While Protecting" in Hamann, Eduarda and Muggah, Robert (eds) *Implementing the Responsibility to Protect: New Directions for International Peace and Security?* Rio de Janeiro: Igarapé Institute, pp. 59–62.
27. Tourinho, M, Stuenkel, Oliver and Brockmeier, Sarah (2016) "'Responsibility while Protecting": Reforming R2P Implementation', *Global Society*, 30(1) 134–150.
28. Statement by H. E. Dilma Rousseff, President of the Federative Republic of Brazil, at the Opening of the General Debate of the 66th Session of the United Nations General Assembly. New York, 21 September 2011. https://gadebate.un.org/sites/default/files/gastatements/66/BR_en_0.pdf Accessed 28 Nov. 2017.
29. Hamann, Eduarda (2012) "Brazil and R2P: A Rising Global Player Struggles to Harmonise Discourse and Practice" in Brosig, Malte (ed) *The Responsibility to Protect – From Evasive to Reluctant Action?* Johannesburg and Pretoria: HSS, ISS, SAIIA, pp. 80–82.
30. Bloomfield, Alan (2015) "India and the Libyan Crisis: Flirting with the Responsibility to Protect, Retreating to the Sovereignty Norm," *Contemporary Security Policy*, 36(1), p. 33.
31. UN Security Council 6491st meeting, 26 February 2011.
32. Hardeep, p. 69.
33. UN Security Council 6491st meeting, 26 February 2011.
34. Ibid.
35. Bloomfield, p. 40.
36. Ibid.
37. Bloomfield, p. 41.
38. Hall, Ian (2013) "Tilting at Windmills? The Indian Debate over the Responsibility to Protect after UNSC Resolution 1973" Global Responsibility to Protect 5, p. 87.
39. UN Security Council, 6531st meeting 10 May 2011.

40. Statement by H.E. Dr. Manmohan Singh, Prime Minister of India at the General Debate of the 66th Session of the United Nations General Assembly on September 24 2011. https://www.pminewyork.org/adminpart/uploadpdf/33994lms80a.pdf Accessed 1 Dec 2017.
41. Verhoeven, Harry (2014) "Is Beijing's Non-Interference Policy History? How Africa is Changing China," The Washington Quarterly, 37(2), 55–70.
42. Ferdinand, Peter (2013) *The Positions of Russia and China at the UN Security Council in the Light of Recent Crises*. EU DG for External Policies of the Union, p. 13.
43. China's evolving foreign policy, The Libyan dilemma, A rising power starts to knock against the limits of its hallowed "non-interference" The Economist, 10 Sep. 2011 http://www.economist.com/node/21528664 Accessed 29 Nov. 2017.
44. "'The West is to be forgotten. We will not give them our oil' – Gaddafi" Russia Today, 16 March 2011. https://www.rt.com/news/libya-oil-gaddafi-arab/ accessed 29 Nov. 2011.
45. Fung, Courtney (2016) Global South solidarity? China, regional organisations and intervention in the Libyan and Syrian civil wars, *Third World Quarterly*, 37(1), 38.
46. Hodzi, Obert (2019) The End of China's Non-Intervention Policy in Africa. Cham: Palgrave Macmillan, pp. 104–106.
47. UN Security Council 6491st meeting 26 February 2011, p. 4.
48. Fung, pp. 33–50.
49. UN Security Council 6498th meeting 17 March 2011, p. 10.
50. Jacobs Andrew (2011) "China Urges Quick End to Airstrikes in Libya" The New York Times, 22 March 2011. http://www.nytimes.com/2011/03/23/world/asia/23beiijing.html
51. China's evolving foreign policy, The Libyan dilemma, A rising power starts to knock against the limits of its hallowed "non-interference" The Economist, 10 Sep. 2011 http://www.economist.com/node/21528664 Accessed 29 Nov. 2017.
52. UN General Assembly H.E. Mr. Yang Jiechi, Minister for Foreign Affairs 26 September 2011. https://gadebate.un.org/en/66/china Accessed 1 Dec. 2017.
53. Verhoeven, Harry (2014) "Is Beijing's Non-Interference Policy History? How Africa is Changing China," *The Washington Quarterly*, 37(2), p. 61.
54. Fasanotti, Federica Saini (2016) "Russia and Libya: A brief history of an on-again-off-again friendship" Washington D.C.: Brookings. https://www.brookings.edu/blog/order-from-chaos/2016/09/01/russia-and-libya-a-brief-history-of-an-on-again-off-again-friendship/ Accessed 29 Nov. 2017.

55. Ibid.
56. Lefèvre, Raphaël (2017) "The pitfalls of Russia's growing influence in Libya", *The Journal of North African Studies*, 22(3), 331.
57. UN Security Council 6491st meeting, 26 February 2011, p. 4.
58. UN Security Council 6498th meeting 17 March 2011, p. 8.
59. The Moscow Times, "Putin Rips 'Medieval Crusade' in Libya" https://themoscowtimes.com/news/putin-rips-medieval-crusade-in-libya-5751 March 22, 2011. Accessed 29 Nov. 2017.
60. Makarychev, Andrey (2011) "Russia's "Libya Debate" Political Meanings and Repercussions" PONARS Eurasia Memo No. 178, September 2011.
61. UN General Assembly 28th plenary meeting 27 September 2011, p. 17.
62. Concept of the Foreign Policy of the Russian Federation, Unofficial translation, Approved by President of the Russian Federation V. Putin on 12 February 2013. http://www.mid.ru/en_GB/foreign_policy/official_documents/-/asset_publisher/CptICkB6BZ29/content/id/122186 Accessed 29 Nov. 2017.
63. Building a Better World: The Diplomacy of Ubuntu White Paper on South Africa's Foreign Policy. Pretoria 13 May 2011.
64. AU PSC 261st Meeting, 23 February 2011, para. 2.
65. UN Security Council 6491st meeting 26 February 2011, p. 3.
66. In 2011 the following 15 countries were elected to the PSC: Benin, Burundi, Chad, Djibouti, Equatorial Guinea, Ivory Coast, Kenya, Libya, Mali, Mauritania, Namibia, Nigeria, Rwanda, South Africa and Zimbabwe. https://au.int/en/organs/psc Accessed 30 Nov. 2017.
67. AU PSC 265th Meeting 10 March 2011, para. 4–5.
68. Ibid., para. 6.
69. Hardeep, p. 84.
70. Hardeep, p. 90.
71. Rossouw, Mandy (2011) "SA's 'no-fly' vote hits turbulence" Mail & Guardian 25 Mar 2011. https://mg.co.za/article/2011-03-25-sas-nofly-vote-hits-turbulence Accessed 30 Nov. 2017.
72. Statement by President Jacob Zuma to the General Debate of the 66th United Nations General Assembly, UN Headquarters, New York, 21 September 2011. http://www.dirco.gov.za/docs/speeches/2011/zuma0922.html Accessed 30 Nov. 2017.
73. Stuenkel, Olivier (2014) "The BRICS and the Future of R2P Was Syria or Libya the Exception?" *Global Journal of the Responsibility to Protect*, 6, 28.
74. Brozus, Lars and Schaller, Christian (2013) "Über die Responsibility to Protect zum Regimewechsel" SWP-Studie 2013/S 13. Accessed at https://www.swp-berlin.org/publikation/responsibility-to-protect-und-regimewechsel/

Glanville, Luke (2013) "In Defense of the Responsibility to Protect" *Journal of Religious Ethics* 41(1), 169–182. Reed, Esther (2012) "Responsibility to Protect and Militarized Humanitarian Intervention: When and Why Churches Failed to Discern Moral Hazard." *Journal of Religious Ethics*, 40(2), 308–334.

75. Reuters "No-fly zone for Libya would require attack: Gates" 2 March 2011. https://www.reuters.com/article/us-libya-usa-pentagon/no-fly-zone-for-libya-would-require-attack-gates-idUSTRE7214EX20110302 Accessed 30 Jan. 2019.
76. APSA Impact Report, The state and impact of the African Peace and Security Architecture (APSA) in 2015, p. 28. Accessed at http://www.ipss-addis.org/y-file-store/resources/publication/20161110_apsa_impact_report_final.pdf
77. Van Nieuwkerk, Anthoni (2007) "A critique of South Africa's role on the UN security council," *South African Journal of International Affairs*, 14(1), 61–77.
78. BRICS Annual Summit, Sanya Declaration, para. 9.
79. Joint Communiqué on the Outcome of the Meeting of BRICS Deputy Foreign Ministers on the Situation in the Middle East and North Africa, Moscow, Russia, November 24, 2011. http://www.brics.utoronto.ca/docs/111124-foreign.html Accessed 1 Dec. 2017.
80. UN General Assembly 28th plenary meeting 27 September 2011, p. 15.

CHAPTER 4

Syria: The World Order Unchallenged or Power Politics Above All Else?

The wars in Syria and Libya unfolded as a consequence of the Arab Spring in early 2011. While the origins of the two conflicts are similar the course of action was taking a very different route. Until today almost a decade later the country is still at war and is regarded as one of the greatest humanitarian crisis in the twenty-first century. The number of international refugees and internally displaced people reached 5.6 million in May 2018 which makes up for roughly one third of the total population.[1] An estimated 500,000 people have died and the use of chemical weapons has been reported frequently.[2] The war often continued not along military frontlines in the countryside but was taking place in urban areas. Cities like Homs or Aleppo became synonyms for urban warfare and targeting civilians. Mediation efforts have often not yielded to tangible progress and ceasefire agreements lasted for some time but could not pacify the entire country. Several chief negotiators have been appointed during the course of the war. Among them were Kofi Annan, Lakhdar Brahimi and Staffan de Mistura.[3] More than in conference rooms a solution was sought on the battle field. The Syrian war remains an example in which the international community failed to contain conflict. The war continues to drag on practically unabated also because of external interferences and great power interests.

The initially peaceful protest against Assad in Spring 2011 quickly turned into a civil war with a regional and international dimension. Defectors from the regular army aimed at building a resistance movement the Free Syrian Army (FSA). Soon terrorist groups infiltrated the country.

© The Author(s) 2019
M. Brosig, *The Role of BRICS in Large-Scale Armed Conflict*, New Security Challenges, https://doi.org/10.1007/978-3-030-18537-4_4

The Al Qaeda off spring Jabhat Al-Nusra committed its first large-scale attack in Syria in December 2011.[4] In the coming years the Islamic State (IS) could gather significant military gains in Iraq and Syria, several rebel groups claimed territory in Syria and a proxy war began to take shape. While the Iranians sponsored Hezbollah and Russia supported Assad, Western powers, Turkey and Arab states wanted him to leave office and started arming opposition groups. Over the years the Assad government was seriously weakened and might have collapsed at some point. Russia's military intervention from September 2015 is generally seen as having prevented this. During the course of 2018 Assad consolidated his power not only because of Iranian and Russian military support but also because of a considerable weakening of Al-Nusra and the IS. However, a peaceful future still appears as a distant dream. Assad's power has been consolidated for now but he appears as too weak to maintain it without external support. The Sunni-Shia divide in the region also shows no signs of ending and the US cancellation of the Iran Nuclear Deal in 2018 provides further insecurity for the Middle East.

Box 4.1 Key Events: Syria

2011	
15 March	Protest starts in southern city of Deraa
10 August	IBSA foreign ministers visit Damascus
18 August	US, UK, France and Germany call on Assad to resign
4 October	Russia and China veto resolution on Syria
12 November	Arab League suspends Syria
2012	
4 February	Russia and China veto resolution on Syria
14 April	UNSC resolution 2042 establishment of military observer mission
21 April	UNSC resolution 2043 establishment of United Nations Supervision Mission in Syria (UNSMIS)
9 July	Geneva Action Group, basic principle for transition
19 July	Russia and China veto resolution on Syria
20 August	Obama use of chemical weapons would be a "red line" that would change his calculus on intervening in the civil war
2013	
21 August	Use of Sarin gas in Damascus kills hundreds
27 September	UNSC Res. 2118 Syria to destroy its chemical weapons stockpile

(*continued*)

Box 4.1 (continued)

2014	
22 May	Russia and China veto resolution on Syria
30 June	Islamic State declares caliphate in Iraq and Syria
23 September	US airstrikes on Islamic State in Syria
2015	
7 August	UNSC 2235, establishment of Joint Investigative Mechanism (JIM) into use of chemical weapons
30 September	Russian military intervention begins
2016	
14 March	Russia announces it will withdraw majority of troops from Syria
8 October	Russia vetoes resolution on Syria
5 December	Russia and China veto resolution on Syria
2017	
4 April	Nerve gas attack in Khan Sheikhoun
6 April	US fires cruise missiles into Syria in retaliation for the Khan Sheikhoun attack
12 April, 24 October, 16, 17 November	Russia vetoes resolution on Syria
28 February, April	Russia and China veto resolution on Syria
2018	
20 January	Turkey military operation against Kurdish fighters
26 February	Russia vetoes resolution on Syria
10 April	Russia vetoes resolution on Syria

THE BRICS RESPONSE

Unlike in the Libyan case in Syria BRICS countries were more than just bystanders to the conflict. They have been actively engaged from the beginning and kept their line of arguments throughout the years. In Libya during the decisive moments of decision-making in the UN BRICS members appeared as little prepared to launch a joint initiative and shape events on the ground. A joint position was the result of the Western-led intervention after it has happened. In the case of Syria a BRICS position emerged early on and generally aimed at preventing a replication of the 'Libyan model'. In this regard BRICS succeeded. In a highly contested arena such as the Middle East the Western and Arab position of removing Assad was blocked by rising powers such as BRICS. This vividly demonstrates their influence in one of the most important armed conflicts of our time.

The focal point of international attention was again concentrating on the UN Security Council as well as on events on ground be they mediation efforts or direct military support for one side or the other. Within the BRICS grouping the relevance and influence of individual members has changed significantly over the years. While at the beginning of the conflict all BRICS members were also Security Council members Brazil was the first to drop out by the end of 2011, to be followed by South Africa and India at the end of the following year. This had to the consequence that Russia and China acquired a more prominent role which can be seen in their frequent use of the veto (four times between 2011 and 2014). With Russia's decision to militarily intervene in Syria, the country has clearly taken the leadership within BRICS. On 13 occasions Russia used a veto since the outbreak of the war.[5] Russia dominates the diplomatic scene as well as the military.

Based on the six in-put conditions what are likely responses by BRICS countries with regard to the war in Syria? Regarding proximity and consequences of the conflict Syria displays different patterns in comparison to Libya. While the latter was mostly confined to the country the Syrian war soon acquired a regional and international dimension. The longer the war continued the more international the conflict became. Although no BRICS country is placed in the direct vicinity to the Middle East, Russia and China are geographically closest to Syria and are worried about Islamist terrorism and separatism in their own countries, either in the Caucasus or Western China. For Brazil India and South Africa no direct threat is emanating from the Syrian war but all BRICS countries have a general concern over terrorist activities and share the interest of curbing it. An active military role could realistically only be played by Russia whose Black Sea fleet is operating in relative proximity to the Syrian coast. Additionally Russia entertains a small naval base and airstrip in Syria. All other BRICS countries do not possess the necessary military hardware or political interest to play an active military role in the conflict. The Syrian war also resonates with the BRICS normative agenda directly as it is addressing questions of global order. The issue of intervention to topple Assad is an essential element of interest for BRICS countries. Here we would expect a strong diplomatic reaction. Materially and economically Syria does not top the list of a first class case for BRICS countries. While Syria is placed in the oil rich Middle East its trade and economic linkages with any of the BRICS countries are unlikely to be a major issue of concern because of the war. Given the severe humanitarian situation in the country we should assume that the BRICS response does not only aim at obstructing initiatives to remove

Assad forcefully but also allow and support multilateral peace negotiations as long as they do not openly challenge Assad. In sum, the Syrian conflict is likely to trigger a strong BRICS reaction because security concerns of two of its members are affected and issues of global order (regime change) are immanently impacted on by the conflict. Given the severity of the crisis we would expect references to multilateralism and humanitarian relief outside of highly contested political issues. Economic reasons for taking positions might only play a secondary role. Clearly Russia is the country with the greatest stakes in the conflict followed by China. The following empirical sections are divided into three parts. The early years 2011–2012, the middle years 2012–2014 and the endgame 2015–2018. Throughout these three phases the role of BRICS is changing, while at the beginning BRICS was most visible as a group providing diplomatic resistance against the West, the center of activity changed from the group as diplomatic actor to Russia as single actor and war fighting party in the conflict. Because of the prominent role Russia and China are playing in Syria the chapter closes with an analysis of their engagement in the conflict.

The Early Phase (2011–2012)

The 2011 BRICS summit which was taking place in April in Sanya does not make any reference to Syria. As events were only starting to unfold and attention was concentrating on Libya during that time the first official BRICS reaction to the Syrian crisis was released in November 2011 during a meeting of the Deputy Foreign Ministers in Moscow. The role of the UN Security Council was emphasized, since it bears the primary responsibility for maintaining international peace and security. It was noted that all parties should strictly implement Security Council decisions. They noted that it was inadmissible to impose solutions on the MENA states through outside intervention in internal political processes. The statement reads:

> The BRICS Deputy Foreign Ministers stressed that the only acceptable way to resolve the internal crisis in Syria is through urgent peaceful negotiations with participation of all parties as provided by the Arab League initiative taking into account the legitimate aspirations of all Syrians. Any external interference in Syria's affairs, not in accordance with the UN Charter, should be excluded. In this context the experience of the international community with regard to developments in Libya needs a thorough review to see if the actions taken were in conformity with the provisions of the relevant resolutions of the UN Security Council.[6]

The link between the Libyan case and Syria is clearly drawn. A repetition of the regime change approach is already ruled out early on. The statement also expresses the fear that adopted resolutions by the Security Council are not followed by action or are overstepping the mandated limits. Western demands of Assad to step down and the later drawing of red lines for intervention by Obama consolidated the BRICS view that military intervention needs to be prevented. This view was also not changed by the LAS first sanctioning Syria and later calling for Assad to resign.[7] As the BRICS countries do not possess the military capabilities to actively deter a Western intervention in order to remove Assad they concentrated on their influence within the Security Council and used sovereignty as a shield against intervention. After Libya it was clear that meticulous attention would be paid to any wording which could potentially open the door to forceful regime change.

In 2011 the Security Council did not find a majority to pass a resolution on Syria. Its first reaction came in the form of a presidential statement under Indian presidency which was adopted unanimously. The statement condemned the violence in Syria, called for an end of hostilities and upholding of Syria's sovereignty. It also finds that the "only solution to the current crisis in Syria is through an inclusive and Syrian-led political process, with the aim of effectively addressing the legitimate aspirations and concerns of the population..."[8]

Shortly after the adoption of the presidential statement a delegation of IBSA countries travelled to Damascus.[9] In this early phase of the conflict it was hoped that domestic reforms initiated by the government and accepted by the opposition would suffice to calm down tensions and would enable a genuine democratic peace process. However, the IBSA and BRICS position became increasingly irreconcilable with the Western and Arab position who insisted on Assad to leave before an inclusive peace process could start. From the IBSA and BRICS perspective the failure of early peace initiatives is at least partly to blame on this uncompromising position of the West to remove Assad. According to the Indian representative to the Security Council this emboldened the opposition to sabotage talks and hardened Assad's position to stay in power because of a lack of acceptable alternatives.[10] In the end, the IBSA initiative was short-lived and had little to no effect on events.

In October 2011 a draft resolution was brought before the Security Council largely supported by the West. It "Demands an immediate end to all violence and urges all sides to reject violence and extremism", reaffirms "the need to resolve the current crisis in Syria peacefully," repeats the importance of Syria's sovereignty and territorial integrity and notices the lack of political reform by the government. Partly the wording of the presidential statement from August was copied into the draft too when referring to a political solution based on a Syria-led inclusive peace process. The draft resolution places the prime responsibility to halt violence on the government. It closes by demanding compliance with the resolution or risking the application of sanctions according to article 41 of the UN Charter.[11]

All BRICS countries opposed the draft resolution. It was vetoed by Russia and China. Brazil, India and South Africa abstained. The statements made after the voting display a fair degree of coherence among BRICS countries but also show some differences. The most critical voice is Russia while Brazil appeared to be more at distance and less fundamental in its comments.

Russia's representative Vitaly Churkin finds that Russia "cannot agree with this unilateral, accusatory bent against Damascus. We deem unacceptable the threat of an ultimatum and sanctions against the Syrian authorities."[12] A similar position is shared by China who sees the threat of sanctions as counterproductive and encouraging the opposition to stay away from negotiations. In the eyes of Russia and China the draft resolution provides for no guarantees that no military intervention to remove Assad is sought. To the opposite, the official statements show concern that the resolution in its current wording can be used against Assad by providing the ground for sanctions. Both countries vetoed the resolutions.

Equally critical are the statements by India and South Africa who decided to abstain. India favors multilateral peace negotiations and called for more time for the government to implement the promised reforms. For India the draft resolution is also too one-sided as it does not explicitly condemn violence from the opposition.[13] South Africa insists on a "holistic" solution equally taking into account the concerns of the government and opposition. Fundamental opposition and deep-seated mistrust against the draft resolution is formulated by the South African representative to the Security Council who is suspicious about "the sponsors' intention to impose punitive measures that would have pre-judged the resolution's implementation. We believe that these were designed as a prelude to further actions. We are concerned that this draft resolution not be part of a hidden agenda aimed at once again instituting regime change, which has been an objective clearly stated by some."[14] Finally the Brazilian statement does not formulate a fundamental opposition but even mentions the establishment of a commission of inquiry into human rights violations and generally favors a political and inclusive solution to the conflict.[15]

In sum, BRICS countries prevented the adoption of the draft resolution out of concerns that it can pave the way and indirectly legitimize Assad's removal from power. These concerns seem to weigh heavier than any other. The exact wording of the draft resolution was maybe not the most controversial issue as the Russian representative finds but the conflict of approaches how to solve the conflict was. The insistence of Western powers that Assad must go shot-down even minimal space for compromise from Russia in the Security Council.[16] From the Russian perspective vetoing the resolution was about teaching the US a lesson. It "can either do regime change or work through the Security Council, but it can't do both."[17] Given the experience from Libya BRICS countries are now uncompromising when it comes to sovereignty rights of the government. Cross references have been made to BRICS and IBSA in the statements after voting. A fairly high degree of coherence could be observed with regard to the rejection of this draft resolution.

A second attempt to pass a Security Council resolution was started in early 2012. Extensive deliberations aimed at taking onboard some of the concerns BRICS members have issued the previous year. For example, no reference has been made to possible sanctions and military enforcement according to chapter VII of the UN Charter is explicitly ruled out. Furthermore, the draft text appears as better balanced. It "demands that all parties in Syria, including armed groups, immediately stop all violence".[18] Reference was made to the LAS transition plan for Syria which was adopted on 22 January with all members except Lebanon agreeing to the plan which foresees Assad to hand-over power to his deputy and start building a unity government.[19]

This time the BRICS grouping was split into two camps. While Russia and China used their veto, India and South Africa voted in favor of the draft which was also supported by all of the remaining members of the Security Council. Russia and China were repeating their complains about the one-sided and biased nature of the draft to the disadvantage of Assad. As the wording of the text has changed considerably and takes account of previous concerns, it becomes obvious that Russia and China principally bloc any resolution which would undermine Assad's power. The disregard for the LAS as well as the 13 other members of the Security Council falls into the response type of mini-lateral hegemonic behavior.

Contrasting Russia and China are Brazil, India and South Africa. India and South Africa both showed satisfaction with the draft resolution and openly endorsed the LAS transition plan. South Africa declared that the current proposal does not resemble any regime change approach and India is content with the resolution ruling out military enforcement but instead giving way for a political solution.[20] In this regard the IBSA countries were favoring a response to the crisis which is less build on power politics but is more integrated into multilateral and regional diplomatic conflict resolution.[21] Consequently, they voted for a General Assembly resolution resembling the failed draft resolution on 21 February 2012 while Russia and China voted against it. The General Assembly resolution was adopted with 137 votes in favor.[22]

Although Russia and China blocked two Security Council resolutions out of fear Assad could be weakened political momentum against the Syrian government was mounting outside the UN framework. Following a French initiative the Group of Friends of the Syrian People was set up in February 2012 comprising around 60 countries but none from the BRICS grouping.[23] The Group of Friends took a much more critical position against Assad and recommended tight sanctions against the regime.[24]

In March 2012 the BRICS Summit was held in New Delhi. Paragraph 21 of the final declaration was solely devoted to the Syrian crisis.[25] Here BRICS countries are calling for an immediate stop of the fighting and a Syrian-led peace process. Initiatives in that direction by the UN and LAS are welcomed. Unsurprisingly the declaration does not criticize the government for its excessive use of force nor is the future of Assad discussed or are sanctions mentioned. However, interesting is that the initiative of the LAS which has taken a critical position against Assad is generally supported but no reference is made to the IBSA visit to Damascus a year earlier. In the end, the Delhi declaration is a compromise between Russia and China who have an interest in not criticizing or sanctioning Assad but protecting him and IBSA. In contrast the IBSA position emphasizes the relevant regional groupings and a multilateral transition process which might have to the consequence Assad leaving power at some point.

Although the UN General Assembly supported the LAS plan it did not materialize. Instead the previously deployed military observer mission by LAS collapsed as Saudi Arabia and Qatar withdrew their support and the initiative for action fell back to the UN Security Council. This time, in April 2012, two resolutions passed the Council (Res 2042, 2043) establishing the United Nations Supervision Mission in Syria (UNSMIS) an unarmed military observer mission of 300 staff. The mission was to observe a ceasefire which was negotiated by the UN's special envoy to Syria former Secretary-General Kofi Annan. Although the ceasefire and negotiations did not provide for a breakthrough, the setting up of an Action Group for Syria facilitated the adoption of the Geneva Communiqué which should become the main point of reference for future peace talks. Annan resigned from his position in summer 2012. The Action Group comprises of the P5 as well as Turkey, Iraq, Kuwait and the EU. The communiqué does not call on Assad to resign but demands political reforms and a genuine democratic transition process. It emphasizes the importance of a peaceful solution to the conflict, highlighting Syria's sovereignty and rejects "any further militarization of the conflict".[26]

Obama's press statement about his "red line" being the use of chemical weapons in the conflict which would lead to "enormous consequences" limited potential space for compromise with Russia and China in the Security Council.[27] Both countries again vetoed a draft resolution from 19 July which threatened Syria with sanctions if it continues to use force against the opposition. Of the four remaining BRICS members in the Security Counciel only India voted in favor of the draft resolution while South Africa abstained. Russia and China repeated its rejection of onesidedly blaming or sanctioning the government of Syria for the continuation of the war. While all four countries supported the extension of the UNSMIS mandate which was also mentioned in the draft, Russia, China and South Africa had issues with it being linked to possible sanctions. A technical resolution extending the mandate of UNSMIS was adopted a few days later pragmatically avoiding contestation between Security Council members.

In sum, the first phase of the Syrian war showed some significant coherence between BRICS countries but also some deviations (see Table 4.1). During the Libyan crisis BRICS countries appeared as less prepared for coordinating and expressing joint positions, this has changed visibly. The joint concern of all BRICS states was that a regime change approach could be repeated and unbalanced accusations and sanctioning of the Assad regime would prepare the ground for a forceful replacement. However, it also became clear that there is a degree of difference between Russia and China and the IBSA countries. While the former acquired the role of a protection force for Assad, India, Brazil and South Africa, although equally critical of Western intervention, followed a more compromising path by, for example, voting in favor of the LAS transition plan. In this vein, Russia

Table 4.1 BRICS voting in UN Security Council 2011–2012

Resolution	Veto	Abstention	Positive
4 Oct 2011, condemnation of Syrian government	Russia, China	Brazil, India, South Africa	
February 2012, LAS peace plan	Russia, China		India, South Africa
Res. 2059 20 July 2012			Russia, China, India, South Africa
Res. 2042 14 April 2012			Russia, China, India, South Africa
Res. 2043 21 April			Russia, China, India, South Africa
19 July 2012	Russia, China	South Africa	India

and China are closer to hegemonic and mini-lateral (strategic) behavior while the IBSA group is closer to cooperative multilateralism within the framework of the UN and in support of regional organizations.

THE MIDDLE YEARS 2013–2014

In the following two years South Africa and India left the Security Council and thus lost some of their influence on decision-making within the UN. Russia and China became the two key countries within the BRICS grouping to shape events actively. Thereby the Russian interest and influence was growing over time. Between 2013 and 2014 the war in Syria entered a new phase. In August 2013 a Sarin gas attack killed several hundred people in Damascus and in June 2014 the IS declared a caliphate stretching across large parts of Iraq and Syria. For Assad and the opposition the war increasingly turned out to become unwinnable. A victory of one side became unlikely because the stalemate on the battlefield was cemented by external supplies in arms, ammunition and sometimes direct military support. A proxy war between those countries supporting Assad (mostly Russia and Iran) and those who wanted him to leave (mostly the West, Arab states and Turkey) prolonged the war. The middle years were characterized by rising Islamist terrorism and a gradual weakening of Assad.

In late March 2013 and one day before the BRICS summit in South Africa LAS filled the suspended membership of Syria with opposition leaders making clear that Arab states do not expect him to return to the LAS.

Assad addressed the BRICS countries directly by appealing to their reformist and anti-colonial position. Assad referred to BRICS as "a just force that seeks to spread peace, security and cooperation among countries away from hegemony, its dictates and oppression which have lasted for decades upon our peoples and nation." and "called upon to exert all possible efforts to end the suffering of the Syrian people,"[28]

The BRICS summit declaration in the end did not make any statements endorsing Assad but condemned human rights violations in Syria. Furthermore, the declaration repeated the call for a Syrian-led political process of which it can be expected that Assad would play a role. The BRICS declaration also opposes a further militarization of the conflict and makes reference to the Geneva Communiqué as a basis for peace talks.[29] What is interesting in this declaration in comparison to the Delhi one is that BRICS does not make any supportive statements toward LAS. Only the joint UN-LAS special envoy Lakhdar Brahimi is supported. The omission of LAS is surely linked to the organization's anti-Assad position which for example was criticized by Russia as undermining political efforts to solve the crisis.[30] This position is increasingly shared by other BRICS members. While in the early phase of the conflict IBSA countries tended to support the LAS this has changed in 2013. A letter from Brazil, India and South Africa to the permanent representative of Qatar to the UN (the country is holding the position of the Secretary-General of the LAS) opposes "the recognition of any opposition group as legitimate representatives of the Syrian people."[31] This view is widely shared among BRICS countries. Language which refers to sovereignty and a Syrian-led political process is usually understood at securing Assad a place at the negotiation table. Reference to the Geneva Communiqué is seen as an instrument against potential regime change approaches.

The use of chemical weapons in the war in Syria in 2013 (and repeatedly in the coming years) increased international tensions substantially. President Obama's red line has been crossed, the US and UK actively thought about military intervention which could have brought a quick end to Assad. The diplomatic scene now shifts mainly to Russia and the US. The challenge for these two countries in 2013 was to find a line which satisfies both countries strategic goals. However, the interests of providing a credible deterrence against the use of chemical weapons, the prevention of regime change and punishment for severe human rights violations of those who committed them appears as almost a mission impossible to reconcile with one another.[32]

Despite these challenges it is noteworthy that the Western-Arab coalition did not intervene militarily with ground troops to oust Assad and that Russia supported by China played an essential role in eliminating chemical weapons owned by Assad. The Western intervention did not materialize not only because Assad agreed to hand over and destroy his chemical weapons but also because Obama and Cameron did not get domestic support for an intervention. The US Congress and Houses of Parliament did not approve such action. Russia played an essential role by facilitating the disarmament of Assad and passing of resolution 2118 in September 2013. Accordingly the destruction of chemical weapons was conducted under the supervision of the Organization for the Prohibition of Chemical Weapons (OPCW). Resolution 2118 paved the way for the OPCW to verify the destruction of chemical weapons. Later on the OPCW should also play an important role investigating alleged uses of chemical substances which continued to be used in the coming years.

With the passing of resolution 2118 Russia prevented a potential military intervention which could have toppled Assad. The West at least could force Assad and Russia to agree to destroy his chemical arsenal. The war itself continued unabated. As Assad was getting weaker but opposition groups were split into many fractions, the IS extended its influence from Iraq into Syria and declared a caliphate in June 2014. As a consequence, US airstrikes targeting IS positions extended into Syria from September. A train and equip program for the Kurdish YPG was agreed by Congress. Increasingly the conflict became protracted with unclear prospects for any warring party.

Again divisions became apparent in the Security Council on the question of international criminal prosecution of war crimes in Syria. Russia and China vetoed a resolution which would have referred the situation to the ICC. By now the rhetoric used to justify their decisions is no surprise. Russia felt that the resolution is unbalanced not explicitly mentioning terrorist organizations and implicitly preparing regime change. According to Vitaly Churkin "The draft resolution was using the Court to inflame political passions for outside military intervention"[33] and thereby preventing a political solution. The Chinese representative argued in the same direction when saying that "Forcibly referring the situation to the Court in the current environment was neither conducive to building trust nor to the resumption of negotiations in Geneva".[34] Although the draft resolution did not mention any particular individuals the fact that Assad committed war crimes and could be hold accountable for them which would inevitably lead to him losing power was enough reason for Russia and China to veto the draft. Their argumentation did not convince the other members in the Security Council who all voted in favor of the resolution. Again the Russian-Chinese mini-lateral coalition acted in a hegemonic way protecting its own interests.

Despite this 2014 has also seen the passing of a number of Security Council resolutions and adoption of presidential statements on Syria.[35] The initial inaction of the previous year has been overcome at least with regard to the passing of resolutions and statements. Widespread agreement could be found in the Security Council with regard to countering terrorism. Resolution 2170 and 2178 engages with the problem of foreign fighters in Syria and calls upon states to step up border controls to curb the growing influx of terrorists into Syria. The fight against terrorism was one of the fields in which BRICS countries as well as the West found some common ground. The rapid extension of the IS into Syria also became a question of survival for Assad. The travelling of thousands of foreign fighters into Syria from Europe and the wider neighborhood posed a domestic security threat for many countries including Russia and China. There was broad agreement on the fight against terrorism in Syria. Beyond the issue of terrorism the Security Council could also pass two resolutions (2139, 2165) addressing humanitarian access to the civilian population. However, immediate positive effects on curbing terrorist activities and an improvement of humanitarian conditions could not be observed.

In the end, Russia and China, the two leading BRICS countries on the Syrian conflict displayed both hegemonic mini-lateralism in order to protect their own interests as well as multi-lateral cooperative behavior. However, cooperative behavior seems to be primarily facilitated in situations in which there was an overlap of common interest with the West (fighting terrorism) but the red line for Russia and China was primarily to protect Assad from sanctions, international criminal prosecution or military intervention to remove him. With the agreement to humanitarian access both countries did not have to compromise on Assad staying in power and could diffuse mounting criticism toward them regarding their power politics over Syria. And disregard for humanitarian issues.

The Endgame 2015–2018

The year 2015 marks the beginning of a turnaround in the Syrian war. With Russia's direct military intervention in favor of Assad the regime was saved from collapsing. The fight against the IS was gradually bearing fruits and with Turkey invading Northern Syria to counter the growing Kurdish influence near its border, by the end of 2018 Assad appeared to have regained power over large parts of the country. Within the BRICS grouping Russia became the most essential country in the Syrian conflict. While at the beginning of the Arab Spring a fairly high level of coherency between BRICS countries could be observed by 2015 it is primarily Russia which shapes events on the ground and takes diplomatic leadership. With holding the BRICS and SCO summits in 2015 in Russia Moscow emerged as leading these groupings on key positions.

However, the beginning of the year has seen a further weakening of Assad with opposition forces, the IS and Al Qaeda as well as Kurdish forces gaining ground at the cost of Assad. Additionally the US train and equip program in support of the opposition started.[36] The erosion of power became obvious. Russia's military intervention in Syria is mainly a reaction to Assad's weakness as his political future was in doubts and Russia would have lost its last ally in the region and would maybe been forced to close down its naval and air base in the country. As Russia's military intervention was conducted at the request of the Syrian government[37] it did not need Security Council approval and could be portrayed as upholding the country's sovereignty. BRICS countries did not challenge this view but also did not openly endorse Russia's military action. However, a credibility gap opened with BRICS rejecting a further militarization of the conflict, insisting on a political settlement and Russia becoming a warring party to the conflict steering peace talks through gains at the battlefield.

At the diplomatic scene the Security Council agreed on resolution 2035 which set up the so-called Joint Investigative Mechanism (JIM) between the UN and OPCW. The JIM has been mandated "to identify to the greatest extent feasible individuals, entities, groups, or governments who were perpetrators, organisers, sponsors or otherwise involved in the use of chemicals as weapons".[38] The resolution is quite important as the previous fact-finding mission (FFM) was only allowed to explore if chemical weapons have been used but not to explore by whom. Russia usually resisted clear attributions to the use of chemical weapons. However, the

JIM proofed to be essential in investigating and determining when, where and by whom these weapons have been used. Between its set up and end in 2017 it produced seven reports in which it identified the government as using chemical weapons in most cases. Russia vetoed the extension of the JIM in late 2017.[39] Eleven votes were cast in favor of the resolution. China abstained. However, in June 2018 the OPCW conference of state parties agreed to extend the mandate of the organization to also explore the source using chemical weapons. During the voting Russia and China voted against this amendment together with 22 other countries, while Brazil, India and South Africa abstained from voting.[40] In this context it is interesting to note that the BRICS summit in July 2018 now agrees to a "comprehensive, objective, independent, and transparent investigations of all alleged incidents" to the use of chemical weapons.[41] Before BRICS summit declarations have condemned the use of these weapons from any party but did not call for an investigation.[42] Here it seems although BRICS members in the OPCW did not support the amendment the later endorsed the overall aim of investigating the use of chemical weapons by the OPCW.

The 2015 BRICS summit in Ufa has been used by Russia to garner support from the grouping. The Ufa declaration expressed "support for the steps of the Russian Federation aimed at promoting a political settlement in Syria"[43] In line with the Russian position is also the rejection of "the politicization of humanitarian assistance in Syria and note the continuing negative impact of unilateral sanctions on the socio-economic situation in Syria"[44] and the "concern of spill-over effects" of terrorist groups in and beyond the Middle East.[45] This rhetoric aided Russian foreign policy goals because it diverts attention away from war crimes committed by Assad and helps Russia to keep him in power by denouncing sanctions as contributing to terrorism and humanitarian assistance as political maneuver in support of Assad's opponents. There is of course no critical word in the declaration against the government. The use of chemical weapons is generally condemned.[46] In sum, Russia's course of action is supported by the BRICS. Before the summit Russia had organized a number of peace talks in Moscow and Astana. This clearly indicates Russia's leadership ambitions.

The military intervention by Russia from late September turned out to be a game changer. Primarily through airstrikes Russia supported the Assad regime. Thereby opposition forces as well as terrorist groups were targeted. This allowed Assad to recapture territory. The recapturing of Aleppo, Syria's second largest town by the end of 2016 visibly showed

Assad regaining strength but at a heavy humanitarian price.[47] Most of the fighting occurred in densely populated urban areas. Syrian and Russian forces faced mounting international critique as the military tactic included the deliberate targeting of civilian areas, the destruction of basic infrastructure, medical facilities, in order to render opposition-held territory unlivable.[48] Because Russia and the US both conducted airstrikes in Syria they agreed on a Memorandum of Understanding on air safety.[49]

In practice US and Russian fighter jets did not intersect in one another's operation. With regard to fighting terrorism they followed complementary goals. Russia's air support for Assad did not only considerably weaken the opposition but the supply of modern air-defense systems also prevents the imposition of any no-fly-zone against the will of the government. A second Libya was not to be repeated. Russian and US ground forces were both operating in Syria but in lower numbers. Russia and the US made further efforts not to directly battle each other. For example a deconfliction line was agreed along the river Euphrates. Although regular Russian troops did not engage in active fighting apart from airstrikes it is assumed that up to 2000 Russian mercenaries are fighting in Syria. A US air attack on pro Assad troops and Russian mercenaries in February 2018 left several Russian nationals dead and demonstrated how easily great power rivalry can escalate into direct confrontation.[50]

Between 2015 and 2018 the Security Council entered its most active phase and passed 14 resolutions on Syria while an additional ten have been vetoed with Russia being the most active veto-user. Despite this mixed result council members (especially the P5) seemed to have found a *modus operandi* which kept the organization going addressing issues of mutual interest (terrorism) and responding to the humanitarian discourse. However, the impact on the ground of the UN remained limited. Diplomatic efforts to solve the crisis rather followed military gains or losses but were not determined by conflict mediation. By the end of 2018 Assad has consolidated his position in the country. Although he is considerably weaker than before the war and is unlikely to fully control the entire country soon any future scenario without him appears as unrealistic.

Because Russia and China are the two countries within BRICS which exert the greatest influence on the conflict the following section explores their individual motivations and positions toward Syria exploring in some detail why these two countries respond so strongly to the conflict in contrast to the IBSA countries.

Russia

Of all the BRICS countries Russia is the geographically closest to the conflict and is the most engaged in Syria. Proximity to the conflict seems to be an important trigger condition in combination with the military capabilities to intervene. Russia has justified its engagement in Syria as a response to a regional security threat at the request of a sovereign state. Its support for Assad is portrayed as a logic defense of a functioning state against terrorist groups which undermine the fragile order in the Middle East.[51] From this perspective the Russian involvement is justified because it fears a spread of terrorism into the Northern Caucasus and a radicalization of Sunni Muslims on its territory. Assad is seen as the only credible power which in the long-run can effectively counter terrorist groups. To which extent this argumentation is convincing and which consequences need to be drawn for Russian foreign policy is a matter of debate. Allison finds that "claims about spillover to the North Caucasus may serve an instrumental purpose"[52] because Sunni terrorism generally undermines Russian influence in the region (see Alawite Assad and Shiite Iran vs Sunni Arab countries allied with the West). In contrast Dannreuther argues that for Russia the conflict in Syria is "a constitutive element in the struggle to defeat Chechen secessionism and to counter the broader threat of Islamist extremism within the Russian Federation."[53] For the moment there is little direct evidence of large numbers of returning foreign fighters constituting a major security threat through separatism or terror attacks in Russia. A wave of terror attacks could be observed in Western Europe for which the IS claims responsibility. Still the building up of a Caliphate by the IS in Syria and Iraq can be seen as a general security threat should it succeed, independent of geopolitical concerns over alliances with Russia.

Proximity to the conflict and Russian military capabilities together allowed the country to play a direct role in the Syrian conflict. The Soviet legacy entailed a bilateral friendship treaty. Moscow entertains two military bases in Syria one airfield in Latakia and a naval base in Tartus. Several thousand Syrian officer were trained in Russian military academies even after the end of the Cold War.[54] The Russian Black Sea fleet based in Crimea was fairly easily to be relocated to the Syrian coast. A naval buildup of 10–15 ships could be observed at the Syrian coast from 2012 and long before the start of airstrikes in September 2015.[55] The Russian naval base in Tartus is rather small consisting of a pier, fuel tanks and barracks for 50–200 sailors.[56] While the military importance of this tiny base is indeed questionable it is one of the few remaining outposts in the region. Russia's naval presence at the Syrian coast also prevented any potential sea embargo and allows Russia to supply weapons to Assad.

Economically Syria is of little importance to Russia. To the opposite it is questionable if Syria can pay back the debt it accumulated over the years in the form of Russian arms supplies.[57] Even before the war Russia had to write off several billion dollars of Soviet era debt related to arms deals. Russia has been Syria's most important arms supplier before the war began. This dependency increased as Assad was losing territory and his power eroded. At the same time the war in Syria has crippled state revenue making it unlikely to pay back debt any time soon. While Assad promised Russian companies will be the first in the line after the war to help rebuild the country it is unclear who will pay for the reconstruction which is estimated to cost between $200–$500bn.[58] Western countries are not eager to pay the bill on Russia's terms alone. In short, there is no economic incentive for Russia to get involved so deeply into Middle Eastern politics. As a major oil producer Russia is not dependent on Arab energy supplies from the region which might also explain why Moscow did not need to take into consideration the LAS position on Assad.

Possibly the best explanation for Russia's engagement in Syria are its geopolitical interests and the opportunity to re-establish Russia as a global powerhouse.[59] Indeed, Russia has achieved most of its foreign policy goals. It saved Assad from being toppled. Without Russian and Iranian air and ground support Assad very likely would not be in power any more. Despite supporting Iran and Assad Russia could stay out of the deepening rift between Sunni and Shia competition in the region. No spill-over effect of Sunni terrorism or separatism could be observed. And even relations with Turkey which supported Assad's departure from power and shot down a Russian fighter-jet have improved significantly while Turkey's relations with the West are strained. Undoubtedly Russia's prestige and claim to great power status was primarily reinforced through its engagement in the Syrian war. Russia successfully confronted the US and Arab states who would otherwise be regarded as more powerful in terms of political and military weight in the region. Russia has done so by using relatively moderate and cost effective means: using its veto in the Security Council to prevent any sanctions or punishment of the government, supplying Assad with arms, preventing a potential sea embargo and no fly-zone and lastly starting an air campaign targeting all forces which challenged the regime. With modest means Russia gained maximum effect.

With regard to BRICS it did play an important role to enhance Russia's strategic goals in the Syrian war. First, the grouping as a matter of principle does not criticize or openly challenge a member's domestic or foreign policy in any of the BRICS statements. If BRICS members do criticize each other it is at a bi-lateral level and would involve key national interests. As this was not the case with the Syrian conflict the BRICS grouping indirectly lends support for Russian positions on Syria. BRICS normative agenda was resonating well with Russian foreign policy goals. BRICS concentration on the Security Council as sole decision-making institution, the linking of compliance to international law primarily with issues of state sovereignty, the rhetoric around unilateral interventions and regime change served Russian interests well. "Rigorous compliance" with the UN Charter as demanded by the Ufa declaration was understood that any action outside the framework of the Security Council was deemed illegitimate. Accordingly, Russia could denounce positions taken by the LAS or other international coalitions or groups which contradict or jeopardize Russian interests. The concentration on the Security Council allowed Russia to block unwanted resolutions through its veto.

The regime change rhetoric was a perfect fit to Russia's geopolitical interests to keep Assad in power. With normative backing from BRICS Russia could fend off any Western-Arab attempts to depose Assad. The anti-colonial reflex of up-holding uncompromised sovereignty almost at any costs was used if not abused by Russia to follow its geopolitical interests. While BRICS countries are quick in pointing to the politization of human rights issues and humanitarian aid in Syria they are rather silent when it comes to a sovereign state committing crimes punishable under the ICC statute and a BRICS member militarily supporting such a government.

China

In terms of proximity to the conflict China does have security, political and economic links to the region and Syria. While there is no direct security threat the traveling of terrorists to and from Syria to China's Western provinces poses a certain concern. Most of the Chinese nationals fighting in Syria against Assad are of Uighur origin, a province which is known for its political unrest.[60] However, the fear for a Jasmine revolution spreading from the Arab Spring to central China is largely unjustified. When only focusing on Syria the importance of the country for China is rather limited.

It, however, becomes much more important when viewing the conflict from a regional perspective. The MENA region is of essential economic importance for China as it is the country's main supplier of crude oil. More than half of China's oil imports are from this region.[61] Thus good relations with Arab states are important to China in order to keep its economy growing which constitutes one of its key domestic priorities. Unlike Russia, China did not run military installations in Syria. The closest military bases to Syria are located in the Gulf of Aden and Djibouti. In sum, considering China's foreign policy trajectory of taking non-interventionist positions and the absence of a direct and significant security threat it would be rather surprising for China to play an active military role in the Syrian conflict or display a diplomatic leadership ambition.

Accordingly China's response to the crisis was mainly confined to the diplomatic sphere and its influence in the Security Council. The first priority was to prevent a repetition of the "Libyan model" of regime change which entailed supporting armed opposition against the government, forming a coalition of the willing to intervene militarily, seek Security Council approval for such action and justify it with reference to protecting civilians and human rights. Such an approach found clear Chinese rejection. The former ambassador to Egypt An Huihou summarizes the Chinese view of the Western role in the conflict as basically hypocritical when saying:

> ...they urge Bashar to stop fighting unilaterally and to withdraw troops from the cities on the one side, whereas arm the oppositions and encourage them to refuse negotiation, to incite more conflicts and cause more casualties. With all these arrangements, they then blame the government for all the violence, with the purpose of justifying their further intervention.[62]

In the case of China the rejection of regime change was not linked to geopolitical issues of great power influence as in the case of Russia but was a principled decision. China repeatedly said it is not looking for a proxy nor establishing a zone of influence.[63] It's voting behavior although protecting Assad is primarily a consequence of the concern over the linkage between intervention and regime change.[64] As a consequence, in case of conflict the protection of sovereignty rights is regarded as more relevant than the protection of civilians.[65] Throughout the crisis China has insisted on a negotiated peace and in single incidents taken diplomatic initiative to work out a peace plan.[66] Like Russia it favored the Geneva Communiqué format over regional groupings or other forms of contact groups. From the Chinese perspective the main reason for political unrest in the region is not political but rooted in under-development and missing economic opportunities. In this context China promotes its BRI as an opportunity for development and cooperation.[67]

The frequent use of the veto in one conflict is unprecedented in Chinese foreign policy history and did surprise Arab nations.[68] The Russian vigor to use the veto to protect Assad from any criticism and intervention was diverting attention away from China and made it easier to veto. Russia and China double vetoed resolutions on six occasions between 2011 and 2017.[69] The difference between Russia and China is that Russia acted more out of geopolitical power interests and China out of principle concern over military interventions. From this perspective the BRICS grouping worked for Russia as a convenient foreign policy instrument through which the country could leverage its goals. For China the BRICS normative agenda reflects well on its preference for uncompromised sovereignty and opposition against the linkage between military interventions on alleged or real humanitarian reasons and regime change targeting Assad. The Chinese position somehow deviated from the Russian with its insistence on political peace talks as the only instrument to solve the crisis.

IBSA

The IBSA countries were not directly involved in the war in Syria and thus their primary response was diplomatic and cooperative focusing on the UN. Economically Brazil and South Africa had no important stakes in the conflict and were also not effected by a potential spread of terrorist activities from the Middle East. Syria does not have any important strategic meaning for these two countries. With regard to India which receives large parts of its oil imports from the region, a major war like the one in Syria is certainly of concern as well as the fight against Islamist terrorism. However, there is no immediate security threat emanating from Syria to India. Thus India's response to the crisis is predominantly diplomatic. The IBSA countries response to the crisis differs from those of Russia and China. While the latter protect the government from any criticism and use their diplomatic influence to keep Assad in power, the IBSA countries took a more nuanced position.

Brazil maybe because it is the most detached from conflict has taken a perspective emphasizing human rights concerns the most prominently within the BRICS grouping. While all BRICS countries emphasize the importance of the UN and seeking a political solution, Brazil finds that one of the main contributing factors to the war is external support for the warring parties which let the country to call for an arms embargo.[70] Brazil also repeatedly called for the criminal prosecution of war crimes committed in Syria. The country voted in favor of the setting up of an Independent International Commission of Inquiry on Syria which since its establishment was chaired by the Brazilian Paulo Sérgio Pinheiro. The commission in contrast to the UN Security Council has explicitly condemned the government forces as well as other groups for human rights violations.[71] A few thousand refugees were granted visas to travel to Brazil for humanitarian reasons.[72] When attacks of chemical weapons occurred Brazil called for an "impartial" inquiry to identify the perpetrators.[73] In the Brazilian case a genuine interest in humanitarian issues seems to be identifiable which contrasts the power politics approach chosen by Russia and the absolute sovereignty approach favored by China. Concerns of illegitimate and forceful regime change are far less articulate in the response to the crisis.

South Africa decided to take a somehow different position. The country has frequently condemned acts of war crimes in Syria committed by different sides. The concern about regime change and the instrumental use of humanitarian issues tends to dominate foreign policy responses. In 2016 the South Africa deputy foreign minister Mfeketo travelled to Damascus on an official state visit, describing bilateral relations as "cordial".[74] One year early Syria's foreign minister travelled to Cape Town meeting Mfeketo. In a press statement during the visit South Africa condemned acts of terrorism and human rights violations by the IS and Al Nusra and other terror groups but did not include Syrian authorities. Instead repeated its rejection "for regime change and external military interference".[75] The experience of Libya has fundamentally shaped South Africa's diplomatic response to the Syrian crisis which is dominated by the deep seated worry about Western military intervention outside the framework of the UN or overstretching UN mandates. While South Africa is not supporting Assad at any costs, like Russia or China do, it seems to value its principled objection to regime change higher than any potential or real war crimes committed by the Syrian government. At least the foreign ministry has difficulties in finding a middle way between the rejection of illegitimate foreign intervention and war crimes committed by the government.

Similar to Brazil and South Africa India lost influence with its departure from the UN Security Council. While in the case of Brazil and South Africa there were practically no significant economic or security links to Syria or the region, for India the region plays a far more important role. Former minister of external affairs Salman Khurshid in 2014 said: "We have substantial interests in the fields of trade and investment, diaspora, remittances, energy and security. Any spill-over from the Syrian conflict has the potential of impacting negatively on our larger interests."[76] Even though this statement is certainly true with regard to oil supplies and terrorism it is interesting to see that India did relatively little to play a somewhat more influential role during the Syrian crisis and after it had to leave the Security Council. After 2013 the ministry of external affairs only made a handful of official comments regarding the situation in Syria. India often avoided to take sides by explicitly condemning violence committed either by the government or particular groups and frequently stressed that "There can be NO military solution to the crisis"[77] and that a negotiated peace is the preferred tool of conflict resolution. Judging from official statements India was of the view that the Syrians themselves have to negotiate an agreement and refers to the crisis as an internal matter.[78] Taking this perspective India, although having some strategic interest in the conflict, decided to only get minimally involved supporting diplomatic initiatives to conflict resolution and providing some modest financial contribution to the UN's humanitarian relief. No initiative was made to claim the role of a key player. India acquired the well-known role of a reluctant hegemon.

Conclusion: The BRICS Grouping and Syria

The longer the war lasted the clearer it became that the BRICS members have different priorities and also responded differently to the conflict. At the beginning of the war the BRICS position was fairly coherent worrying about a replication of the Libyan model in which sanctions are used to isolate the government and opposition groups are armed to remove Assad. Consequently, BRICS members all serving on the Security Council in 2011 rejected unilateral action only targeting the government. The BRICS group response resembles those of the cooperative response types taking a neutral stance to conflict parties and emphasizing multilateral reactions within the confines of the UN system.

Over time, however, the IBSA countries, Russia and China diverged from this common route. Table 4.2 summarizes the different responses of individual BRICS countries and their main motivation for it. India, Brazil and South Africa had to leave the Security Council and therewith lost important formal decision-making power to work through the UN system. The IBSA mediation initiative bore no fruits and thus the influence of Russia and China with its veto power was increasing within the BRICS group as the war was intensifying. This also let to a change in response to the crisis. Gradually Russia and China favored a neo-imperialist and hegemonic response to the crisis instead of a cooperative one. The premier goal was not neutral conflict mediation but playing power politics in the case of Russia in order to redeem great power status which resulted in protecting Assad from any criticism, sanctions or forceful replacement at almost any costs. At the diplomatic level Russia and China double vetoed a number of draft resolutions. Lastly Russia responded the most forceful by actively becoming a conflicting party in the war and moving toward neo-imperial behavior which was occasionally punctuated by multilateralism (fighting terrorism, mediation, humanitarian relief). China played a hegemonic role using its diplomatic weight in the Security Council vetoing any resolution which could undermine the survival of Assad. Its main motivation was not great power politics but a deep reaching wariness over sovereignty and non-intervention. South Africa, Brazil and India not possessing the privilege of veto power or significant enough resources to change the direction of the conflict can all be categorized as responding cooperatively to the crisis emphasizing the importance of multilateral solutions within the established framework of the UN. Despite this they do vary in approach, ambition and motivation. South Africa's main motivation was to stop the erosion of sovereignty rights as seen in the Libyan example. Brazil favored multilateral responses to the crisis based on humanitarian concerns and articulated a responsibility to sanction human rights violations. Finally India favored multilateralism as a means to maintain state sovereignty and enable non-military solutions to the conflict.

Table 4.3 provides an overview of the six in-put variables and their relative strength. Assuming that the stronger the in-put conditions are (+++ vs. ---) the stronger (more coercive) the response is confirmed when looking at Russia, China vs. South Africa and Brazil. Both Russia and China display greater vulnerabilities to the conflict and have significant capabilities at their disposal than South Africa and Brazil. Hence their response to the crisis is different as described above. Interesting is the case

Table 4.2 Mapping of response types and motivation: Syria

Country	Russia	China	South Africa	Brazil	India
Response type	Neo-imperialist (temporary)	Hegemonic (leadership)	Cooperative (active)	Cooperative (active)	Cooperative (passive)
Main motivation	Reclaiming great power status, strategic interests, occasional multilateralism	Sovereignty and non-intervention, occasional multilateralism	Upholding multilateralism based on sovereignty and non-intervention	Upholding multilateralism, humanitarian concerns	Upholding multilateralism, non-military, non-interventionist solution

Table 4.3 Trigger variables and countries: Syria

	Russia	China	South Africa	Brazil	India
Proximity	+ +	+	– – –	– – –	+
Capability interests	+ +	+	– – –	– – –	–
Type of conflict	+ + +	+ + +	+ + +	+ + +	+ + +
Economics	+	+ +	– – –	– – –	+ +
BRICS agenda	+ +	+ +	+ + +	+	+ +
Humanitarian norms	– –	– –	+	+ +	+

+ and – indicate various degrees of importance or lack thereof of the trigger variables

of India which displays greater vulnerabilities than South Africa and Brazil but its response remains similar to its IBSA partners. In all countries we can also see a positive alignment to the BRICS normative agenda of a multi-polar world order of sovereign equal states which explains the prominence with which the topic was dealt with at BRICS summit meetings. Humanitarian concerns seemed not to have played a dominant role. Only Brazil showed above the average diplomatic initiative to sanction war crimes.

Notes

1. Source: UNHCR https://data2.unhcr.org/en/situations/syria accessed 11 June 2018.
2. Specia, Megan (2018) "How Syria's Death Toll Is Lost in the Fog of War" The New York Times 13 April 2018. https://www.nytimes.com/2018/04/13/world/middleeast/syria-death-toll.html accessed 11 June 2018.
3. Lundgren, Magnus (2016) "Mediation in Syria: initiatives, strategies, and obstacles, 2011–2016," *Contemporary Security Policy* 37(2) 273–288.
4. Humud, Carla, Blanchard, Christopher and Nikitin, Mary Beth (2017) *Armed Conflict in Syria: Overview and U.S. Response*. Washington D.C. Congressional Research Service, p. 6.
5. UN Dag Hammarskjöld Library: Security Council – Veto List https://research.un.org/en/docs/sc/quick accessed 11 June 2018.
6. Joint Communiqué on the Outcome of the Meeting of BRICS Deputy Foreign Ministers on the Situation in the Middle East and North Africa, Moscow, Russia, 24 November 2011.
7. Sly, Liz (2012) "Arab League calls on Syria's Assad to step down" The Washington Post, 22 January 2012. https://www.washingtonpost.com/

world/middle_east/arab-league-calls-on-syrias-assad-to-step-down/2012/01/22/gIQAajYhJQ_story.html?noredirect=on&utm_term=.de19dd2bc10b accessed 22 June 2018.
8. UN Security Council, Statement by the President of the Security Council, 3 August 2011.
9. Brazilian Ministry of Foreign Affairs (2011) "Statement to the Press from IBSA about consultations held in Syria – Damascus," August 10, 2011. http://www.itamaraty.gov.br/en/press-releases/14334-declaracao-a-imprensa-do-ibas-sobre-consultas-mantidas-na-siria-2 accessed 22 June 2018.
10. Hardeep, p. 125.
11. UN Security Council, draft resolution 612, 4 October 2011.
12. UN Security Council, 6627th meeting 4 October 2011, p. 3.
13. Ibid., pp. 6–7.
14. Ibid., p. 11.
15. Ibid.
16. Charap, Samuel (2013) "Russia, Syria and the Doctrine of Intervention", *Survival*, 55(1), p. 37.
17. Ibid., p. 40.
18. UN Security Council, draft resolution 77, 4 February 2012, p. 3.
19. Saleh, Yasmine and Noueihed Lin (2012) "Arab League proposes new plan for Syrian transition" Reuters 22 January 2012. https://www.reuters.com/article/us-syria/arab-league-proposes-new-plan-for-syrian-transition-idUSTRE8041A820120122 accessed 13 June 2018.
20. UN Security Council, 6711th meeting 4 February 2012, p. 8.
21. Higashi, Daisaku (2013) "Battle at the UN Security Council on Peace Enforcement in Libya and Syria: Focusing on the Strategies of BRICS" Doushisha University, Global Studies. http://global-studies.doshisha.ac.jp/attach/page/GLOBAL_STUDIES-PAGE-EN-73/80560/file/OS2013_5.pdf accessed 18 June 2018.
22. UN General Assembly, Resolution 66/253. The situation in the Syrian Arab Republic, 21 February 2012.
23. Abdenur, Adriana (2016) "Rising Powers and International Security: the BRICS and the Syrian Conflict" *Rising Powers Quarterly*, 1(1), p. 114.
24. Group of Friends of the Syrian People: 1st Conference Chairman's Conclusions from the First Conference of the Group of Friends of the Syrian People ("the Friends' Group") held in Tunis on February 24, 2012. http://carnegie-mec.org/diwan/48418?lang=en accessed 13 June 2018.
25. BRICS Summit Declaration, New Delhi, 29 March 2012, p. 21.
26. Final communiqué of the Action Group for Syria, 30 June 2012.
27. President Barack Obama, Remarks by the President to the White House Press Corps, 20 August, 2012.

28. Gladstone, Rick and Droubi, Hala (2013) "Assad Sends Letter to Emerging Powers Seeking Help to End Syrian War" The New York Times 27 March 2013. https://www.nytimes.com/2013/03/28/world/middleeast/syrias-developments.html accessed 14 June 2018.
29. eThekwini Declaration 27 March 2013, p. 26.
30. Gladstone and Doubi.
31. IBSA letter to permanent representative of Qatar to the UN, 18 April 2013.
32. Edwards, Brett and Cacciatori, Mattia (2018): The politics of international chemical weapon justice: The case of Syria, 2011–2017, *Contemporary Security Policy*, 39(2), 280–297.
33. UN Security Council Referral of Syria to International Criminal Court Fails as Negative Votes Prevent Security Council from Adopting Draft Resolution 22 May 2014, p. 5.
34. Ibid., p. 6.
35. Odeyemi, Christo (2016) "Re-emerging Powers and the Impasse in the UNSC over R2P Intervention in Syria," *Strategic Analysis*, 40:2, 131.
36. Humud, et al. para. 8.
37. "Syria's Assad wrote to Putin over military support: statement" Reuters 30 September 2015. https://www.reuters.com/article/us-mideast-crisis-syria-putin-idUSKCN0RU17Y20150930 accessed 22 June 2018.
38. UN Security Council, Resolution 2235, para. 5, 7 August 2015.
39. UN Security Council, Draft Resolution 970, 17 November 2017, https://research.un.org/en/docs/sc/quick
40. OPCW, Conference of the States Parties, 27 June 2018. https://www.opcw.org/fileadmin/OPCW/CSP/C-SS-4/en/css403_e_.pdf accessed 30 July 2018.
41. BRICS Summit Declaration, Johannesburg 25–27 July 2018, p. 46.
42. BRICS Summit Declaration, Xiamen, 4 September 2017, p. 41.
43. BRICS Summit Declaration, Ufa, 9 July 2015, p. 36.
44. Ibid.
45. Ibid., para. 38.
46. Ibid., para. 36.
47. Aljazeera (2016) "Syria's government recaptures all of Aleppo city" 22 December 2016 https://www.aljazeera.com/news/2016/12/syria-government-recaptures-aleppo-161222184428465.html accessed 18 June 2018.
48. International Crisis Group (2016) "Russia's Choice in Syria" Crisis Group Middle East Briefing N°47, Istanbul/New York/Brussels, 29 March 2016. https://www.crisisgroup.org/middle-east-north-africa/eastern-mediterranean/syria/russia-s-choice-syria accessed 19 June 2018.

49. U.S., Russia Sign Memorandum on Air Safety in Syria, 20 October 2015, https://www.defense.gov/News/Article/Article/624964/us-russia-sign-memorandum-on-air-safety-in-syria/ accessed 18 June 2018.
50. Reuter, Christopher (2018) "The Truth About the Russian Deaths in Syria" Spiegel Online 2 March 2018. http://www.spiegel.de/international/world/american-fury-the-truth-about-the-russian-deaths-in-syria-a-1196074.html accessed 18 June 2018.
51. Allison, Roy (2013) "Russia and Syria: explaining alignment with a regime in crisis" *International Affairs* 89(4), p. 809.
52. Ibid., p. 819.
53. Dannreuther, Roland (2012) "Russia and the Middle East: A Cold War Paradigm?" *Europe-Asia Studies*, 64(3), p. 545.
54. Allison, p. 802.
55. Russia Today (2013) "Russia to expand Mediterranean fleet to 10 warships – Navy chief" Russia Today 13 September 2013. https://www.rt.com/news/navy-warship-syria-mediterranean-800/ accessed 19 June 2018.
56. Kramer, Andrew (2012) "Russian Warships Said to Be Going to Naval Base in Syria" The New York Times 18 June 2012. https://www.nytimes.com/2012/06/19/world/europe/russian-warships-said-to-be-going-to-naval-base-in-syria.html accessed 19 June 2018.
57. Allison, p. 805.
58. Kathrin Hille, Henry Foy and Max Seddon (2018) "Russian business first in line for spoils of Syrian war" Financial Times, 2 March 2018. https://www.ft.com/content/c767cfba-1c9a-11e8-aaca-4574d7dabfb6 accessed 20 June 2018.
59. Frolov, Vladimir (2017) "Two Years on, the Stakes of Russia's War in Syria Are Piling (Op-ed) Russia may have helped Assad win the war, but crucial decisions lie ahead" *The Moscow Times* Sep 29, 2017. https://themoscowtimes.com/articles/two-years-on-the-stakes-of-russias-war-in-syria-are-piling-59112 Accessed 20 June 2018.
60. Blanchard, Ben (2017) "Syria says up to 5000 Chinese Uighurs fighting in militant groups" Reuters 11 May 2017. https://www.reuters.com/article/uk-mideast-crisis-syria-china/syria-says-up-to-5000-chinese-uighurs-fighting-in-militant-groups-idUSKBN1840UP accessed 21 June 2018.
61. Dusek, Mirek and Kairouz, Maroun (2017)" Is China pivoting towards the Middle East?" World Economic Forum 4 April 2017. https://www.weforum.org/agenda/2017/04/is-china-pivoting-towards-the-middle-east/ accessed 21 June 2018.
62. Huihou, An (2012) "The Turmoil in the Middle East and North Africa, and Western Neo-Interventionism" 270–285.
63. Speech by H.E. Xi Jinping President of the People's Republic of China At the Arab League Headquarters "Work Together for a Bright Future of

China-Arab Relations" Cairo, 21 January 2016 http://english.cntv. cn/2016/01/22/ARTIadCQDyVQjG0ADCkR2tcl160122.shtml accessed 21 June 2018.
64. Fung, Courtney (2018) "Separating Intervention from Regime Change: China's Diplomatic Innovations at the UN Security Council Regarding the Syria Crisis" *The China Quarterly* 235, 693–712.
65. Swaine, Michael (2012) "Chinese Views of the Syrian Conflict" *Chinese Leadership Monitor* No 39 https://www.hoover.org/research/chinese-views-syrian-conflict accessed 21 June 2018.
66. Patey, Luke and Malmvig, Helle (2016) "Geopolitics and non-western intervention in Syria, China, the Syrian conflict, and the Threat of Terrorism" Policy Brief DIIS·Danish Institute for International Studies, December 2016. http://pure.diis.dk/ws/files/710591/China_the_Syrian_conflict_and_the_threat_of_terrorism_webversion.pdf accessed 21 June 2018.
67. Speech by H.E. Xi Jinping, see above.
68. Interview Prof Wu, Bing Bing, Peking University 27 December 2017.
69. UN Dag Hammarskjöld Library: Security Council – Veto List https://research.un.org/en/docs/sc/quick accessed 21 June 2018.
70. Brazil, Ministry of Foreign Affairs: Geneva ll International Conference on Syria – Montreaux, January 22, 2014 – Intervention by Deputy Foreign Minister, Ambassador Eduardo dos Santos, January 22, 2014. http://www.itamaraty.gov.br/en/press-releases/3605-international-conference-of-syria-geneva-ii-montreaux-january-22-2014-speech-by-deputy-foreign-minister-ambassador-eduardo-dos-santos accessed 23 July 2018.
71. Resolution adopted by the Human Rights Council at its seventeenth special session S-17/1. Situation of human rights in the Syrian Arab Republic.
72. Watts, Jonathan (2015) "A long way from home: Syrians find unlikely refuge in Brazil" The Guardian 11 March 2015. https://www.theguardian.com/world/2015/mar/11/syrians-refuge-brazil-latin-america-war-refugees accessed 23 July 2018.
73. Brazil, Ministry of Foreign Affairs: "Use of chemical weapons in the Syrian province of Idlib" 4 April 2017. http://www.itamaraty.gov.br/en/press-releases/16045-use-of-chemical-weapons-in-the-syrian-province-of-idlib accessed 23 July 2018.
74. South Africa, Department of International Relations and Cooperation: Deputy Minister Mfeketo is in Syria on an official visit. 18 May 2016. http://www.dirco.gov.za/docs/2016/syri0518.htm accessed 23 July 2018.
75. South Africa, Department of International Relations and Cooperation: Deputy Minister Mfeketo met her Syrian counterpart for bilateral consultations. 4 August 2015. http://www.dirco.gov.za/docs/2015/syri0806.htm accessed 23 July 2018.

76. India, Ministry of External Affairs: External Affairs Minister's Statement at the International Conference on Syria (Geneva-II) January 22, 2014. https://www.mea.gov.in/Speeches-Statements.htm?dtl/22765/External_Affairs_Ministers_Statement_at_the_International_Conference_on_Syria_GenevaII accessed 24 July 2018.
77. Ibid.
78. India, Ministry of External Affairs: Address by Minister of State for External Affairs Shri E. Ahamed at High-level International Humanitarian Pledging Conference for Syria. January 30, 2013. https://www.mea.gov.in/Speeches-Statements.htm?dtl/21138/Address_by_Minister_of_State_for_External_Affairs_Shri_E_Ahamed_at_Highlevel_International_Humanitarian_Pledging_Conference_for_Syria accessed 24 July 2018.

CHAPTER 5

Ukraine: Moving Borders Changing Orders?

The conflict in the Ukraine maybe more than any other conflict discussed in this study touches upon global order questions. Of the four conflicts explored it is the least violent. Between its outbreak in late 2014 and September 2018 the Uppsala Conflict Data Program (UCDP) lists 6366 fatalities.[1] For the attention the conflict receives internationally these numbers are comparatively moderate. In other words, it is not the intensity or severity of the conflict which makes the Ukrainian crisis standing out. It is its propensity and character challenging the dominant Western order which makes it an ideal test case for exploring the influence of rising powers on global order questions. The international political dimension of the Ukrainian crisis is indeed further reaching than those of the other three case studies. While the interests of Western countries and emerging powers were at odds over Libya and Syria direct confrontation was avoided. Western countries did not back Syrian opposition forces through sending ground forces at a scale that would have threatened Assad's survival and led to a direct confrontation between the US and Russia. Russia's leading role in Syria was tolerated in the end, though not by choice. The civil war in South Sudan also lacks a broader global order dimension. This is fundamentally different in the case of the Ukraine. While in Libya and Syria one side backed off, in the Ukrainian crisis both Russia and the West maintain their position.

© The Author(s) 2019
M. Brosig, *The Role of BRICS in Large-Scale Armed Conflict*, New Security Challenges, https://doi.org/10.1007/978-3-030-18537-4_5

Although the situation is reminiscent of Cold War times, there is no Cold War II on the horizon. Three elements shaping the Cold War are now missing. First, there is no competition between ideological systems. Second, the conflict has no nuclear dimension. Third, the conflict does not take place in a global order shaped by bi-polarity. The last point is of course the most relevant condition for this chapter. However the ongoing conflict will be solved and whatever the consequences are global order questions will not just be an issue between Russia and the West as it was during the Cold War. The standoff between Russia and the West over the Ukraine will also be fought in the international arena over the opponent's ability to create authority and legitimacy for their positions and action on the ground. In a multi-polar system this is a rather complex undertaking.

The Ukrainian crisis is a delicate case for BRICS countries for two reasons. First it involves one of its members directly. In all other cases the security implications from war were rather indirect; this time one of its members is deeply involved in war fighting right at its borders. Second, the violation of Ukraine's territorial integrity deeply infringes upon classical sovereignty rights. BRICS countries traditionally attach great importance to these and have frequently criticized the West for acting neo-imperially when intervening militarily. Thus the political stakes for BRICS countries and global order questions about the rightness of action are the highest in the case of the Ukraine.

How the Conflict Unfolds

The sources for conflict were building up over a number of years since the Ukraine declared independence following the demise of the Soviet Union. Historically, culturally and geographically the Ukraine will remain closely linked to Russia independent of how the current conflict is finally solved. This inter-connectedness makes it nearly impossible for Russia to turn a blind eye to Ukrainian politics. At the heart of the conflict are not Russian-Ukrainian cultural bounds but the competition between Western economic and political ascendancy in the form of the EU as well as US influence in the form of NATO versus Russia's claim of authority in the post-Soviet region. Lastly, the Ukrainian crisis and subsequent war are a symptom of the inability of Western countries and Russia to have built a reliable post-Soviet order which balances and takes account of each other's interests and security concerns. The Ukraine's in-between position between the EU's Europe and Russia's Eurasia is a geopolitical fact. Drawing it in only one direction, East or West, nurtures conflict without giving either side a strategic advantage in the long run. As in many other violent conflicts, the signs for disaster were visible before the conflict broke out but have been poorly understood nor has either side been concerned about conflict prevention.

The history of the Crimean peninsula has been a rather dynamic one. It has been conquered by Russia in the eighteenth century; the Crimean war in the nineteenth century has seen military conflict between imperial powers (Turkey, France, Britain) and Russia; during the Russian Revolution in the early twentieth century it changed hands many times between the Red Army and tsarist troops. During the Second World War it was occupied by Nazi Germany from 1942 to 1944. In 1954 the Soviet Union transferred the territory to the Ukrainian Soviet Socialist Republic (SSR). It remained part of independent Ukraine after the collapse of the Soviet Union. However, its population is mostly Russian-speaking and Russia's Black Sea fleet is stationed in Sevastopol and could not easily be relocated. The Crimean peninsula is the geostrategically most important location for Russia in the region, as it is synonymous for projecting naval power at its Southern border. Not to forget a North Atlantic Treaty Association (NATO) member state, Turkey, lays opposite Russia's Southern sea border and control of Crimea means controlling access to the Sea of Azov with its harbor in Mariupol.

In May 1997 Russia and the Ukraine adopted a friendship treaty. In Article 3 both countries agreed to recognize each other's "(…) sovereign equality, territorial integrity, inviolability of borders, peaceful settlement of disputes, nonuse of force or threat of force, including economic and different ways of pressure, the right of the people to dispose freely of the destiny, non-interference to internal affairs (…)."[2] Also in 1997 Russia agreed to lease the now exterritorial naval base on Crimea for 20 years. The end of the lease and insecure future of the Russian fleet on Ukrainian territory were surely seen as a major strategic problem in Russia. Indeed, the destiny of the Russian fleet and thus geopolitical influence in the region were also linked to the political direction Ukrainian politics would take.

The 2004 elections have been the most controversial until then. Viktor Yushchenko and Viktor Yanukovych engaged in a fierce power battle triggering the Orange Revolution in which civil society enforced the cancelation of supposedly rigged elections in favor of Yanukovych, a pro-Russian candidate. Finally Yushchenko emerged as winner of the rerun elections in December. During his presidency until 2010 the Ukraine started leaning toward the West. In September 2008 the Ukrainian Prime Minster Yulia Tymoshenko declared her intention not to extend the Russian lease contract beyond 2017.[3]

In 2008 NATO considered the application of Georgia and the Ukraine for membership which was fiercely resisted by Russia and portrayed as a direct security threat by Putin.[4] Increasingly Russia was disillusioned from its engagement with the West. From Moscow's view its approach of pragmatic cooperation with the West on issues of terrorism after 9/11[5] and Medvedev's attempt to build a new transatlantic security architecture[6] were not bearing any tangible political fruits. To the contrary, NATO membership was further extending eastward. In 2004 Bulgaria and Romania joined NATO and with Georgia and Ukraine on the brink to follow Russia would have been the only non-NATO country at the Black Sea but its most valuable military asset in the Ukraine. The idea that the Russian navy might either need to leave Crimea or be "out-crowded" by NATO in Sevastopol was a scenario which can be assumed to be perceived as difficult or unacceptable in Russia.

The Ukrainian-Russian relations were strained over other issues as well. In 2005 and 2008 the dispute over gas prices and transfer fees through Ukrainian pipelines escalated and Russia stopped pumping gas to its neighbor.[7] This had far-reaching consequences beyond the Ukraine. Many Eastern European countries and now EU members have a near 100% dependency on Russian gas. The use of energy supplies as a pressure tool to get control of the transit pipelines by buying the Ukrainian state-owned company Naftogaz was not received as a friendly act and nurtured fears of Russian domination and started a debate around the EU's energy security. The dispute lingered on five years and was ended only after a change of government and the election of Viktor Yanukovych. He agreed on a 25-year lease for the Russian Black Sea fleet in exchange for a discounted price of Russian gas. The pro-Russian president initially eased relations with Russia but later should be chiefly involved in escalating the crisis.

Before the Ukrainian crisis turned violent and Yanukovych left office a bidding competition began between the EU and Russia. Both sides aimed at tying the Ukraine to their economic zone. While Russia was building the Eurasian Union the EU was offering the adoption of an Association Agreement. At the same time the state of Ukraine's economy was deplorable; the end of the command economy did not bring about great improvements in living standards. The US economist Rosefielde describes the Ukrainian economy with harsh words as "one of unstable, successive kleptocratic regional clan coalitions that prioritize venality over national welfare."[8] Indeed, its gross national income (GNI) per capita was standing at $6920 in 1990 and at $7550 in 2010. Its population was shrinking from 52 m to 45 m.[9] With the beginning of the war the Ukrainian economy was almost collapsing and declined drastically from $183bn (2013) to just $91bn in 2015.[10]

Both the EU and Russia offered loans in addition to the integration of the Ukraine into their economic zone. While the EU's offer was linked to just under a billion dollars of loans Russia offered $15bn and reduced gas prices. In 2013 Russia showed its muscles by introducing new customs regulations which brought Ukrainian exports to Russia to a standstill. In fact, even the pro-Russian Yanukovych was hesitant to join the Eurasian Union right away. But relations with the EU started to cool down. The Association Agreement with the EU was planned to be signed in 2013 but was postponed to 2014. In November 2014 the EU Summit convened in Vilnius, Lithuania, and the signing of the EU Association Agreement was expected to be a historic achievement of the EU's eastern partnership program. However, the mix of Russian political and economic pressure and incentives of loans without political conditionality to reform the Ukrainian political system led Yanukovych to decline signing the agreement. The consequences of this decision triggered the Euromaidan protest which led to the toppling of Yanukovych, followed by Russia's annexation of Crimea and a protracted war in which Russia supports secessionist movements in Eastern Ukraine.

Mass protest in Kiev's central square, the Maidan, were starting in late November 2013 and lasted around three months until Yanukovych left office and fled to Russia (see timeline of events in Box 5.1). With him fleeing the country he also abandoned an EU-brokered power-sharing deal with the opposition and played no political role anymore.[11] Shortly before Yanukovych left, the Ukrainian parliament (Rada) voted to remove him. During the time of the Maidan protest the international atmosphere was becoming increasingly tense. Western high-ranking officials visited the protest camps in Kiev frequently. As protesters showed no sign of giving up, a change in government and turn away from Russia became more likely. In February 2014 violence in Kiev led to the death of 88 people, further increasing Western pressure on Yanukovych.[12] A leaked conversation between the US Assistant Secretary of State Victoria Nuland and US ambassador to the Ukraine Geoffrey Pyatt revealed that the US was already planning a future without Yanukovych.[13] This opened accusations against the US of actively seeking regime change. While many Western countries did support the Maidan protesters, it is not clear how far this support was reaching beyond public rhetoric.

Box 5.1   Key Events: Ukraine

1921	Establishment of Ukrainian Soviet Social Republic
1954	Crimea transferred to Ukraine
1991	Declaration of Independence
1994	Leonid Kuchma becomes president
1997	Treaty on friendship, cooperation and partnership between Ukraine and the Russian Federation
	Russia leases Ukrainian naval base on Crimea for 20 years
2002	Ukraine bids for NATO membership
2004	Orange Revolution, Viktor Yushchenko becomes president
2010	Viktor Yanukovych becomes president
	Kharkiv Pact, Russian lease of naval base on Crimea for 25 years
2013	
21 Nov.	Yushchenko opts against association treaty with EU, takes up Russian offer
24 Nov.	Mass protest begins in Kiev
2014	
21 Feb.	Power-sharing agreement signed between opposition and Yushchenko
22 Feb.	Parliament votes to remove Yushchenko, who flees the country
23 Feb.	Oleksandr Turchynov becomes interim president
27 Feb.	Russian soldiers start infiltrating Crimea
1 Mar	Russian Duma approves use of force on Ukraine
15 Mar	Russia vetoes draft UN Security Council resolution
16 Mar.	Referendum in Crimea to join Russia
18 Mar.	Russia officially annexes Crimea
21 Mar	OSCE deploys Special Monitoring Mission (SMM)
21 Mar	Ukraine signs Association Agreement with EU
24 Mar	BRICS foreign ministers reject expulsion of Russia from G20
27 Mar	UN General Assembly adopts resolution on territorial integrity of the Ukraine
7 Apr.	In Eastern Ukraine pro-Russian protesters occupy government buildings in Kharkiv, Donetsk and Luhansk
25 May	Poroshenko becomes president
17 July	Malaysian Airlines jet shot down over Eastern Ukraine
5 Sep.	First Minsk peace deal
2015	
12. Feb.	Package of Measures for the Implementation of the Minsk Agreements
29 July	Russia vetoes draft UN Security Council resolution
2016	
19 Dec.	UN General Assembly adopts resolution on Crimea
2017	
1 Sep.	Association Agreement with EU enters into force

(*continued*)

Box 5.1 (continued)

2018
31 Aug. Pro-Russian rebel leader Alexander Zakharchenko is killed in Donetsk
25 Nov. Standoff at Strait of Kerch
17 Dec. UN General Assembly adopts resolution on militarization in Sea of Azov

With the EU power-sharing deal signed on 21 February, collapsing only one day after, the conflict over the Ukraine continued to escalate. Less than a week later Russian soldiers started infiltrating Crimea. On 1 March the Russian parliament approved sending troops to the Ukraine. At the same time US President Obama warned Russia about invading the Ukraine.[14] With Russian troops controlling Crimea Russia organized a referendum on the secession from the Ukraine and joining the Russian Federation. The referendum was held on 16 March with nearly 96% of voters supporting secession.[15] Two days after the referendum Russia accepted the vote and integrated Crimea into the Russian Federation.

The de facto annexation of Crimea against the will of the Ukraine and in violation of the UN Charter and the 1997 Friendship Treaty increased tensions further, within the Ukraine and between the West and Russia. The US and EU quickly introduced economic sanctions against Russia and aimed to diplomatically isolate the country. While the annexation of Crimea occurred without bloodshed, Ukraine's Eastern regions bordering Russia and populated mainly by Russian-speakers soon turned into a battle field. The regions of Luhansk and Donetsk declared their independence from Ukraine. These internationally non-recognized territories until today remain outside the control of Kiev.

From March 2014 the Organization for Security and Cooperation in Europe (OSCE) sent out an initially small Special Monitoring Mission (SMM) of less than a 100 observers which increased to 1247 in September 2018.[16] International efforts to negotiate a ceasefire agreement started soon in 2014 and were concentrating on the so-called Normandy format (Russia, Ukraine, the US, France, Germany). These talks resulted in the adoption of the Minsk Protocol on 5 September 2014 which is until now the most important point of reference for a negotiated solution. The Minsk Protocol was followed by a number of additional documents: the Minsk Memorandum (19 September 2014), the Minsk Implementation Agreement (12 February 2015) and four auxiliary documents: the Addendum to the Minsk Package of Measures (29 September 2015), the Decision on Mine Action (3 March 2016), the Decision on Full Cessation of Live-Fire Exercises (3 March 2016) and the Framework Decision on Disengagement (21 September 2016).[17] With the adoption of this framework of ceasefire agreements which had the goal to deescalate and separate warring parties as well as to withdraw heavy weaponry from the front line, the SMM was tasked to monitor the implementation. The Minsk Protocol also requires Kiev to decentralize power and speaks of "self-government" of Luhansk and Donetsk.[18] The issue of constitutional reform and federalization of the Ukraine has been an issue which Russia pushed for. Over the years the various ceasefire agreements have been broken many times. For example between 20 August and 2 September 2018 the SMM lists 8000 ceasefire violations.[19] Numbers for other months are equally high. Daily updates of ceasefire violations are published on the SMM website.[20] While it is true that the Minsk Protocol is often criticized for being a failure it at least prevented a full-scale escalation and inter-state war with Russia.[21]

The outbreak of armed secessionism in the East, the annexation of Crimea and Yanukovych fleeing for Russia have left the country in turmoil and in a state of disorganization and deep internal divisions. Oleksandr Turchynov was appointed interim president until elections in May were held which Petro Poroshenko won. De facto the Ukraine was close to collapsing economically and in no condition to effectively defend its territory. With the Russian annexation of Crimea the country also lost its navy and its armed forces were in a poor condition. At the beginning of the war only 6000 of the 140,000 Ukrainian troops were effectively operational and no match for the Russian incursion.[22]

The considerable economic, military and political weakness of Kiev allowed Russia to leverage control over the country's future.[23] Although Russia never officially recognized the breakaway regions, it has been complicit in supporting them and supplying enough military equipment to prevent Ukrainian troops to regain control. Regular Russian troops, volunteers and paramilitary units are operating in the Ukraine irregularly.[24] Russian military activities are increasingly well documented. A maximum of 10,000 troops is estimated to have operated in Eastern Ukraine in 2014, 28,000 troops are deployed in Crimea and several ten thousand troops are now permanently located at the Ukrainian border.[25] The downing of a civilian aircraft with 298 passengers on board in July 2014 further deteriorated relations between the West and Russia, as it turned out that the plane was shot down by a Russian missile and most passengers were Dutch.[26]

After events in 2014 developed most dramatically with a change in government, a crumbling economy and Russia's incursions into Ukrainian territory, the conflict in the following years and until now displays little signs of moving either way. Russia does not aim at annexing further parts of its neighbor's territory nor is Kiev able to reclaim control. The conflict appears to be frozen. Talks around deploying a UN peacekeeping mission to the country which might be more effective in implementing and monitoring the Minsk Protocol or a potential future peace agreement are also not going off the ground.[27]

The BRICS Response

The conflict in the Ukraine is the only case of the four explored in which a BRICS member is sharing a common border with a country experiencing large-scale armed confrontation. The security implications are the most immediate for one member, Russia, which, although is officially in denial, is a warring party in the conflict through its (partly) concealed support of Russian separatists in the Donbas. With Russia being closely linked to the conflict and practically all other members being at distance internal disparities over how to respond to the crisis might be the largest in this case. The close historical linkages between the Ukraine and Russia almost make the Ukrainian case a Russian domestic issue. While it is clearly not, it is beyond doubt that the Ukrainian crisis touches upon vital Russian national interests. In situations in which first-class (uncompromising) national interests are involved the BRICS group is avoiding antagonism among its members. The preferred strategy to circumvent political confrontation is to keep silent and not respond in any polarizing manner. For example the Chinese-Indian border dispute is not discussed, nor is the Tibetan question or disputes over the South China Sea. BRICS countries tend not to discuss or criticize each other over contentious (domestic) issues among themselves. The absence of, for example, punitive instruments in the BRICS foreign policy toolbox such as sanctions or suspensions serves two purposes. First, they are generally seen as problematic and an instrument of hegemonic politics which runs counter to the BRICS normative agenda of demanding a more equal world order free of domineering politics by the West. Second, on the surface it provides BRICS with the impression of group coherency and unity. Given the international dimension of the Ukrainian crisis a non-reaction was a non-option. However, the official response was still somehow meager.

We can find reference to the crisis in two summit declarations: in 2014 and 2015. At the Fortaleza summit in Brazil BRICS countries agreed on the following:

> We express our deep concern with the situation in Ukraine. We call for a comprehensive dialogue, the de-escalation of the conflict and restraint from all the actors involved, with a view to finding a peaceful political solution, in full compliance with the UN Charter and universally recognized human rights and fundamental freedoms.[28]

The search for a peaceful solution based on political negotiations is a formula BRICS uses as a standard phrase. It appears in all four conflicts studied. Reference to the UN is also used most frequently by BRICS countries because its emphasis on sovereignty correlates with the BRICS position on sovereign equality in the global order and it cements Russia's and China's position within the Security Council. What is interesting with regard to the paragraph above is less what was mentioned and referred to explicitly but more what has been omitted.

While in the cases of Libya and Syria BRICS countries have been defenders of territorial integrity and classical state sovereignty rights, no such rhetoric is mentioned in the case of the Ukraine. The annexation of the Crimea constitutes a rather clear case violating the territorial integrity of the Ukraine committed by a BRICS member. This stands in contradiction to BRICS emphasis on non-violent conflict resolution and respect for state sovereignty. In order not to disguise this contradiction the 2014 Fortaleza declaration refers to sovereignty and territorial integrity of Syria in paragraph 37 but does not mention it in the case of the Ukraine.

The contradictions which emerged around the issue of sovereignty and territorial integrity are not easily solved. BRICS members had to find a balance between avoiding normative hypocrisy, getting Russia to agree on the summit declaration and voicing concerns if any of the rest of the group. Omitting criticism while referring to the UN Charter in general terms provided somehow a middle path. The summit declaration of course did not criticize Russia as the final text needs to be agreed by all five BRICS countries. While it does not voice critique it also does not endorse Russian action on the Ukraine. As the West applied sanctions against Russia and expelled it form the G8 the BRICS relative silence on the crisis can count as a diplomatic advantage for Russia. The BRICS group even prevented the exclusion of Russia from the G20 which was scheduled to meet in Australia in November 2014.[29]

In 2015 the BRICS summit was convening in the Russian city of Ufa. In the context of the Ukrainian crisis and the meeting in Russia the BRICS summit was holding particular importance for Russia. As was to be expected it neither criticized Russia nor endorsed its politics over the Ukraine and no reference was made to state sovereignty. The summit agreed on the following text:

> We reiterate our deep concern about the situation in Ukraine. We emphasize that there is no military solution to the conflict and that the only way to reconciliation is through inclusive political dialogue. In this regard we call on all parties to comply with all the provisions of the Package of Measures for the Implementation of the Minsk Agreements, adopted in February 2015 in Minsk by the Contact Group on Ukraine, supported by the leaders of Russia, Germany, France and Ukraine and endorsed by the UN Security Council in its resolution 2202.[30]

BRICS maintained their emphasis on non-coercive means to conflict resolution and issued their endorsement for the Minsk agreements and the respective Security Council resolution supporting it. By lending support to the Minsk agreement BRICS accepted the Normandy format and the SMM as taking the lead in conflict mediation. What is interesting is that no BRICS summit endorsed the UN General Assembly vote on the Ukraine from March 2014.[31] The respective resolution refers to the threat and use of force against the territorial integrity of the Ukraine as well as calling for a political solution of the conflict and declaring the referendum in Crimea illegal.

The reason why BRICS documents do not mention this resolution cannot only be referred to Russian rejection. No BRICS country voted in favor of this resolution. While Russia, unsurprisingly voted against it, the remaining BRICS countries abstained. The resolution was adopted by 100 in favor, 11 objections, 58 abstentions and 24 not voting.[32] From these results we can conclude that BRICS countries in general do not feel that the crisis in the Ukraine should be framed in terms of violation of territorial integrity or aggression against a sovereign country. However, this does not mean that Russian policies toward the Ukraine are supported but hints to a view that there might be reasonable causes behind Russia's behavior.

In sum, the BRICS group response to the crisis can best be characterized as falling in the category of passive cooperation. BRICS is not assuming a leading or hegemonic role promoting an alternative to existing conflict mediation but is supportive of the Normandy format and SMM as central actors for conflict resolution. The passive cooperative response reflects on the relative remoteness of the conflict for most BRICS countries which do not attach direct security, political or economic relevance to the crisis. The comparatively reluctant engagement of BRICS also works out for Russia which does not need to fear harsh rhetoric or punitive measures over the annexation of Crimea. The partly passive response also reflects on a slight, even though in a rather concealed manner, non-approval of Russian action over the Ukraine. However, any potential critique remains unarticulated. The following section explores individual responses to a greater detail.

Russia

The Ukrainian conflict constitutes a national security priority. In this regard the Ukrainian case study stands out in comparison to the other conflicts. No other case study has reached the priority level for any BRICS member as Ukraine for Russia. The large common border, a sizable Russian-speaking population in the Ukraine (17%) and Crimea (65%), a naval base and the availability of a large number of ground troops in the region facilitated the Russian decision to intervene in the Ukraine. Military capabilities are easily available and could be moved without considerable risk of losing the upper hand on the battlefield or fear of external intervention. Geographic proximity and readily available military assets only confronting a weakened Ukraine enabled Russia to move quickly and decisively.

Its response to the Ukrainian crisis fits into the category of neo-imperial behavior which is characterized by the unilateral use of force, being a conflict party in the crisis, a temporary or permanent intrusion and occupation of territory (see Fig. 2.1). Multilateral fora are used to appease international concerns over the conflict; coercive means of foreign policy are dominating this response type. The annexation of Crimea and the support for proxy fighters in the Donbas region visibly illustrate the power politics dimension.

This most coercive response to the crisis which was in the first place a domestic political crisis of the Ukraine correlates with Russian foreign policy interests which are seen in Moscow as legitimate and uncompromising. Before the Ukrainian crisis broke out Russia defined its sphere of security and the instruments which it is willing to use to tackle them rather openly. In February 2012 Putin spoke about purposefully provoked conflicts next to Russia's borders. Without explicitly mentioning them it can be assumed that reference to colored revolutions and Western endorsement of them is actually meant. Putin continues: "Under such conditions, Russia cannot rely on diplomatic and economic methods alone. (…) Our Armed Forces, special services and other security agencies should be prepared to provide quick and effective responses to new challenges. It is a necessary requirement for Russia to feel secure and for our partners to listen carefully to what our country has to say in various international formats."[33]

In Russia's foreign policy the post-Soviet region occupies a special place as it is defined as near abroad, or zone of interest in which Russia claims a certain privilege. Dominance in the post-Soviet region is seen as essential for two reasons. First, it consolidates the claim of being a great power, and second it perceives its neighboring countries as a buffer zone against unwanted external influence.[34] In situations in which vital security interests are violated Russia preserves the right to unilaterally take action including the use of coercive means. For the Ukraine being the most relevant country in the post-Soviet space Russia vehemently rejects NATO membership, sees EU association with suspicion and opposes colored revolutions because they are not only undermining Russian influence but are also seen as domestically challenging the Russian political system. Colored revolutions are categorized as security threat to Russia because they are interpreted as a soft kind of Western intervention. Valery Gerasimov, the General Chief of Staff of the Armed Forces, categorizes them as new Western means of warfare.[35]

Popular revolutions as they happened in a number of Eurasian countries are generally denounced as driven by external actors aiming to diminish Russian interests. Socio-economic and domestic grievances are not perceived to be the main drivers leading to political unrest. The Russian reading of events finds some resonance among BRICS countries. This can be referred back to the experience of Western regime change in Libya and Syria which is seen by BRICS as illegitimate intervention prepared or supported by Western countries instigating domestic unrest against otherwise stable governments. As BRICS countries do not interfere if one of their members' key interests are involved and the Russian rhetoric could link up to the BRICS agenda, no serious opposition was to be expected. To the contrary, similar to the Syrian case Russia could use hegemonic power on the Ukraine, establish itself as a great power in a multi-polar world order and connect to the BRICS normative agenda by claiming to resist neo-imperial Western domination.

The conflict in the Ukraine and with Russia is mostly driven by political and security questions. Economic issues are relevant and inter-linked with politics but have not been the single most important condition. The gas dispute between the Ukraine and Russia reached its peak before the conflict and the dispute over customs tariffs is not directly linked to the annexation of Crimea or Russian separatism in the Donbas. The economic relations between the two countries display an asymmetric relationship to the advantage of Russia. The Ukraine is relatively more dependent on Russia than the latter is on the Ukraine. While exports to the Ukraine only make up some 2% of Russian overall exports, Russian imports to the Ukraine make up 17%. Russia is Ukraine's largest trading partner.[36]

Still the Ukraine is of greater geo-economic importance because Russian gas is pumped through the country to the EU. Revenue from gas exports through the Ukraine exceeds benefits from direct trade and the Ukraine profits economically as much from transit fees as from direct trade with Russia. In the past, the Ukraine has been the main transit country to the West. This is gradually changing. With the crisis emerging both sides aim at reducing mutual dependencies.[37] Russia is building new pipelines bypassing Eastern Europe (Nord Stream 1 + 2) and the Ukraine is also importing gas from its Western neighbors.

In the case of the Ukraine humanitarian concerns for getting engaged played no genuine role. Russia's response to the conflict was not motivated by genuine humanitarian concerns but humanitarian rhetoric was used instrumentally to defend action. This usually refers to Russia's attempts to justify military action on the basis of protecting Russian-speakers living in the Ukraine.[38] In March 2014 Putin said: "Protecting these people is in our national interests. This is a humanitarian mission. (…) we cannot remain indifferent if we see that they are being persecuted, destroyed and humiliated."[39] The use of humanitarian grounds for Russian engagement was primarily an instrument to disperse negative international responses denouncing Russian action as violating international law and portraying Russia as a rightful actor who is only protecting its fellow countrymen. Until today no ethnic cleansing, targeting or systematic prosecution has actually happened.

Russia sought to legalize its action through different rhetorical assertions. One such attempt was to argue that in the case of Crimea the population was only exercising its right to self-determination in accordance with the UN Charter article 1. In the Security Council the Russian representative even argued that "in the majority of cases, the realization of peoples' right to self-determination is achieved without the agreement of the central authorities of the State."[40] However, these arguments are lacking legal grounding and are not covered by the UN Charter as it violates the territorial integrity of the Ukraine; any secession of Crimea without authorization by the Ukraine is a clear violation of international law.

At the Security Council Russia vetoed the adoption of a resolution reiterating the territorial integrity of the Ukraine and declaring the planned referendum in Crimea "has no validity" and cannot change the status of the peninsula.[41] The resolution was sponsored by 42, mostly Western, countries, none of them from BRICS. In the Security Council the resolution was supported by 13 members while China abstained and Russia vetoed it. In order to provide legitimate reasons for the annexation Russia argued that while the referendum expresses the will of the people, the government in Kiev fell victim of a coup d'état including national radicals and thus cannot exercise rightful action over its territory.[42] Russia also argued that Yanukovych invited Russia to stabilize the country and provide military assistance.[43] Both arguments do not provide a legal coverage for the Russian incursion into the Ukraine. First, Yanukovych left the country on his own, and second, according to the constitution only the Ukrainian parliament can issue a request for military assistance.[44]

While Russia could protect itself from criticism in the Security Council, it does not have a strong supportive position in the General Assembly. On 27 March the General Assembly adopted a resolution very similar in text as the vetoed one: declaring the referendum has no validity. In paragraph two the resolution "Calls upon all States to desist and refrain from actions aimed at the partial or total disruption of the national unity and territorial integrity of Ukraine, including any attempts to modify Ukraine's borders through the threat or use of force or other unlawful means."[45] The resolution was adopted with 100 votes in favor. Unsurprisingly Russia voted against it and the remaining BRICS members abstained. The resolution had practically no effect on the ground. It was adopted nine days after Russia officially incorporated Crimea into the Russian Federation. It, however, showed that the majority of countries disapprove the annexation. A notable omission is the BRICS group.

How Russia annexed Crimea and got involved in supporting separatists in the Donbas was openly admitted. According to President Putin planning to regain Crimea started on 22 February with Yanukovych leaving office. Putin also admitted deploying troops to the peninsula.[46] With regard to the Donbas Russia opted for more concealed action of hybrid warfare: supporting separatists but not recognizing them officially. In December 2015 Putin declared: "We've never said there are no people there who deal with certain matters, including in the military area, but this does not mean that regular Russian troops are present there."[47] Through these hybrid warfare tactics Russia could claim not to be a warring party but at the same time involving the Ukraine in a war which it cannot win and thus exert control over the country's destiny.

On the diplomatic front the Normandy format led to the negotiation of several peace agreements known as Minsk Protocol (from 5 September 2014 onward). The Security Council adopted resolution 2202 on 17 February 2015 in support of the implementation of the Minsk agreements. The resolution was adopted unanimously, also reaffirming the territorial integrity of the Ukraine, a wording Russia was avoiding in other documents. In this context Russia could portray itself as a cooperative actor using multilateral diplomacy to end the conflict. After the adoption of the resolution the Russian representative to the UN seized the moment mentioning Russia's peaceful intention, focusing on political dialogue, rejecting unilateral action, supporting the Minsk Protocol and supporting the OSCE monitoring mission.[48] However, at the same time Russia is keeping the conflict going and shows no signs of undoing the annexation of Crimea. While Russia does show cooperative behavior it is mostly driven by tactical considerations and the instrumental use of cooperation for easing tensions with Western countries. In fact, Western sanctions and sharply falling oil prices put the Russian economy under pressure but do not constrain Russian military operations or political ambitions seeking great power status.[49]

Relations with the West deteriorated further over the downing of a Malaysian Airlines plane in Eastern Ukraine. The issue came to the Security Council in July 2015 with mostly Western countries and Malaysia submitting a draft resolution which aimed at establishing an international criminal tribunal investigating the causes of the crash.[50] Russia vetoed the resolution and China abstained. At the UN the battle over the right interpretation of events continued and shifted to the General Assembly again because of the Russian veto in the Security Council. In late 2016 the General Assembly adopted a resolution "Condemning the temporary occupation of part of the territory of Ukraine" and "reaffirming the non-recognition of its (Crimea) annexation" by Russia.[51] The resolution was adopted with only 70 votes in favor, 76 abstentions and 26 votes against.

The BRICS countries almost voted coherently against the resolution; only Brazil abstained.

The resolution was rather confirming the BRICS perception which Russia actively nurtured: that the West is again bullying a non-Western country and disrespecting one of its members on issues of national priority. The following statement by Putin links up perfectly to the BRICS normative agenda which aims at overcoming Western paternalism.

> They are constantly trying to sweep us into a corner because we have an independent position, because we maintain it and because we call things like they are and do not engage in hypocrisy. But there is a limit to everything. And with Ukraine, our western partners have crossed the line, playing the bear and acting irresponsibly and unprofessionally.[52]

As we will see below this rhetoric was partially accepted by BRICS countries. While countries did not fully endorse the Russian position BRICS countries did not join the West by condemning the annexation of Crimea and Russian incursion in the Donbas. One reason for this was surely that although the annexation of Crimea was illegal, BRICS countries thought that Russia has legitimate security concerns over the Ukrainian crisis.

In 2018 tensions over the access to the Sea of Azov increased markedly leading to Russia blocking Ukrainian ships and a short sea encounter between Russian and Ukrainian vessels at the Strait of Kerch.[53] While the incident did not escalate to a military encounter, the blocking of the Strait of Kerch effectively deprives the Ukrainian harbor town of Mariupol from access to the sea. As a consequence of the situation a third UN General Assembly resolution was drafted calling on Russia to cease the occupation of Crimea and identifying and condemning Russia as the main source for militarization in the region. The resolution was adopted with only 66 countries in favor but 72 abstaining and 19 voting against it.[54] All BRICS countries voted against the resolution except Brazil which abstained. An Iranian amendment to the draft proposal which "[u]rges both States to exercise restraint and respect for each other's sovereignty and inviolability of borders" which could have been more acceptable to the BRICS group was not adopted.[55]

As of today the conflict in the Ukraine can best be described as frozen conflict. There are no signs that either side would militarily be able to gain the upper hand or the conflict would abate. The SMM continues to report thousands of violations of the ceasefire agreements.

China

As regards China, the conflict in the Ukraine has no direct or immanent security consequences for the country. There are also no Chinese military facilities near the conflict which could be affected. The strongest links between the Ukraine and China can be observed in the economic sphere. The Chinese BRI also cross-cuts Eurasia and the Ukraine. Chinese-Ukrainian trade is small in terms of its overall seize. In 2016 Chinese imports reached $2.2bn (mostly iron ore, seeds oil, corn) and exporting goods of the same value.[56] However, China has started investing in transport infrastructure following the BRI. Here investment also focused on Crimea because of its geostrategic position in the Black Sea. With the conclusion of a strategic partnership between China and the Ukraine in 2011 and the adoption of a development plan for the strategic partnership (2014–2018) investment in Crimea was concentrating on renovating and upgrading the shipping infrastructure, such as a liquefied gas terminal, but also a modern airport.[57] With the annexation of Crimea these plans could not be realized with the Ukraine. Pragmatically China adjusted to the new situation. Investment is now concentrating on harbor infrastructure in mainland Ukraine in the Sea of Azov in Mariupol and Berdyansk as well as upgrading the Ukrainian road system and investing in the energy and agricultural sectors. In 2018 China announced investments of $7bn in the country.[58]

In the end, the war did not deter or stop Chinese investment. To the opposite, with Russia not being welcome in the Ukraine new business opportunities are opening up for both sides. For China the Ukrainian acceptance of the BRI is important as the country forms a pivotal land bridge to Europe and Russia is treating the BRI with skepticism. Outside of Central Asia the Ukraine is the first nation which endorsed the BRI.[59] Chinese investment in coal-to-gas technology may in the future reduce dependency on Russian gas imports. In this regard China assists the Ukraine in diversifying its trade relations beyond the antagonistic Russia versus EU relationship.

From a purely economic side there was little incentive or pressure coming from the conflict which clearly would have forced China to take sides. The annexation of Crimea led to an adjustment of investments. There is, however, no equivalent replacement for the Crimean peninsula. Investment in Mariupol is politically more risky because Russia controls access to the Sea of Azov and should relations between the Ukraine and Russia deteriorate sharply economic loses cannot be ruled out. Despite this Chinese investors are willing to take these risks.

On the political front China's first response to the crisis was following traditional pathways of non-intervention and neutrality which is often resulting in China not taking sides and abstaining from voting in situations of political confrontation. In fact, by securing and developing its economic interests in the Ukraine, as well as by maintaining the increasingly close relations with Russia, China profits from keeping a lower profile and avoiding further polarization of the conflict.

Table 5.1 provides an overview of Chinese voting patterns in the UN on key documents relating to the conflict. China voted in favor of only two resolutions (2166, 2202). In both cases they were adopted unanimously and broad-based international support was visible. Resolution 2166 called for an investigation of the downing of a Malaysian Airline plane over Eastern Ukraine and resolution 2202 is supporting the Minsk Protocol. Both decisions are rather uncontroversial and do not force China to take sides. In the case of General Assembly resolutions 71/205 and 73/589 which were clearly identifying and condemning Russia as occupying force, China voted against them. The two draft Security Council resolutions which were vetoed by Russia (189 and 562) saw abstention by China. It also abstained in the UN General Assembly vote on the territorial integrity of the Ukraine (68/262).

Table 5.1 Chinese voting on Ukraine

Document	Topic	Date	Vote
UNSC draft res 189	Declaring referendum in Crimea invalid	15 March 2014	Abstain
UNGA res 68/262	Territorial integrity of Ukraine	27 March 2014	Abstain
UNSC res 2166	Investigation of Malaysia Airlines crash	21 July 2014	In favor
UNSC res 2202	Support for Minsk agreement	17 February 2015	In favor
UNSC draft res 562	Establishing a criminal tribunal following Malaysia Airlines crash	29 July 2015	Abstain
UNGA res 71/205	Condemning occupation of Crimea	16 December 2016	Against
UNGA res 73/589	Calls on Russia to end occupation of Crimea	17 December 2018	Against

Traditionally China has emphasized non-intervention, sovereignty and territorial integrity as cornerstones of its foreign policy. Fear of secessionist movements within China (Tibet or Xinjiang), the one-China policy (Taiwan) and external contestation led to the insistence on these classical state sovereignty rights. With regard to the Ukrainian crisis China applied a more flexible non-dogmatic interpretation of it also showing some ambiguities. With its abstention on the Security Council draft resolution on the referendum on Crimea and abstention to the General Assembly resolution on the territorial integrity of the Ukraine, China tacitly accepted Russia's annexation of the peninsula.[60] That it voted against condemning the occupation of Crimea in 2016 fits into this line.

Still Chinese officials maintain that their support for the territorial integrity of the Ukraine is unbroken. China has justified its position on two arguments: First, a condemnation or even sanctioning of Russia would be counter-productive in seeking a political solution to the conflict, and second, the crisis has been exacerbated by Western external interference into domestic Ukrainian issues.[61]

While initially China gave the impression of being a neutral observer to the conflict, its position was gradually inclining toward a Moscow-friendly view but without openly endorsing annexation. In late November 2014 a high-ranking Chinese diplomat, Gui Congyou, told Russian media:

> We are against any nationality gaining independence through referendums. As far as Crimea is concerned, it has very special features. We know well the history of Crimea's affiliation, (…) China reacts with full understanding to the challenges and threats Russia has faced in connection with the Ukrainian issue and supports Moscow's approach to its settlement. We are not interested in an armed conflict on the Ukrainian territory and wish to see the issue settled by political means. We are against external intervention in Ukraine's internal affairs through government coups.[62]

The above statement is not without contradictions. On the one hand, China rejects independence by referendum, favors a political solution and opposes interference in domestic affairs. On the other hand, it does not condemn the annexation of Ukrainian territory or Russian support for armed separatists in the Donbas. These contradictions might result first from Chinese fear of separatism in China and the Chinese wish to reunite with its "breakaway province" but de facto independent Taiwan.

At first sight, the Ukrainian case might not easily fit into the BRICS normative agenda for a reformed political order based on sovereign equality. In fact, the use of neo-imperialist instruments as the annexation of territory or the support of armed separatists in a neighboring country is a tactic which BRICS countries would fiercely reject if applied on them. However, the BRICS reading of events is a different one. Punitive measures or strongly worded diplomatic statements against Russia are seen as not helping to solve the conflict but are also not justified. Russia's hegemonic position in the region is seen as legitimate. The Russian response to the crisis is seen as tolerable because it was provoked by the West which uses colored revolutions as an instrument not to spread democracy but to extend its sphere of influence at the cost of Russia and steering turmoil. Consequently, Russia is not perceived as an aggressor but rather as a hegemon acting within its recognized sphere of influence. The BRICS normative agenda fits in with regard to their distaste for punitive measures and emphasis on multi-polarity in which Russia plays a pivotal role.

Categorizing the Chinese response to the Ukrainian crisis is no easy undertaking. China does show support for multilateral conflict resolution by voting in favor of resolution 2202 in support of the Minsk process. In this regard, China's response can be categorized as passive cooperative as it does not show initiative to get directly involved in conflict mediation and is satisfied with other regional powers taking the initiative. Its response to the crisis and tacit toleration of Russian neo-imperialist power politics rather point to hegemonic tendencies in which great powers are granting themselves a degree of exceptionalism from established global rules such as the inviolability of borders and non-intervention.

India

Geographically and economically the Ukraine is outside India's strategic ambit. The conflict does not pose any immediate or direct threat. Investment levels are low and no significant number of Indian nationals are living and working in the conflict zone. The Indian response to the crisis is akin to that of China and other BRICS countries and can be categorized as passive cooperative. Regarding Crimea India has neither criticized Russia nor endorsed its annexation. On 6 March 2014 the Indian Ministry of External Affairs responded to the events in the Ukraine by referring to the importance of having "a legitimate democratic process."[63] This statement implies that the current government (after Yanukovych left) is not seen as legitimate. While India did not interpret events as covert regime change, a certain unease can be read between the lines as of how the government was changed. Shivshankar Menon, National Security Adviser, said one day later: "There are legitimate Russian and other interests involved and we hope they are resolved."[64] In the remainder of the statement India called for a diplomatic solution to the conflict.

During a telephone conversation between Putin and Prime Minister Singh, on 18 March 2014, the Indian position became slightly more pronounced. The prime minister "emphasized the consistent position India had on the issues of unity and territorial integrity of countries" and speaks of "legitimate interests of all countries in the region" which should be recognized in a political settlement of the conflict.[65] In other words, India opposes secession movements but tolerates Russian action. The reasons for this are several.

In comparison to the Ukraine, Russia is of greater relevance to India. It is the country's largest arms supplier and also plays an important role in the energy sector. Apart from its general skepticism of using punitive measures for achieving political goals it is unlikely that sanctioning Russia will facilitate a political solution but instead can undermine BRICS as a group. And lastly India aims to avoid a situation in which it is forced to take sides and clearly align to the Western camp. India has voted against UN General Assembly resolution 71/205 from 2016 and abstained on resolution 68/262. More generally taking sides would undermine the country's independent and neutral position to the conflict and run counter to it favoring a multi-polar world order in which Russia plays an important role for India.[66] Attempts to punish or isolate Russia are therefore not desirable. Additionally India has rhetorically supported the Minsk Protocol[67] but does not show any individual initiative to mediate the conflict. Therefore, the Indian response can best be described as passive cooperative.

Although the events in the Ukraine have no direct security impact on India, they may shift global power positions to the detriment of the country. Continued tensions between Russia and the West may lead to Russia and China strengthening their cooperation. This has indeed been quite visible in recent times, for example, with the largest Russian military exercise since the end of the Cold War in September 2018 in which Chinese troops had been invited. With China and Russia becoming close associates the strategic space for India is shrinking in Asia.[68]

South Africa

The South African response to the conflict has been described as rather "low key."[69] This should not be surprising as there are very little direct effects for South Africa emanating from the conflict. Given South Africa's geographical remoteness from the crisis there are no linkages to the conflict. Economically Russia and the Ukraine also play a minor rule. Only for wheat imports the Ukraine is the most important trading partner.[70] Accordingly, South Africa's response to the crisis is akin to that of India and can be categorized as cooperative but passive. Still the conflict in the Ukraine is of relevance because it affects Russia as a BRICS member and it affects issues of global order.

Indicative of the relatively low priority South Africa is giving the Ukraine is the low number of official statements the Department of International Relations and Cooperation (DIRCO) was issuing. In total only two rather short press statements have been issued. On 2 March DIRCO issued its general concern over the security situation in the Ukraine and called for a peaceful solution.[71] With the annexation of Crimea South Africa responded with a second statement published one day after the General Assembly adopted its resolution on the territorial integrity of the Ukraine and the referendum in which South Africa abstained. The 28 March statement was longer:

> South Africa calls upon both the Russian Federation and Ukraine to engage in dialogue and cooperation in the interest of the stability of the broader region. (...) South Africa is of the view that the escalation of hostile language, the imposition of sanctions and counter-sanctions, the use of threat of force and violent actions do not contribute to the peaceful resolution. (...) We further encourage regional initiatives aimed at resolving the crisis and in this regard welcome the deployment of the Organisation for Security and Cooperation in Europe's (OSCE) Special Monitoring Mission to Ukraine.[72]

What is interesting in the statement is that it does not mention territorial integrity or sovereignty, as, for example, the Indian response was doing. A regional mediated solution is favored and the SMM explicitly mentioned. Sanctions regimes are referred to as potentially harmful for conflict resolution. The use of force is denounced as destructive instrument. In the statement South Africa avoids direct mentioning of perpetrators but refers directly to Russia and the Ukraine as conflicting parties. South Africa does not condemn the annexation of Crimea and thus voted against General Assembly resolution 71/205.

As the junior partner within BRICS South Africa is rather unlikely to take on a member from the grouping directly and criticize it for its action. South Africa would have isolated itself in a grouping toward which it attaches great importance and whose membership was not self-evident given its small size and limited capacity of power projection in the concert of greater powers.[73] South Africa's emphasis on a multi-polar world certainly made it reluctant to join a Western-led campaign to isolate Russia and apply sanctions. South Africa's own foreign policy tradition is centered on conflict mediation and power-sharing deals which it applied in its own region, Southern Africa, for example in Zimbabwe.

Brazil

Links between Brazil and the conflict are as weakly developed as in the case of South Africa. There are no direct or indirect security effects from the conflict nor is Brazil having any significant economic interests. It is rather through the BRICS membership that it is linked to the conflict but not because of individual interests. The 2014 annual BRICS summit was taking place in Fortaleza and the summit even if not explicitly endorsing Russian action over Crimea was signaling that BRICS would not join Western sanctions and diplomatic efforts to isolate Russia. Despite this Brazil's response to the crisis was almost muted. The Foreign Ministry only issued one note in February 2014 at the peak of the standoff between Yanukovych and protesters but did not respond to the annexation of Crimea. The 2014 note reads as follows:

> The Brazilian government is following with concern the deterioration of the political and institutional framework in Ukraine and expresses deep regret over the deaths in Kiev. The Brazilian Government urges all parties to dialogue. The political crisis in Ukraine should be addressed by the Ukrainians themselves peacefully and on the basis of respect for institutions and human rights.[74]

The emphasis on settling the political standoff by Ukrainians reveals an unease with external interference into the conflict. This is mostly directed against Western countries' support for the opposition. During her September speech at the UN General Assembly President Rousseff reiterated that the use of force will not lead to the solution of conflict and that military interventions deteriorate conflicts.[75] This statement referred mostly to Western interventions in Iraq and Libya but it also mentioned the Ukraine. Given the Russian military incursion into the Donbas and annexation of Crimea one could value this statement as a disapproval of the use of force by Russia in the conflict over the Ukraine.

However, this did not lead to Brazil voting in favor of the three General Assembly resolutions on the Ukraine. On all three occasions (2014, 2016, 2018) Brazil abstained. While in 2014 (referendum question) all BRICS countries abstained apart from Russia which voted against it, in 2016 (condemning the occupation) and 2018 (calling on Russia to end the occupation of Crimea) all BRICS countries voted against the resolution apart from Brazil. As the only BRICS country Brazil was rejecting not to criticize Russia over the annexation of Crimea. Explaining this slightly different position Stuenkel argues that "Brazil's stance on recent events in Ukraine is part of a hedging strategy by rising powers that are keen to preserve ties to the U.S., but are also acutely aware that the global order is moving towards a more complex type of multipolarity, making it necessary to maintain constructive ties with all poles of power."[76] Additionally mounting domestic pressure on Rousseff was leaving less space for ambitious foreign policy positioning. Siding with BRICS while not antagonizing Western powers correlates with the limited relevance the conflict was having for Brazil. This resulted in a passive but cooperative response to the crisis.

CONCLUSION: BRICS AND THE CRISIS IN THE UKRAINE

The Ukrainian crisis is the only case in which a BRICS member state is involved in a large-scale armed conflict in its direct vicinity and which resulted in the annexation of territory from another country. At the same time, there were no direct negative security effects for any of the other BRICS members emanating from the conflict. The Western support for protesters in Kiev against the pro-Russian government was seen by all BRICS countries as unduly interference into domestic affairs. BRICS neither endorsed Russian action over the Ukraine nor did the group or individual countries condemn Russia. BRICS tolerated Russian action not because it was seen as legitimate in a narrow legal sense but because it was seen as belonging to Russia's core sphere of influence which BRICS members grant to each other without expected interference from the group. The fairly small size of BRICS also makes it difficult to issue criticism against a single member without undermining the group as such unlike the case of Russia's expulsion from the G8. In this context BRICS showed solidarity with Russia by rejecting Russia's exclusion from the G20 format. In general BRICS declarations do seldom or never discuss security issues which are of vital national interest such as Kashmir, Taiwan or the South China Sea. The Ukraine is seen as being part of Russia's essential foreign policy strategy which is built on Russian predominance in the post-Soviet region. This is as such accepted by BRICS countries. Equally domestic politics are not discussed or commented by BRICS members. De facto BRICS countries almost treat the Ukrainian conflict as a domestic Russian issue on which the grouping does not issue strong comments or critique.

Tables 5.2 and 5.3 summarize the response of BRICS countries as well as display potential trigger variables. In general the BRICS response to the Ukrainian crisis is the most unequal among the four conflict studies. While Russia's response fits into the category of neo-imperial behavior all remaining members decided to take a rather passive position but lending rhetorical support for the Minsk process and tolerating Russian action.

If we contrast the response types with the potential causes for action we can see that nearly all trigger variables speak strongly in favor of Russia. The Ukraine is in direct neighborhood and falls within core security and political interests. Russia also commands over significant resources to project power, militarily and economically, and has used them in the conflict. The conflict remained rather localized which played to the advantage of Russia which could frame the issue as a Russian/Ukrainian one in which external interference was not welcome. In this context Russia could even

Table 5.2 BRICS response types and motivation: Ukraine

Country	Russia	China	South Africa	Brazil	India
Response type	Neo-imperialist (direct, permanent)	Cooperative (passive)	Cooperative (passive)	Cooperative (passive)	Cooperative (passive)
Main motivation	Dominating post-Soviet region	Investment saving rhetorical support for multilateral peace negotiations	No genuine interests, rhetorical support for multilateral peace negotiations	No genuine interests, almost no response	No genuine interests, rhetorical support for multilateral peace negotiations

Table 5.3 Trigger variables and countries: Ukraine

	Russia	China	South Africa	Brazil	India
Proximity	+ + +	+	– – –	– – –	– – –
Capability, interests	+ + +	–	– – –	– – –	– – –
Type of conflict	–	–	–	–	–
Economics	+ +	+	–	– – –	– –
BRICS agenda	+ +	+ +	+ +	+ +	+ +
Humanitarian norms	– –	– –	+	+	+

+ and – indicate various degrees of importance or lack thereof of the trigger variables

invoke the BRICS normative agenda. Although the Russian military incursions are in violation of key BRICS normative positions on classical sovereignty rights, the response to the crisis was reinterpreted as defending legitimate Russian interests and fending off Western soft interventionism opposing Yanukovych. This was putting the Ukrainian conflict in one line with Libya and Syria in which BRICS is opposing Western regime change. While BRICS countries widely share Russia's critique against the one-sided Western support of protesters which indeed led to the fall of a pro-Russian government, there was no open endorsement but mere toleration of Russia's annexation of Crimea and involvement in the Donbas.

The rather muted response of BRICS to the conflict may also be explained by the relative remoteness of the conflict, its confined regionalized consequences and little economic relevance for the majority of BRICS countries. Openly criticizing Russia would potentially have strained relations within BRICS for little gain but risking the BRICS project as such. The unwritten rules within BRICS do not expect group members to discuss contentious domestic issues but respect essential national interests of the other. Judged from this perspective the relative silence of BRICS regarding the Ukrainian crisis is little surprising. To which extent BRICS have sacrificed their otherwise principled insistence on sovereign equality and a rules-based world order, rejecting military interventions and Western hypocrisy, is another question.

Notes

1. http://ucdp.uu.se/#country/369 accessed 10 September 2018.
2. The treaty of friendship, cooperation and partnership between the Russian Federation and Ukraine of 31 May 1997. https://cis-legislation.com/document.fwx?rgn=4181 accessed 10 September 2018.

3. "No Russian fleet in Ukraine beyond 2017 -Ukrainian PM" 24 September 2008. https://www.unian.info/society/148224-no-russian-fleet-in-ukraine-beyond-2017-ukrainian-pm.html accessed 10 September 2018.
4. Erlanger, Steven (2008) "Putin, at NATO Meeting, Curbs Combative Rhetoric" The New York Times, 5 April 2008. https://www.nytimes.com/2008/04/05/world/europe/05nato.html accessed 10 September 2018.
5. Tsygankov, Andrei (2016) "Russia's Foreign Policy change and Continuity in National Identity", Chapter 5 "The World after September 11 and Pragmatic Cooperation". Lanham, Boulder, New York, London: Rowman & Littlefield, 135–176.
6. President of Russia, "The draft of the European Security Treaty" http://en.kremlin.ru/events/president/news/6152 accessed 10 September 2018.
7. Tsygankov, Andrei (2015) "Vladimir Putin's last stand: the sources of Russia's Ukraine policy", *Post-Soviet Affairs* 31 (4), p. 283.
8. Rosefielde, Steven (2017) *The Kremlin Strikes Back Russia and the West after Crimea's Annexation.* Cambridge: Cambridge University Press, p. 167.
9. World Bank, Country profile Ukraine. http://databank.worldbank.org/data/views/reports/reportwidget.aspx?Report_Name=CountryProfile&Id=b450fd57&tbar=y&dd=y&inf=n&zm=n&country=UKR accessed 10 September 2018.
10. World Bank, https://data.worldbank.org/country/ukraine accessed 10 September 2018.
11. Agreement on the Settlement of Crisis in Ukraine, *The Guardian*, 21 February 2014. https://www.theguardian.com/world/2014/feb/21/agreement-on-the-settlement-of-crisis-in-ukraine-full-text accessed 11 September 2018.
12. UCDP Ukraine: http://ucdp.uu.se/#country/369 accessed 11 Sep. 2018.
13. Chiacu, Doina and Mohammed Arshad (2014) "Leaked audio reveals embarrassing U.S. exchange on Ukraine, EU" Reuters 7 February 2014, https://www.reuters.com/article/us-usa-ukraine-tape/leaked-audio-reveals-embarrassing-u-s-exchange-on-ukraine-eu-idUSBREA1601G20140207 accessed 11 September 2018.
14. Lally, Kathy, Englund, Will and Booth, William (2014) "Russian parliament approves use of troops in Ukraine" 1 March 2014 *The Washington Post*. https://www.washingtonpost.com/world/europe/russian-parliament-approves-use-of-troops-in-crimea/2014/03/01/d1775f70-a151-11e3-a050-dc3322a94fa7_story.html?noredirect=on&utm_term=.712de78376c0 accessed 11 September 2018.

15. Collett-White, Mike and Popeski, Ronald (2014) "Crimeans vote over 90 percent to quit Ukraine for Russia" Reuters 16 March 2014. https://www.reuters.com/article/us-ukraine-crisis/crimeans-vote-over-90-percent-to-quit-ukraine-for-russia-idUSBREA1Q1E820140316 accessed 11 September 2018.
16. OSCE, SMM, Status Report 2 September 2018. https://www.osce.org/special-monitoring-mission-to-ukraine/392816?download=true accessed 11 September 2018.
17. Haug, Hilde (2016) "The Minsk Agreements and the OSCE Special Monitoring Mission Providing Effective Monitoring for the Ceasefire Regime" Security and Human Rights 27, p. 345.
18. See Implementation Agreement from 12 February 2015.
19. OSCE, SMM, Status Report 2 September 2018.
20. http://www.osce.org/ukraine-smm/reports
21. Golanski, Robert (2016) "One year after Minsk II: consequences and progress" *European View*, 15, 67–76.
22. Klein Margarete (2018) *Russlands Militärpolitik im postsowjetischen Raum Ziele, Instrumente und Perspektiven*. SWP-Studie 19, p. 16.
23. Roesefield (2017).
24. Bushuev, Mikhail (2015) "Evidence mounting of Russian troops in Ukraine" *Deutsche Welle* 4 March 2015. https://www.dw.com/en/evidence-mounting-of-russian-troops-in-ukraine/a-18294255 accessed 11 September 2018.
25. Sutyagin, Igor (2015) "Russian Forces in Ukraine" RUSI Briefing Paper, p. 4.
26. Birnbaum, Michael (2018) "Dutch-led investigators say Russian missile shot down Malaysia Airlines Flight 17 over Ukraine in 2014" *The Washington Post* 24 May 2018. https://www.washingtonpost.com/world/dutch-led-investigators-say-russian-military-missile-shot-down-flight-mh17-over-ukraine-in-2014/2018/05/24/1e2ff92e-5f3c-11e8-8c93-8cf33c21da8d_story.html?utm_term=.86e49be871d3 accessed 11 September 2018.
27. Grono, Magdalena and Brunson, Jonathan (2018) "Peacekeeping in Ukraine's Donbas: Opportunities and Risks" *International Crisis Group*, 6 March 2018. https://www.crisisgroup.org/europe-central-asia/eastern-europe/ukraine/donbas-peacekeeping-opportunities-and-risks accessed 11 September 2018.
28. BRICS Fortaleza Declaration, 2014, para. 44.
29. BRICS Ministers Meet on the Sidelines of the Nuclear Security Summit in the Hague 24 March 2014. http://www.brics.utoronto.ca/docs/140324-hague.html accessed 12 September 2018.
30. Ufa Declaration, 2015, para. 43.

31. UN General Assembly, Resolution 68/262, 27 March 2014. "Territorial integrity of Ukraine".
32. United Nations Bibliographic Information System (UNBISNET) http://unbisnet.un.org:8080/ipac20/ipac.jsp?profile=voting&index=.VM&term=ares68262 accessed 12 September 2018.
33. Vladimir Putin (2012) "Being strong: National security guarantees for Russia" Russia Today, 19 February 2012. https://www.rt.com/politics/official-word/strong-putin-military-russia-711/ accessed 14 September 2018.
34. Klein (2018), pp. 7–11.
35. Ibid., p. 11.
36. Data drawn from https://atlas.media.mit.edu/en/profile/country/ukr/ and https://atlas.media.mit.edu/en/profile/country/rus/ accessed 14 September 2018.
37. Pirani, Simon and Yafimava, Katja (2016) "Russian Gas Transit Across Ukraine Post-2019: pipeline scenarios, gas flow consequences, and regulatory constraints" Oxford Institute for Energy Studies.
38. Allison, Roy (2014) "Russian 'deniable' intervention in Ukraine: how and why Russia broke the rules" *International Affairs*, 90 (6), 1262, 1264, 1266.
39. Vladimir Putin (2014) "Vladimir Putin answered journalists' questions on the situation in Ukraine" 5 March 2014. http://en.kremlin.ru/events/president/news/20366 accessed 17 September 2018.
40. UN Security Council 7138th meeting, 14 March 2014.
41. UN Security Council, S/2014/189, para. 5, 15 March 2014.
42. Ibid.
43. Allison (2014), p. 1264.
44. Ibid.
45. UN General Assembly, 68/262. Territorial integrity of Ukraine, 27 March 2014.
46. BBC News, Putin reveals secrets of Russia's Crimea takeover plot, 9 March 2015. https://www.bbc.com/news/world-europe-31796226 accessed 17 September 2018.
47. Vladimir Putin (2015) "Vladimir Putin's annual news conference" http://en.kremlin.ru/events/president/news/50971 17 December 2015, accessed 14 September 2018.
48. UN Security Council, 7384th meeting 17 February 2015.
49. Rosefielde (2017), pp. 129–151.
50. UN Security Council, 29 July 2015, draft resolution S/2015/562.
51. UN General Assembly, resolution A/71/205/Add.3, 19 December 2016, "Situation of human rights in the Autonomous Republic of Crimea and the city of Sevastopol (Ukraine)."

52. Vladimir Putin (2014) "Address by President of the Russian Federation" 18 March 2014. http://en.kremlin.ru/events/president/news/20603 accessed 17 September 2018.
53. BBC News "Russia-Ukraine sea clash in 300 words" 30 November 2018. https://www.bbc.com/news/world-europe-46345697 accessed 22 Jan 2019.
54. UN "General Assembly Adopts Resolution Urging Russian Federation to Withdraw Its Armed Forces from Crimea, Expressing Grave Concern about Rising Military Presence" 17 December 2018. https://www.un.org/press/en/2018/ga12108.doc.htm accessed 22 Jan 2019.
55. UN General Assembly, A/73/L.68, 13 December 2018.
56. Data drawn from: https://atlas.media.mit.edu/en/profile/country/ukr/ accessed 18 September 2018.
57. Qiang, Liang (2014) "Multiple Game in the Ukraine Crisis", p. 280.
58. Brooke, James (2018) "With Russia on the Sidelines, China Moves Aggressively into Ukraine" http://www.atlanticcouncil.org/blogs/ukrainealert/with-russia-on-the-sidelines-china-moves-aggressively-into-ukraine 5 January 2018, accessed 18 September 2018.
59. Qiang, Liang (2014), p. 278.
60. Kuznetsov, Dmitry (2016) "China and the Ukrainian Crisis: From 'Neutrality' to 'Support' for Russia" China Report 52 (2), p. 101.
61. UN Security Council 7138th meeting 15 March 2014, Liu Jieyi Chinese representative.
62. "China against declaration of independence at referendums" 21 November 2014, http://tass.ru/en/world/760944 accessed 18 September 2018.
63. India, Ministry of External Affairs, 6 March 2014. "Recent developments in Ukraine", https://www.mea.gov.in/press-releases.htm?dtl/23041/Recent_developments_in_Ukraine accessed 19 September 2018.
64. "Russian interests in Crimea 'legitimate': India" The Times of India, 7 March 2014. http://timesofindia.indiatimes.com/articleshow/31557852.cms?utm_source=contentofinterest&utm_medium=text&utm_campaign=cppst accessed 19 September 2018.
65. "Putin calls up Manmohan Singh after Russia annexes Crimea" The Times of India, 18 March 2014. http://timesofindia.indiatimes.com/articleshow/32252937.cms?utm_source=contentofinterest&utm_medium=text&utm_campaign=cppst accessed 19 September 2018.
66. Chacko, Priya (2015) "Why India doesn't support Western sanctions on Russia" *East Asia Forum* 6 may 2014. http://www.eastasiaforum.org/2014/05/06/why-india-doesnt-support-western-sanctions-on-russia/ accessed 19 September 2018.

67. "India-Russia Joint Statement After PM Narendra Modi Meets President Vladimir Putin" NDTV 15 October 2016. https://www.ndtv.com/india-news/full-text-india-russia-joint-statement-after-pm-narendra-modi-meets-president-vladimir-putin-1474578 accessed 19 September 2018.
68. Mohan, Raja (2015) "India: The Quest for Balance in Asia" in Hett, Felix and Wien, Moshe (eds) *Between Principles and Pragmatism Perspectives on the Ukraine Crisis from Brazil, India, China and South Africa*. Berlin: Friedrich-Ebert-Stiftung, p. 6.
69. Allison, Simon (2015) "South Africa: Treading a Fine Line" in Hett, Felix and Wien, Moshe (eds) Between Principles and Pragmatism Perspectives on the Ukraine Crisis from Brazil, India, China and South Africa. Berlin: Friedrich-Ebert-Stiftung, p. 10.
70. Sanderson, Sertan (2014) "How South Africa's economy is affected by the Ukraine crisis" 6 March 2014. https://www.thesouthafrican.com/battlefield-of-ukraine-war-in-south-africa/ accessed 19 September 2018.
71. South Africa, DIRCO, "SA calls for a peaceful resolution to the situation in Ukraine" 2 March 2014. http://www.dirco.gov.za/docs/2014/ukra0303.html accessed 19 September 2018.
72. South Africa, DIRCO, "Press Statement on the Situation in Ukraine", 28 March 2014. http://www.dirco.gov.za/docs/2014/ukra0328.html accessed 19 September 2018.
73. Sidiropoulos, Elizabeth (2014) "South Africa's response to the Ukrainian Crisis" Noref Policy Brief—June 2014.
74. Brazil, Ministry of Foreign Affairs, Situation in Brazil, Nota 4319 February 2014. http://www.itamaraty.gov.br/en/press-releases/3579-situation-in-ukraine accessed 24 September 2018.
75. President of the Federative Republic of Brazil, Dilma Rousseff on the occasion of the General Debate of the 69th General Assembly of the United Nations—New York, September 24, 2014. http://www.itamaraty.gov.br/en/speeches-articles-and-interviews/president-of-the-federative-republic-of-brazil-speeches/5836-statement-by-the-president-of-the-federative-republic-of-brazil-dilma-rousseff-at-the-general-debate-of-the-69th-general-assembly-of-the-united-nations-new-york-september-24th-2014 accessed 24 September 2018.
76. Stuenkel, Oliver (2014) "Why Brazil has not criticised Russia over Crimea" The Norwegian Peacebuilding Resource Centre, May 2014.

CHAPTER 6

South Sudan: BRICS Active Mediator or Bystander to Conflict?

The last conflict to explore is the continued civil war in South Sudan. In terms of violence and human suffering it equals those conflicts discussed in earlier chapters. Fully accurate casualty numbers are difficult to obtain and vary widely. The Armed Conflict Location & Event Data Project (ACLED) counts some 22,000 battle-related deaths since the war broke out.[1] A recent study by the London School of Hygiene and Tropical Medicine estimates that up to 382,000 people have died because of the war (including indirect causes).[2] Some 2.5 million refugees (25% of the population) had to flee their home and found refuge in neighboring countries.[3] Another 4.2 million have been displaced within South Sudan and 7 million people count as "severely food insecure."[4] The degree of humanitarian crisis, the partition from Sudan in 2011 which was accompanied by significant international efforts to support a peaceful future, the investment of Chinese and Indian companies into the oil sector and cordial relations of South Africa's ruling party, the African National Congress (ANC), with the Sudan's People Liberation Movement (SPLM) in South Sudan provide suitable conditions to trigger a BRICS response to the conflict. Evidence of it can be found in summit declarations in 2014 and 2015 in which one paragraph each is dedicated to the conflict and its solution. However, the conflict in South Sudan does not play an equally important role or triggered equally strong reactions by BRICS members as the conflicts in Libya, Syria and Ukraine have done. While the intensity of war remains high, it does not figure equally high in foreign policy

© The Author(s) 2019
M. Brosig, *The Role of BRICS in Large-Scale Armed Conflict*, New Security Challenges, https://doi.org/10.1007/978-3-030-18537-4_6

priorities of BRICS countries and thus their response to the conflict appears as more individualistic than on the other three cases explored.

In the case of South Sudan BRICS countries are very differently affected by the conflict which might explain why there is relatively little group response. Brazil practically has no connections to South Sudan; it is neither politically nor economically of any importance. For Russia South Sudan is of little to no geostrategic interest. For India and China the situation is different. South Sudan forms part of India's Eastern African area of economic and political interest within the Indian Ocean. India is also invested in the oil sector. It is the largest troop contributor to the UN Mission in South Sudan (UNMISS). Of all BRICS countries China is playing the greatest role in the conflict. It is practically dominating the oil industry and is playing an increasingly important role facilitating conflict mediation and has extended its role with providing peacekeepers for the UN mission. Lastly, South Africa, while not directly affected by the consequences of the war, continues to play an important role as mediator through regional organizations such as the AU. Inter-party relations between the SPLM and ANC have developed over decades. As a leading African country South Africa aims to make a visible contribution to conflict resolution. In sum, the BRICS response to the conflict is more individualized than group-oriented and can be characterized as passive cooperative response. Conflict resolution is in general sought to take place within the various multilateral structures of regional organizations and the UN. A domineering hegemonic or neo-imperial approach by a single actor is not visible.

The next section provides an overview of main events during the civil war. In contrast to the other three cases which have been actively shaped by external actors, the conflict in South Sudan is essentially internally driven and thus the inner conflict dynamics are important to understand to make sense of the external (BRICS) response. The subsequent sections will explore the BRICS group response to the crisis and then go through individual reactions.

CONFLICT DYNAMICS IN SOUTH SUDAN

The outbreak of the civil war is usually attributed to a leadership contest within the SPLM which was brewing throughout 2013 and escalated in December of that year into armed conflict in the capital Juba. However, the outbreak of violence in 2013 forms part of a much longer chain of armed conflict in Sudan. Indeed, today's civil war is rooted in the decade-long war the South was fighting to become an independent country. Therefore it makes sense to go deeper into the conflict history. Within the territory of Sudan which became independent in 1956, as the first African country, several wars took place which intersected with one another and lasted for decades. In fact, the country hardly knows longer periods of uninterrupted peace (see Box 6.1). The recent civil war in South Sudan is only one among many wars which took place in Sudan. The Southern desire to break away from the North is as old as the country itself. The first Sudanese civil war took place from 1955 to 1972 but did not result in the establishment of an independent Southern state. In the late 1970s oil was discovered in what is today South Sudan. It took decades until the oil wealth could be drilled and a pipeline was built. Only with the beginning of the millennium production increased gradually, creating growing revenues and reaching a peak in 2009.[5]

Box 6.1 Key Events: South Sudan

1955–1972	First Sudanese Civil War
1956	Sudan becomes independent
1978	Oil discovered in Sudan
1983	Foundation of Southern People's Liberation Movement/Army (SPLM/A)
1983–2005	Second Sudanese Civil War
1995	China National Petroleum Company (CNPC) invests in oil sector
2005	Comprehensive Peace Agreement (CPA) preparing autonomy and independence
2005	John Garang leader of the SPLM/A dies in plane crash; Salva Kiir replaces him
2011	
February	Violence in Jonglei state erupts
May	Sudan occupies border to disputed region of Abyei
July	South Sudan becomes independent
2012	
January	South Sudan shuts down entire oil production
January	China presents Five-Point Plan to ease tensions and resume oil production
April	South Sudan temporarily occupies oil-rich Heglig
September	AU mediates oil agreement
2013	
March	Resumption of oil production
July	Kiir dismisses entire cabinet including Vice President Machar
December	Fighting breaks out in Juba, beginning of a civil war

(continued)

Box 6.1 (continued)

2014	
January	First round of mediation leads to ceasefire agreement, which is broken quickly
January	China presents five-point peace plan
April	Fighting spreads to oil-rich city of Bentiu
April	IGAD-led peace talks begin in Addis Ababa
May	UN Security Council adopts resolution 2155, UNMISS gets protection of civilians mandate
June	Kiir and Machar agree to work on transitional government
2015	
January	China deploys peacekeeping battalion to South Sudan
March	UNSC adopts resolution 2206, targeted sanctions
August	IGAD mediation leads to a peace deal, power-sharing agreement
2016	
April	Unity government established
July	Intense fighting in Juba; unity government collapses; Machar gets wounded, leaves country
November	Riek Machar under house arrest in South Africa
2017	
December	IGAD establishes the High Level Revitalization Forum (HLRF)
2018	
January	South Sudan and South Africa agree on MoU on defense
March	Machar leaves South Africa
July	UNSC adopts resolution 2428, arms ban
August	New power-sharing agreement between Machar and Kiir

Crucial for the emergence of the independent South Sudan was the second civil war and the establishment of the SPLM under its rebel leader John Garang in 1983. A protracted war finally resulted in a comprehensive peace agreement (CPA) in 2005.[6] The CPA granted South Sudan some degree of autonomy and the possibility of a referendum on independence after an interim period. Additionally, the South was integrated in a government of national unity in Khartoum and received half of the revenue Sudan was gaining by selling its oil.[7] The sudden death of Garang shortly after the signing of the CPA brought Salva Kiir into leadership position. A referendum was held in 2011 which resulted in a landslide victory for independence. On 9 July 2011 South Sudan became an independent country. Between the signing of the CPA and independence the South earned some $13bn in oil revenue which was mainly spent to extend the payroll of the Sudan People's Liberation Army (SPLA). By 2011 the SPLA enlisted 240,000 soldiers and 90,000 militia and policemen toward which it distributed its oil rent.[8] While by its name the CPA was comprehensive and detailed it did not address a number of critical issues.

As oil production was creating several billions of income for Sudan leading to an oil boom in Khartoum and increased spending of the South it was not clear how the oil wealth would be distributed once South Sudan becomes an independent country. Seventy-five percent of oil production was in the South but the pipeline pumping the oil to Port Sudan to ship it overseas is exclusively going through Sudan. A clear border still had to be established between the two countries and the future of the disputed Abyei region was unresolved. The imperfect CPA fueled conflict with the North after independence. While the war for independence was formally over with the CPA it de facto continued even after 2011. Military encounters between the North and South intensified in 2011 and 2012. In May 2011 Sudan interfered in Abyei and South Sudan temporarily occupied the oil fields in Heglig in Sudan. The quarrel over transmission fees through Port Sudan escalated and led South Sudan to shut down its entire oil production in January 2012; it returned to production only in 2013 which was later again interrupted by the new civil war. In fact oil revenue never reached previous levels. In 2016 oil covered 99% of South Sudan's total export, practically all of it going to China and accounted for $1.34bn of revenue.[9]

The link between oil and conflict has been formulated most explicitly by Alex de Waal.[10] He argues that the SPLM/A during the war of independence and through the CPA has established a kleptocratic and neo-patrimonial system of governance which was designed to loot the country's natural wealth and distribute it through a complex patronage system. The militarized nature of this system which was concentrating on the SPLM/A was bearing great security risks. In order to gain independence from the North the security payroll was overstretched to gain loyalty of soldiers against an otherwise too powerful enemy. With gaining independence and the oil shutdown the system of payoffs came under strain and gave rise to leadership rivalry. As leadership in the SPLM was linked to leadership of the SPLA, the power struggle almost immediately turned into a war. While the oil wealth was important to gain independence from Sudan, the dwindling revenue fueled conflict between Kiir and Machar.

Certainly the causes of war cannot exclusively be determined by reference to economic incentives or the absence of them. Two other lines have been discussed frequently. These are the persisting and long-lasting divisions in the internal structure of the SPLM/A and the ethnic dimension the conflict soon acquired. From early on the SPLM/A was never structured in a way which centralized control over its various commanders. It is often described as a decentralized organization with semi-autonomous units and fragmented leadership. The split between Kiir and Machar might indeed be a result of lacking integration within the SPLM/A.[11] Already in the 1990s the SPLA split and Machar and others left the movement. They formed part of a number of Khartoum-backed Southern militias which received arms and money from Sudan during the civil war. After returning to the SPLM Machar became the number two within the movement and vice president of the country after independence. His attempt to rally for leadership within the SPLM which was seen as automatically becoming president of the country was effectively blocked by Kiir, who dissolved his cabinet and postponed crucial party meetings. In the absence of political and civilian instruments for mediating inner party conflicts the competition between the two leaders turned violent in December 2013.

It has also been argued that the civil war bears a dangerous ethnic dimension. Indeed revenge killings between Dinka and Nuer, the two groups aligned to Kiir and Machar, could be observed and loyalty to military commanders is often organized along ethnic lines. However, the main motivation for the outbreak of violence is most likely to be found in the internal SPLM leadership competition. Economic incentives and ethnic affiliations are fueling the conflict and complicate its settlement. Accordingly most international mediation efforts are concentrating on power-sharing agreements re-building the *status quo ante* before December 2013.

Mediation efforts started only a few days after the war began and involved a group of neighboring countries within the Intergovernmental Authority on Development (IGAD), a regional organization comprising eight countries at the Horn of Africa including South Sudan. In late December the prime minister of Ethiopia and president of Kenya visited Juba and met Kiir as well as detained members of the SPLM, pushing for the start of peace talks. At a special IGAD summit a team of envoys from Ethiopia, Kenya and Sudan was put together.[12] However, a ceasefire negotiated in January 2014 collapsed quickly. The same happened to a ceasefire agreement negotiated in May.[13] In the meantime the UN increased its troop size twice to finally 13,000 troops and 2001 police of its operation UNMISS and added an explicit protection of civilians mandate to it.[14] By the end of 2014 the AU established a high-level committee consisting of the presidents of Algeria, Chad, Nigeria, Rwanda and South Africa in support of IGAD as well as an AU High Representative for South Sudan.[15] Additionally the so-called Troika of the US, the UK and Norway as well as China got involved in conflict mediation.

In February 2015 the two sides agreed in principle on the establishment of a transitional unity government and the intention to negotiate a peace deal.[16] However, as concrete progress toward peace remained elusive international pressure to end the conflict was mounting. The Security Council unanimously adopted targeted sanctions (travel ban and asset freeze) and was "strongly condemning" both sides for failing to form a transitional government and end hostilities.[17] In August 2015 a breakthrough was reached with the signing of the Agreement on the Resolution of the Conflict in the Republic of South Sudan (ARCSS).[18] By April 2016 Machar was expected to return to Juba and take the position of a vice president in a unity government. Constitutional reforms and elections were expected to be scheduled later. A Joint Monitoring and Evaluation Commission (JMEC) was established to oversee the implementation of the agreement.

While expectations were high the realities of war soon kicked in. A UN protection site in Malakal was attacked in February 2016 and, although Machar did return to Juba, hostilities broke out in July. He had to flee the capital and was chased and attacked in an assassination attempt which he could escape but got wounded.[19] After July he left South Sudan for the Democratic Republic of Congo (DRC), Sudan and South Africa for medical treatment.[20] In his absence Kiir replaced him as vice president with Taban Deng Gai. Machar's visit to South Africa turned out to become an unplanned long stay away from South Sudan. During his South African visit in late 2016 he was de facto kept under house arrest during 2017 but released later in 2018.[21]

The year 2017 was a lost year for peace. Although Machar was forced to stay outside of South Sudan, it did not revive the peace process and the civil war continued. To the opposite, with Taban Deng Gai replacing Riek Machar in the so-called SPLM in Opposition (IO) the anti-SPLM movement revealed deep internal splits and even fighting erupted between pro-Machar and pro-Taban factions as well as fighting between the SPLM/A and SPLM-IO.[22] The pro-Machar group made their participation in further peace talks conditional on the lifting of his house arrest.[23] In December an agreement on the cessation of hostilities, protection of civilians and humanitarian access was agreed. But it was built on shaky grounds. Given the continuous insecurity and repeated failures to progress IGAD established the High Level Revitalization Forum (HLRF) with the aim to either get the ARCSS implemented or broker a new deal.

The international community again increased pressure on the belligerents. IGAD introduced targeted sanctions against individuals violating the ceasefire in March 2018. The UN Security Council first decided in May to extend its existing sanctions regime and later in July adopted resolution 2428 after another ceasefire agreement collapsed right after it was adopted. This resolution finally introduced a general arms embargo as a punitive measure because of missing progress in peace talks. This step was seen as controversial within the Security Council and only received the minimal approval of nine affirmative votes against six abstentions, among them Russia and China. Those countries abstaining articulated their concerns around disbelief that punitive measures would be counter-productive for peace talks and that the arms embargo would effectively impact on Kiir more than on Machar as the latter receives supply from informal channels which are difficult to sanction through formal resolutions.[24] In the end, the mounting international pressure and tireless diplomacy of IGAD countries led to a renewed signing of a power-sharing agreement in August 2018 which was essentially built on the ARCSS.[25]

Given the seemingly endless cycle of ceasefire and peace agreements it remains to be seen if the most recent agreement is given a chance to survive. The international community invested significantly in a diplomatic solution to the conflict. Interventionist instruments such as sanctions or military pressure were used rather reluctantly. An IGAD protection force which was mandated at 4000 troops operating alongside UNMISS never materialized as effective instrument to contain armed conflict. This leads to another problem with the IGAD-led mediation process. Given their member states' different interests in South Sudan a neutral arbitration and effective monitoring and supervision of ceasefire and power-sharing conditions are complicated. Uganda was early on sending troops in support of Kiir and Sudan is expected to be aligned to Machar. As it stands the root cause of the conflict, leadership competition within a further disintegrating SPLM, has not been solved by power-sharing agreements. Conflict dynamics remain very much domestically driven with outside actors having rather little influence over events. This distinguishes the war in South Sudan fundamentally from the other conflicts explored in previous chapters.

The BRICS Group Response to South Sudan

The group response to the conflict remains largely diplomatic and supportive of existing mediation initiatives by regional organizations and the UN. There is no explicit BRICS attempt visible which aims at making a separate contribution. However, a detailed look at the summit declarations referring to South Sudan reveals that BRICS although not claiming their own space deviate to some extent from Western initiatives to conflict mediation. The Fortaleza (2014) and Ufa (2015) declarations are devoting a whole paragraph to South Sudan while the Xiamen declaration (2017) refers to the crisis only in general terms. All other declarations do not mention South Sudan. In the Fortaleza declaration BRICS countries are explicitly condemning violence against civilians and refer to all parties of the conflict, not taking sides or issuing any preferences.[26] A solution to the conflict is seen only through an "inclusive political dialogue."[27] Support is given to the IGAD mediation process and the building of a government of national unity. The Ufa declaration repeats all of the above points but becomes more urgent in language condemning "all ceasefire violations" and calling upon the "political will" of conflicting parties to end violence.[28] A degree of frustration is visible with the lack of progress on the ground despite the agreement of numerous ceasefire and power-sharing deals. The lack of progress and continuous cycles of violence and broken peace agreements might indeed have led to the disappearance of South Sudan from summit declarations.

The overall language of the two paragraphs resembles those of the UN and regional organizations demanding protection of civilians, ending hostilities, access to humanitarian aid and supporting conflict mediation. In this regard BRICS operates well within what might be described as generally expected response to the outbreak of a violent conflict. What is interesting with regard to these statements is not only what has been mentioned but also what is missing. The issue of sanctions has not been touched upon. Although the UN Security Council adopted targeted sanctions and a general arms embargo was discussed and it was clear that war crimes have been committed by both sides as an AU Commission of Inquiry in South Sudan found,[29] punitive measures were not seen as the right instrument to exert pressure on the warring parties. This position varies from those taken by the West and in particular the US. Washington most actively called for a sanctions regime and implemented it unilaterally before they were adopted by the UN. Even though Russia and China did not use their veto to prevent the adoption of sanctions against South Sudan, they voiced principled reservations about their utility and appropriateness as they were seen as imposing external power to a domestic problem. Consequently, support for sanctions was not always unerring. Despite a ban a SPLA general could travel to China and partake in a defense workshop.[30]

To which extent sanctions have been a useful instrument is still up to debate. They have certainly enforced the signing of peace agreements in 2015 and 2018. Still the implementation of them remains difficult and many negotiated agreements failed quickly after they have been adopted. The issue of sanctions in the case of South Sudan is far less urgent for BRICS countries as in the other cases explored. What is different with regard to Libya and Syria is that the application of sanctions does not coincide with external Western military intervention, nor does it intend or imply a regime change approach. The sanctions are meant to pressure Kiir and Machar into power sharing reestablishing the *status quo ante*. Despite this one can observe a general reluctance to actively use punitive measures as a tactical instrument for peace negotiations by BRICS countries.

The conflict in South Sudan did not affect BRICS countries directly; there was no direct security threat for any of the group members. Economically the country is of some importance for China and India due to their investments in the oil sector but Sudanese oil never occupied a dominant role in oil imports for these countries. South Sudan also only displays to a rather limited degree the potential to alter or affect questions of global order or great power politics which distinguishes it from conflicts in Libya, Syria and Ukraine. The conflict dynamics are to a fair degree confined to South Sudan and the region. Issues of external military interventions (from outside the direct neighborhood), proxy wars or regime change play no role. It is rather domestic conflict dynamics which shape the international response than the international response is able to shape the conflict. The BRICS group response to the conflict is somehow reluctant, not domineering or blocking alternative approaches. A slightly passive cooperative response type within existing multilateral organizations best characterizes BRICS engagement. At the level of the five group members the responses do vary slightly from active conflict engagement (China, South Africa), to passive and opportune engagement (India, Russia) and practically no response (Brazil). The following section explores individual country reactions to the crisis, starting with China.

China

Of the five BRICS members China is the most involved in South Sudan. It is the largest foreign investor in the country and in June 2018 contributed 1030 soldiers to UNMISS[31]; it is also involved in conflict mediation. This active Chinese role is unprecedented for a conflict far away from its home region. While in many violent conflicts China opted for keeping a low profile this is different with regard to South Sudan. South Sudan is often characterized as an experimental test case for China's role in peace and security questions on the African continent.[32] In terms of response types China's reaction to the conflict falls within the active cooperative category emphasizing multilateral and politically neutral behavior. The main reason why China is so actively involved is certainly linked to its long-standing investment in the Sudanese oil sector which started in 1995 and pre-dates the partition of Sudan and the South Sudanese civil war. While the effects of the war have no direct impact on China's national security its multibillion investment in the country and safety of Chinese workers are directly affected.

The economic importance of South Sudan for China needs to be seen from various angles. From a purely economic perspective of getting access to oil in order to keep the Chinese economy growing South Sudan might be judged as being of lesser importance. Between 1999 and 2011 Sudan accounted for 5.5% of China's oil imports and only 2.6% of its total oil consumption.[33] In the following years the importance of (South) Sudanese oil decreased further as China's oil consumption and imports increased. In 2011 China imported around 5 million barrels of oil per day; in 2017 this number increased to 8.4 million barrels.[34] During the same period the South Sudanese production declined from around 325,000 to just 130,000 barrels per day.[35] During the shutdown of the production it was even lower. In other words, Sudanese oil never reached the position in which it was critical for China. Additionally Patey argues that Chinese investment in the oil sector did not directly "lock-up" oil for China, because it was mainly sold on international markets.[36]

Still Chinese investment is anything but trivial. Within South Sudan it is the single most dominant actor and revenue from oil exports remains the largest source of income. It seems almost inevitable that China plays an important role and that the course of the civil war directly impacts Chinese investment. While the overall importance of Sudanese oil for China is relative, the Sudan investment is of greater importance for the

China National Petroleum Company (CNPC), China's largest oil company. When taking over the oil business from Western companies in the late 1990s CNPC was accepting a fairly high degree of risks. Western companies left because of the insecure environment and mounting public pressure on Sudan which used increasing oil revenues among other things for its war in Darfur. The importance of (South) Sudan for CNPC should not be underestimated. Until 2007 it invested $7bn and for the company it was the first and largest overseas project. When oil production reached its maximum output the Sudanese oil field made up 40% of CNPC's international oil production. As Patey argues, "Sudan was more than just another investment on the company's portfolio: it was a venture of crucial strategic importance for CNPC's international expansion."[37] While Sudanese oil might not be of the greatest strategic relevance, CNPC investment was a crucially important step for developing China's international energy security strategy. As Chinese oil consumption was quickly outstripping its domestic supply international investments were becoming essential. Most likely because of this situation China becomes more engaged in security issues and conflict management in South Sudan. Following the oil industry around 100 Chinese companies from various sectors were operating in the country before the war broke out.[38] However, the years leading up to independence, the short years after and during the civil war since 2013 have been anything but easy to manage.

Traditional Chinese principles of non-interference, developmental peace[39] and non-coercive diplomacy are clearly challenged by its South Sudan experience.[40] Oil wealth did not bring development nor could it stop fighting but was rather nurturing conflict; staying aloof when Chinese investments and its nationals are under direct threat would not pay off and a principled exclusion of punitive sanctions from peace negotiations might be unable to commit the conflicting parties to agree on a ceasefire and later peace deal. China carefully but gradually adjusted its foreign policy according to these challenges.

China's engagement in South Sudan needs to be seen from the legacy of Chinese engagement with Sudan. For example, China played an important role in convincing President Bashir to accept a peacekeeping mission in Darfur in 2007. Initially the SPLM perceived China as being too closely allied with Khartoum; this changed over time and with South Sudan becoming independent. Links between the SPLM and the Communist Party of China (CPC) were established and cadres trained and invited to Beijing. Although diplomatic relations were quickly established with

South Sudan becoming independent, this did not give Beijing much leverage over events on the ground. The sudden oil shutdown in 2012 and China's rejection to finance an alternative oil pipeline circumventing Sudan did not improve mutual relations. Before the shutdown, South Sudan changed the contractual obligations it inherited from Sudan to CNPC for the case of a production stop, freeing the country from any compensation payments.[41] South Sudan even expelled high-ranking Chinese businessmen in the oil sector.

With the outbreak of the war China quickly supported the UN with the extension of the existing peacekeeping mission. The respective resolutions 2132 and 2155 were adopted with Chinese consent and no abstention. China's handwriting is directly visible in resolution 2155 which mentions the protection of oil installations twice.[42] In fact the key strategic motivation for China's rather unusual involvement in peace mediation was the protection of its nationals and assets in South Sudan.[43] Despite this primarily economic motivation Chinese peace initiatives were received favorably by key regional actors such as Ethiopia and Sudan.[44] China increased its military footprint in UNMISS considerably since the outbreak of the war. In December 2013 340 soldiers served in the UN mission; this increased to just over 1000 in April 2015.[45]

On the diplomatic front China kept its standard position of calling for a peaceful solution to the conflict based on political mediation without privileging one side or the other. Indeed both SPLM and SPLM-IO members traveled to China in different capacities. The initial mediation steps were taken by IGAD, with China repeatedly supporting it. China's special representative for African Affairs, Zhong Jianhua, accompanied IGAD-led peace talks from early on and initially formulated only a modest role for China. He said, "We are not the party to propose our own initiative, at least at this stage. So, we urge all parties concerned to respect an African solution proposed by African parties."[46]

A more explicit attempt to get directly involved in peace talks could be observed with the initiative of Foreign Minister Wang Yi, who presented a four-point peace plan in January 2015 at an IGAD consultation meeting.[47] Such explicit initiatives still remain exceptional. In most situations the officially promoted idea of fostering "Chinese solutions" is linked to political crisis management, using non-punitive instruments, highlighting the primacy of developmental peace and portraying China as a responsible power.[48] However, as peace talks failed in early 2015, the Security Council agreed for targeted sanctions with the adoption of resolution 2206. The resolution was adopted unanimously. In August 2015 a peace agreement and power-sharing deal were reached. China supported the deal. It became a signatory to the ARCSS and was assigned a role in its monitoring through the JMEC. However, as before the power-sharing agreement failed. While in principle China remains skeptical about sanctions it voted in favor of Security Council resolution 2241 which extends the UNMISS mandate and reiterates the willingness to use sanctions against peace spoilers as well as condemns attacks against oil installations.[49]

China's role in South Sudan did not only receive heightened international attention because it is deviating from its traditional approach of strict non-interference in armed conflicts. The shipping of arms to the country sparked some controversy. In July 2014 the SPLA received arms and ammunition worth $20.7m from the China North Industries Corporation (Norinco).[50] As the SPLA-IO does not have access to official state-to-state weapons market, the shipment could be interpreted as a one-sided support of one group within a civil war. Despite this, there are some doubts that this shipment of arms was a deliberate attempt of taking geopolitical influence. The order was most likely placed before the outbreak of the war and the active arming of the SPLA would have thwarted political mediation efforts and created international opposition against China's role in South Sudan generally speaking.[51] China declared a moratorium on arms sales to South Sudan and after the Norinco shipment the UN panel of experts on South Sudan which is monitoring arms sales has not reported any Chinese arms deals to South Sudan.[52]

To which extent China is only playing the role of a neutral arbitrator or major actor engaging in geopolitics needs to be explored further. Surely China's main interest in South Sudan is about protecting its oil and other investments and keeping its nationals safe. In practice, China has been contributing to armed conflict either willingly, through neglect of the conflict, or out of misreading (South) Sudanese politics. Arms shipments to Sudan have a longer history. With oil revenues increasing Chinese arms exports increased as well.[53] When South Sudan became independent this practice continued but was now nurturing a civil war. It is also no secret that the governance structures in South Sudan have been a major contributing factor to the conflict. As described above the oil money feeds a kleptocratic military elite which rules through fear, violence and distributing oil wealth to its supporters. Ignoring these realities is negligent at best. Inviting the South Sudanese army chief, who is banned to travel by the UN, to a two-week-long workshop in Beijing in peace times might fall within China's military diplomacy approach[54]; in war times this is not the case. There is tension between China's diplomatic and rather short-term efforts to reduce violence through political negotiations and its inability to address the structural deeper laying causes of conflict. In this context China is often portrayed as a newcomer missing experience and comprehensive strategic thinking in conflict resolution.[55]

As the ARCSS collapsed and mediated solutions became increasingly more difficult to achieve because of increasing factionalism and Machar being kept in South Africa, the issue of a general arms embargo was referred to the Security Council in July 2018 after peace talks failed again. While China voted for resolutions 2206 and 2241 which implemented targeted sanctions, it in the past and after adopting resolution 2428 voiced principled concerns over the usefulness of sanctions. These fall within two categories.

First, the Chinese ambassador to the UN "maintained that sanctions should serve only as a means, not an end in themselves."[56] This statement refers not only to the conflict as such but equally to the measures to address it. In this regard South Sudan is seen as a conflict in which questions of global order and their execution do play a role. Sanctions as a means of the powerful against a sovereign state are generally seen as problematic. In the case of South Sudan, the US declared a unilateral arms embargo already in February and was lobbying for a UN resolution.[57] In opposition to targeted sanctions a general arms embargo is of a greater dimension and Chinese reluctance to agree to it is more fundamental.

Second, China would not act against the wishes of regional organizations which have taken the lead in conflict mediation. Its main role was often to be a table-setter providing the venue and support for negotiations for the warring parties and regional actors. In the case of an arms embargo the AU and IGAD as well as individual African countries voiced concerns that an arms embargo would complicate peace talks. In other words regional organizations did not fully endorse embargo plans. As a consequence, China abstained together with five other countries during the vote.

In sum, China's response to the crisis falls within the category of active cooperation. It got involved in conflict mediation to a substantial degree which was unforeseen in the country's history. The main trigger for this behavior can be found in Chinese economic interest. On issues of global order and security the conflict did play only a marginal role for China. Even deep-rooted skepticism against sanctions did not lead China to veto Security Council resolutions implementing such sanctions. This forms a stark contrast to the frequent veto use on Syria. While indeed China does not have many resources (military, political) to play a dominant role in the conflict in terms of geopolitical footprint, it is developing these capacities through getting involved in UN peacekeeping, supporting conflict mediation and increasing its investment in key infrastructure in the wider region including the opening of a military base in Djibouti. The way in which China is indirectly contributing to the conflict might be more a consequence of lacking understanding, experience and negligence to (South) Sudanese conflict dynamics than real strategic behavior to garner geopolitical influence.

South Africa

Since 1994 South Africa holds close links to (South) Sudan. Former and current Presidents Thabo Mbeki, Jacob Zuma and Cyril Ramaphosa have all been involved in conflict mediation.[58] Diplomatic links between the countries and ruling political parties are well-developed and long-standing. Since the outbreak of the civil war Bashir, Kiir and Machar all traveled to South Africa and South African high-ranking politicians and diplomats are regularly visiting Khartoum and Juba. South Africa's engagement with the South Sudan conflict pre-dates the outbreak of violence in December 2013. Apart from close diplomatic ties South Africa is also invested in the mining sector, telecommunications and brewery business (SAB Miller invested $70m).[59]

As in the case of the other four BRICS countries South Africa is not directly affected by the war in South Sudan, there are some 3500 km between Juba and Johannesburg, nor does South Africa have the capacities to become a single dominant actor to play a hegemonic role. While its economic investment is not trivial it is also not relevant enough to explain the country's above-average engagement to the crisis. The most convincing explanation rests in the long-standing inter-party relations between the ANC and SPLM and South African ambition to be a continental champion of peace which is eager to share its experience of conflict resolution through mediation.[60] The protracted and multiple conflicts in Sudan provided this opportunity. The response to the crisis can be categorized as largely active cooperation within existing multilateral institutions in Eastern Africa (IGAD) and the continent (AU).

Already during its time in exile and soon after the foundation of the SPLM the ANC established close ties to it. Before and after South Sudan's independence South Africa trained 1600 SPLM cadres in the security and justice area, education and public administration.[61] South Africa also played an instrumental role supporting the CPA in 2005.[62] There is undoubtedly great South African sympathy for the liberation struggle of the SPLM.[63] Since 2011 Thabo Mbeki chaired the AU High Level Implementation Panel on Sudan (AUHIP) which was a follow-up from the AU High Level Panel on Darfur. The AUHIP was tasked to deal with the unresolved issues the CPA was leaving. It later played an important role in ending hostilities between Sudan and South Sudan as well as the oil shutdown in 2012.[64] The AUHIP closely interacts with IGAD and the UN. South Africa also made a substantial contribution to the UN Hybrid Operation in Darfur (UNAMID). Up to 1000 soldiers were deployed but recalled after 2015.[65] South Africa has not contributed any personnel to UNMISS. In 2012 South Africa shortly became South Sudan's largest weapons supplier.[66] While in general China and Russia were among the most important arms dealers in that particular year, they did not export weapons to South Sudan and thus the selling of ten armored personnel carriers (APC) made up the largest share of South Sudanese arms imports.[67]

In 2009 Mbeki was forced to resign and, after a caretaker government of Kgalema Motlanthe, Jacob Zuma became president and Cyril Ramaphosa his deputy. In this capacity Ramaphosa became South Africa's chief mediator in February 2014. He facilitated intra-party talks within the SPLM with the goal to overcome leadership competition.[68] Unfortunately these efforts bore no fruits. South Africa was also a guarantor for the ARCSS from August 2015 along with neighboring countries, IGAD, the UN, the Troika, the EU, AU and China.

While mediation efforts were many and practically all of them failed, South Africa started playing a more important role with keeping Riek Machar under house arrest in Johannesburg from late 2016 until his departure in early 2018. This move might have been motivated by regional powers in Eastern Africa and US pressure on Sudan and Ethiopia to put Machar on ice. In the end, the absence of Machar from South Sudan did not help peace talks but increased internal factionalism within the SPLM-IO, complicating peace talks. Due to Machar's involuntary absence and South Africa concluding a defense agreement with South Sudan,[69] it has been argued that South Africa has abandoned its position as neutral arbitrator and is siding with Salva Kiir.[70] Still South Africa is not claiming any leadership or hegemonic role. Initiative and conflict dynamics remain regional and domestic which South Africa is working with but not imposing solutions and lobbying for them.

India

India's relations to the African continent are long-standing dating back several centuries. Especially between Eastern Africa and Western India in the Indian Ocean region relations have developed vibrantly.[71] Up to one million people of Indian origin are estimated to live in Africa. India's rising economy, increased trade with Africa and the need to have access to resources and markets are key drivers in India's Africa outreach.[72] Behind China India is the second largest investor in the South Sudanese oil sector. Traditionally India plays an important role in UN peacekeeping. In UNMISS it provided the largest contingent of 2407 troops as of June 2018.[73]

With this mix of relative proximity of the conflict to a strategically important region, economic investment and substantial military contribution to peacekeeping in South Sudan, one would expect that India has an interest to play a visible maybe even leading role in conflict management. However, this cannot be said. India's engagement in the conflict only falls within the cooperative passive type of response options. The country is rather a follower than a leader, not aiming to set its own standards but willing to support regional leadership and act under global multilateral organizations such as the UN. India's response in this case falls neatly into Destradi's conceptualization of a reluctant hegemon acting with hesitance and lacking initiative of its own.[74]

Economically speaking access to oil reserves is of near-absolute importance for India. Its dependency on imports forces the country to seek overseas investments and diversify its portfolio to balance risks and opportunities. For India its investment in South Sudan did not mark the beginning of a new overseas chapter. India's Oil and Natural Gas Corporation (ONGC) can look back at several decades of international experience but often failed to succeed.[75] Access to Sudanese oil fields was most uncertain and succeeded only with strong diplomatic backing from New Delhi and because Sudan did not want to give China near-full control over its oil wealth.[76]

From 2003 onward oil was exported to Mumbai from Port Sudan. For ONGC Sudanese oil made up some 46% of its overall production until 2010.[77] Before the partition of Sudan ONGC invested some $3bn in the country.[78] However, the overall importance of Sudanese oil for India should not be overrated. Its share of oil imports did not even reach 1%. It peaked in 2010, making up only 0.54% and a net value of $425m. In that year India imported oil worth $79.1bn. Nigeria was the second largest supplier making up 11% of imports worth nearly $9bn.[79] In other words, the Indian investment in the oil sector never reached the level of a crucially important source of energy.

During the 2012 oil shutdown India showed some diplomatic initiative to secure its investment. It appointed a special envoy to Sudan and South Sudan, the trade expert Amarendra Khatua.[80] It is unclear what specific role Khatua played as the breakthrough between the two countries was negotiated by the AU and South Africa's Mbeki. In contrast to other BRICS countries India upgraded its consulate in Juba to embassy level relatively late: eight months after South Sudan became independent.[81] Before the outbreak of the civil war in Juba India's newly appointed special envoy Raghavan paid South Sudan a visit preparing Kiir's planned trip to India later in the year and promising capacity building programs for the young nation.[82]

With the outbreak of violence India did not step up its diplomatic efforts in conflict resolution as China or South Africa did. Its first concern was guided at protecting its nationals. The Ministry of External Affairs expected Indian soldiers serving under UNMISS to help evacuate fellow compatriots.[83] Since the beginning of UNMISS India made a substantial contribution to the mission, even larger than that of China or any other contributing nation. Still this substantial contribution was not used to play a larger and more influential role during the long-lasting and often failing peace mediation process. While in the case of China its increased contribution to UN peacekeeping can be assumed to be linked to its economic interest, this is different in the Indian case.

India for a long time has been the UN's chief contributor to peacekeeping missions. Since the beginning of the organization India deployed to nearly every mission. In this context South Sudan is no exception or beginning of a new era as it is for China. For India peacekeeping is also an expression of South-South developmental solidarity and is linked to maintaining a certain type of world order which India prefers. Here peacekeeping is no direct expression of narrow geostrategic or economic interest. While acting through the UN India gets involved in managing security matters. This bears several advantages for the country. It conforms to its foreign policy position of being a reluctant power and the absence of a greater strategic plan for its further afar international relations. The UN is primarily a multilateral organization built on cooperation of many nations and Indian leadership is not automatically needed but contribution to burden-sharing is highly welcome. It allows getting involved in managing security issues outside of unilateral or mini-lateral coalitions of the willing.[84] In this regard India seems to be content with its role as multilateral peacekeeper in South Sudan without feeling the need to take a more proactive role without being explicitly asked to assume such a role.

Russia

For Russia the conflict in South Sudan is of little to no importance. There are no direct consequences from the conflict for Russia and the conflict is geographically remote. Access to oil resources has no importance and sub-Saharan Africa generally plays no important strategic role for Russia.[85] Although Russia was one of the main arms suppliers to South Sudan, the volume of weapon sales has been rather small. In contrast to Syria and Ukraine in which vital Russian interests have been touched, this cannot be claimed for the conflict in South Sudan. Consequently, Russia takes no genuine interest in the conflict or its solution. Russia is involved in South Sudan primarily through its membership in international organizations or groupings such as the UN Security Council or BRICS.[86] Russia deploys only 16 staff to UNMISS (mostly police).[87] It makes no contribution to conflict mediation. Its response type to the crisis can best be described as passive cooperative. Passive because it does not propose any significant conflict resolution initiatives on its own and cooperative because it does not block or impose initiatives affecting South Sudan through its veto in the Security Council.

Through its voting and positioning in the Security Council Russia occupies an important position. The combination of sanctions with peace talks has been identified as generally problematic. Even when Russia voted for sanctions as in the case of resolution 2206 it voiced reservations. The Russian representative Iliichev after adopting the resolution said: "[W]e think that the practical implementation of the measures planned for the sanctions regime would be counter-productive, at least so long as there is still hope to resolve the conflict through negotiations."[88] Whether this position comes from a genuine concern over lacking progress in peace talks or is seen as an opportunity to counter Western calls for sanctions is a matter of debate.

When the Security Council adopted the arms ban in July 2018 following a US draft proposal, the Russian representative Polyanskiy was keen in lashing out against the US accusing it of "mindlessly" brandishing the sanctions stick.[89] Russia argued that the arms embargo would primarily hit Kiir and thus is indirectly a partisan move in support of the SPLM-IO. Polyanskiy continued: "[A]s for Russia, we did not support and will not support a policy of imposing decisions on independent countries and regions that suit forces outside the region for domestic political or other reasons." A few days later the Foreign Ministry stepped up its rhetoric and spoke of Western "blackmailing" and disregard for African positions. In this tirade the key goal seems to rather be to discredit sanctions as a Western tool to undermine African solutions. These arguments are grossly distorted if not manipulative. A pretext was looked for and found. Despite this harsh rhetoric Russia did not use its veto which it was not hesitating to use in the cases of Syria and Ukraine. South Sudan may not be important enough to further strain relations with the West and other countries. Indeed the African members to the Council were split on the decision of the arms ban. While Ethiopia as well as Equatorial Guinea was most vocally against the ban, Cote d'Ivoire voted in favor. In the end, after the sanctions were adopted peace talks resumed and a new power-sharing deal was agreed.

Brazil

In the case of Brazil and South Sudan, the story is short. Given that Brazil is geographically the most detached from the conflict within the BRICS grouping and has no economic or other strategic interest in the country and has no permanent seat at the Security Council, it is no surprise that it did not respond to the crisis in any significant way. The maximum Brazil was contributing was declaratory support for the UN, AU and IGAD negotiating in South Sudan.[90] Brazil also endorsed in principle the idea of power sharing and emphasized the importance of seeking a political solution.[91] But no direct involvement in peace talks occurred. The most direct engagement was Brazil's support of just 18 staff to UNMISS.[92] The overall reaction to the crisis comes close to a non-response. At best it can be regarded as cooperative but passive.

Conclusion: BRICS and Crisis in South Sudan

The BRICS group response to the conflict in South Sudan can best be described as passive cooperative. There is not much variation between BRICS countries (Table 6.1) and thus the BRICS group provides a fairly coherent picture. In the two instances in which BRICS summit declarations dedicate paragraphs to the crisis BRICS is not seeking a role for itself but is supporting existing mediation efforts by regional organizations and UN peacekeeping. BRICS are largely supportive of multilateral peaceful solutions. They only voiced concerns over sanctions as a pressure tool to overcome deadlock in peace talks after ceasefire and power-sharing agreements have failed (repeatedly) and thus the BRICS declarations neither condemn nor endorse UN sanctions. Despite criticism raised most prominently by Russia and to a lesser degree by China, both countries never used their veto to boycott resolutions which they have done frequently in the case of Syria.

The reason why BRICS is not claiming a more active role might best be explained by the absence of any direct security threat from the crisis for any of the five countries and the character of the crisis itself which does not provide many opportunities to link it to the BRICS normative agenda. In contrast to Libya or Syria, in South Sudan conflict is not linked to issues of externally induced regime change but centers around internal SPLM divisions which turned violent. In this kind of situation the BRICS agenda which calls on equal participation in world affairs, seeks political solutions for armed conflicts and is sovereignty sensitive does not overlap or contradict existing efforts to solve the crisis in South Sudan.

Table 6.1 Mapping of response types and motivation: South Sudan

Country	Russia	China	South Africa	Brazil	India
Response type	Cooperative (passive)	Cooperative (active)	Cooperative (active)	Cooperative (passive)	Cooperative (passive)
Main motivation	No genuine interests but using conflict as opportunity for politicking	Investment saving through multilateral peace negotiations, facilitator role	Champion of African solutions, modest economic interests, facilitator role	No genuine interests but providing declaratory support for multilateral peace talks	Reluctant hegemon, economic interests, seeking multilateralism solutions

As mentioned there is not much variation between BRICS countries when it comes to responding to the South Sudanese crisis. All countries are largely cooperative; they do vary only in the degree of cooperative engagement. China and South Africa are most actively involved in conflict mediation or provide significant resources for the UN peacekeeping mission. Russia, India and Brazil behave cooperatively but do not show individual initiatives on their own. They mostly go along the mainstream. India is deploying a substantial amount of peacekeepers but does not claim any leadership role in South Sudan. Brazil is the most passive, only lending declaratory support for conflict resolution, and Russia gets involved in South Sudan merely through sitting on the Security Council.

What is interesting here is that although the response to the crisis is mostly the same, the trigger variables for the response types do vary between countries (Table 6.2). For example while China, South Africa and India do have the most economic interest in South Sudan, India does not play an active role in conflict mediation. For India most indicators would imply a much more active role, but the country remains to be a reluctant power. In contrast, China seems to have overcome its traditional passive behavior. It does have the capacity to respond, economic interests are obvious and its preference for peaceful conflict settlement is fully compatible with BRICS positions. Brazil's passivity seems to be hardly surprising. Most trigger variables are negative. There is no incentive to get more involved beyond mostly declaratory support for existing peace efforts. In the case of Russia a similar picture emerges. A faraway internal armed conflict does not suffice to respond stronger. This forms a clear contrast to Russian involvement in Syria and Ukraine in which vital interests are involved.

Table 6.2 Trigger variables and countries: South Sudan

	Russia	*China*	*South Africa*	*Brazil*	*India*
Proximity	– – –	+	– – –	– – –	+
Capability interests	–	+ +	+ +	– – –	+ +
Type of conflict	– –	– –	+	– – –	– –
Economics	– –	+	+	– – –	+
BRICS agenda	+	+	+	+	+ +
Humanitarian norms	– –	– –	+ +	+	+

+ and – indicate various degrees of importance or lack thereof of the trigger variables

Lastly with South Africa, though most variables are in positive territory only geographically the conflict does not compel South Africa to respond. Given that most variables are positive one would even assume that the country would get involved more substantially by, for example, claiming a regional leadership role or deploying a much higher number of peacekeepers through the UN. The current economic situation does not allow South Africa to play a more active military role.

Notes

1. Data drawn from: https://www.acleddata.com/data/ accessed 13 August 2018.
2. Checchi, Francesco et al. (2018) *Estimates of crisis-attributable mortality in South Sudan, December 2013–April 2018: A statistical analysis*. Department of Infectious Disease Epidemiology, Faculty of Epidemiology and Population Health, London School of Hygiene and Tropical Medicine. https://crises.lshtm.ac.uk/wp-content/uploads/sites/10/2018/09/LSHTM_mortality_South_Sudan_report.pdf accessed 5 October 2018.
3. Data drawn from https://data2.unhcr.org/en/situations/southsudan accessed 13 August 2013.
4. Report of the Secretary-General on South Sudan, 14 June 2018, para. 25.
5. De Waal, Alex (2015) *The Real Politics of the Horn of Africa Money, War and the Business of Power*. Cambridge, Malden: Polity, p. 102.
6. See the full text of the CPA at: https://reliefweb.int/report/sudan/comprehensive-peace-agreement-between-government-republic-sudan-and-sudan-peoples
7. Patey, Luke (2014) *The New Kings of Crude China, India, and the Global Struggle for Oil in Sudan and South Sudan*. London: C. Hurst & Co, p. 210.
8. De Waal, Alex (2014) "When Cleptocracy becomes Insolvent: Brute Causes of the Civil War in South Sudan" *African Affairs* 113/452, p. 355.
9. Data drawn from: https://atlas.media.mit.edu/en/profile/country/ssd/ accessed 13 August 2018.
10. De Waal, Alex (2014).
11. Johnson, Douglas (2014) "Briefing: The Crisis in South Sudan" *African Affairs* 113/451, pp. 300–309.
12. Motsamai, Dimpho (2017) "Assessing AU mediation envoys The case of South Sudan" Pretoria: Institute for Security Studies, *East Africa Report*, Issue 10, February 2017, p. 6.
13. BBC News, "South Sudan rivals Kiir and Machar agree peace deal" 10 May 2014. https://www.bbc.com/news/world-africa-27352902 accessed 14 August 2018.

14. See UN Security Council Resolutions, 2132, 2155, 2252.
15. Motsamai, p. 7.
16. Areas of Agreement on the Establishment of the Transitional Government of National Unity (TGoNU) in the Republic of South Sudan. http://www.sudantribune.com/IMG/pdf/1_feb_2015_agreement.pdf accessed 14 August 2018.
17. UN Security Council resolution 2206, 3 March 2015.
18. IGAD, Agreement on the Resolution of the Conflict in the Republic of South Sudan, Addis Ababa 17 August 2015 http://www.sudantribune.com/IMG/pdf/final_proposed_compromise_agreement_for_south_sudan_conflict.pdf accessed 14 August 2018.
19. Knopf, Kate Almquist (2016) Ending South Sudan's Civil War. Council on Foreign Relations, Council Special Report No. 77 November 2016, p. 5.
20. Machier, Tor Madira (2017) "Who detains Machar in South Africa?" Sudan Tribune 29 December 2017. http://www.sudantribune.com/spip.php?article64371 accessed 14 August 2018.
21. Allison, Simon (2017) "Riek Machar's lonely 'exile' in SA" Mail & Guardian 21 July 2017. https://mg.co.za/article/2017-07-21-00-riek-machars-lonely-exile-in-sa accessed 14 August 2018.
22. UN Security Council, 8166th Meeting (PM)Cessation of Hostilities Agreement Violations Persist in South Sudan, Under-Secretary-General Tells Security Council, 24 January 2018. https://www.un.org/press/en/2018/sc13176.doc.htm accessed 14 August 2018.
23. UN Security Council, Letter dated 12 April 2018 from the Panel of Experts on South Sudan addressed to the President of the Security Council, para. 29.
24. UN Security Council 8310th meeting 13 July 2018.
25. BBC News, South Sudanese celebrate peace deal signed by Kiir and Machar, 6 August 2018. https://www.bbc.com/news/world-africa-45077389 accessed 14 August 2018.
26. BRICS Fortaleza Declaration, 2014, para. 33.
27. Ibid.
28. BRICS Ufa Declaration 2015, para. 45.
29. Final Report of the African Union Commission of Inquiry on South Sudan, 15 October 2014. http://peaceau.org/uploads/auciss.final.report.pdf accessed 16 August 2018.
30. Oduha, Joseph (2018) "South Sudan army chief defies UN travel ban with visit to China" The East African. http://www.theeastafrican.co.ke/news/ea/South-Sudan-army-chief-defies-UN-ban-with-China-visit/4552908-4715152-m84ct/ accessed 16 August 2018.
31. Data drawn from https://peacekeeping.un.org/en/troop-and-police-contributors accessed 17 August 2018.

32. Large, Daniel (2018) "Sudan and South Sudan: A Testing Ground for Beijing's Peace and Security Engagement" in Alden et al. (eds) *China and Africa Building Peace and Security Cooperation on the Continent*. Cham: Palgrave Macmillan, pp. 163–178.
33. Patey, p. 118.
34. Data drawn from https://www.ceicdata.com/en/indicator/china/crude-oil-imports accessed 17 August 2018.
35. "South Sudan oil production to resume in September: minister" Sudan Tribune 30 July 2018. http://www.sudantribune.com/spip.php?article65949 accessed 17 August 2018.
36. Patey, p. 119.
37. Patey, p. 111.
38. Crisis Group International (2017) China's Foreign Policy Experiment in South Sudan, Asia Report No. 288, 10 July 2017, p. 8.
39. Xuejun, Wang (2018) "Developmental Peace: Understanding China's Africa Policy in Peace and Security" in Alden et al. (eds) *China and Africa Building Peace and Security Cooperation on the Continent*. Cham: Palgrave Macmillan, pp. 83–100.
40. Alden, Chris and Yixiao, Zheng (2018) "China's Changing Role in Peace and Security in Africa" in Alden et al. (eds) *China and Africa Building Peace and Security Cooperation on the Continent*. Cham: Palgrave Macmillan, pp. 39–66.
41. Patey, p. 229.
42. UN Security Council, Resolution 2155, 27 May 2014, para. 21
43. Hodzi, Obert (2019) *The End of China's Non-Intervention Policy in Africa*. Cham: Palgrave Macmillan, p. 191.
44. Ibid., p. 190.
45. Data drawn from https://peacekeeping.un.org/en/troop-and-police-contributors accessed 17 August 2018.
46. Martina, Michael (2014) "South Sudan marks new foreign policy chapter for China: official" 11 February 2014. https://www.reuters.com/article/us-china-southsudan/south-sudan-marks-new-foreign-policy-chapter-for-china-official-idUSBREA1A0HO20140211 accessed 17 August 2018.
47. UN Security Council 7396th meeting 3 March 2015. Liu Jieyi.
48. Ministry of Foreign Affairs, Peoples Republic of China, Foreign Minister Wang Yi Meets the Press, 8 March 2015. http://www.fmprc.gov.cn/mfa_eng/zxxx_662805/t1243662.shtml accessed 20 August 2018.
49. UN Security Council, Resolution 2241, 9 October 2015, para. 34.
50. Interim report of the Panel of Experts on South Sudan established pursuant to Security Council resolution 2206 (2015), 21 August 2015, para. 70.
51. Large, Daniel (2016) "China and South Sudan's Civil War, 2013–2015" *African Studies Quarterly* 16(3–4), p. 41.

52. For an overview of reports please see: https://www.un.org/sc/suborg/en/sanctions/2206/panel-of-experts/work-mandate
53. China's Arms Sales to Sudan, Fact Sheet (2007) Human Rights First, https://www.humanrightsfirst.org/wp-content/uploads/pdf/080311-cah-arms-sales-fact-sheet.pdf accessed 20 August 2018.
54. Zhixoing, Shen (2018) "On China's Military Diplomacy in Africa" in Alden et al. (eds) *China and Africa Building Peace and Security Cooperation on the Continent*. Cham: Palgrave Macmillan, pp. 101–122.
55. Chun, Zhang and Kemple-Hardy, Mariam (2015) From conflict resolution to conflict prevention: China in South Sudan. Saferworld https://www.saferworld.org.uk/downloads/pubdocs/from-conflict-resolution-to-conflict-prevention%2D%2D-china-and-south-sudan.pdf accessed 20 August 2018.
56. UN Security Council 8210th meeting, 13 July 2018, Ma Zhaoxu.
57. US Department of State, "U.S. Arms Restrictions on South Sudan" 2 February 2018. https://www.state.gov/r/pa/prs/ps/2018/02/277849.htm accessed 20 August 2018.
58. Motsamai, Dimpho (2017) "Assessing AU mediation envoys: The case of South Sudan" Pretoria: Institute for Security Studies, East Africa Report, Issue 10, February 2017.
59. Khadiagala, Gilbert (2018) "South Africa in Eastern Africa: Kenya, Tanzania, Uganda and Sudan/South Sudan" in Adebajo, A and Virk, K (eds) *Foreign Policy in Post-Apartheid South Africa Security, Diplomacy and Trade*. London, New York: I.B. Tauris, p. 228.
60. Curtis, Devon (2018) "South Africa's Peacemaking Efforts in Africa: Ideas, Interests and Influence" in Adebajo, A and Virk, K (eds) Foreign Policy in Post-Apartheid South Africa Security, Diplomacy and Trade. London, New York: I.B. Tauris, 69–92.
61. South Africa: Department: International relations and Cooperation, Media Statement, Mr. Ramaphosa visits South Sudan, 05 March 2014. http://www.dirco.gov.za/docs/2014/south-suda0305.html accessed 20 August 2018.
62. Nathan. Lauri (2010) "Interests, ideas and ideology: South Africa's Policy on Darfur" *African Affairs*, 110, 438 (1), p. 59.
63. Cheryl Hendricks and Amanda Lucey (2013) "South Africa and South Sudan Lessons for post-conflict development and peacebuilding partnerships" ISS Policy Brief 49, December 2013.
64. Khadiagala, p. 228.
65. Data drawn from: https://peacekeeping.un.org/en/troop-and-police-contributors accessed 20 August 2018.
66. Ferrie, Jared (2016) "Would an arms embargo on South Sudan work?" IRIN 12 July 2016. https://www.irinnews.org/news/2016/07/12/would-arms-embargo-south-sudan-work accessed 20 August 2018.

67. Stockholm International Peace Research Institute (SIPRI). http://armstrade.sipri.org/armstrade/page/trade_register.php accessed 20 August 2018.
68. Khadiagala, p. 229.
69. Martin, Guy (2018) "More detail on SA's defence agreement with South Sudan" DefenceWeb, 24 April 2018. http://www.defenceweb.co.za/index.php?option=com_content&view=article&id=51462:more-detail-on-sas-defence-agreement-with-south-sudan&catid=56:diplomacy-a-peace&Itemid=111 accessed 20 August 2018.
70. Pedneault, Jonathan (2018) "There are better ways for SA to assist South Sudan than military cooperation" Mail & Guardian 5 February 2018. https://mg.co.za/article/2018-02-05-there-are-better-ways-for-sa-to-assist-south-sudan-than-military-cooperation accessed 20 August 2018.
71. Xavier, Constantino (2015) "Unbreakable Bond Africa in India's Foreign Policy" in Malone, D. et al. (eds) *The Oxford Handbook of Indian Foreign Policy*. Oxford: Oxford University Press, pp. 566–578.
72. Narlikar, Amrita (2010) "India's rise to power: where does East Africa fit in?", *Review of African Political Economy*, 37(126), pp. 451–464.
73. Data drawn from: https://peacekeeping.un.org/sites/default/files/5_mission_and_country_4.pdf accessed 21 August 2018.
74. Destradi, Sandra (2017) "Reluctance in international politics: A conceptualization" *European Journal of International Relations* 23(2), p. 329.
75. Patey, p. 132.
76. Ibid., p. 144.
77. Ibid., p. 153.
78. Parachar, Sachin (2012) "Indian envoy in South Sudan on oil mission" *The Economic Times* 2 April 2012. https://economictimes.indiatimes.com/news/politics-and-nation/Indian-envoy-in-South-Sudan-on-oil-mission/articleshow/12500931.cms accessed 21 August 2018.
79. Data drawn from: https://atlas.media.mit.edu/en/visualize/tree_map/hs92/import/ind/show/2709/2010/ accessed 21 August 2018.
80. Parachar, 2012.
81. India, Ministry of External Affairs, "Consulate General of India in Juba, South Sudan upgraded to Embassy level" March 13, 2012. https://www.mea.gov.in/press-releases.htm?dtl/19108/Consulate_General_of_India_in_Juba_South_Sudan_upgraded_to_Embassy_level accessed 21 August 2018.
82. India, Ministry of External Affairs, "Visit of Special Envoy of India for Sudan and South Sudan, Shri P.S. Raghavan to South Sudan" 8–9 August, 2013. https://www.mea.gov.in/press-releases.htm?dtl/22059/Visit_of_Special_Envoy_of_India_for_Sudan_and_South_Sudan_Shri_PS_Raghavan_to_South_Sudan_89_August_2013 accessed 21 August 2018.

83. India, Ministry of External Affairs, "Official Spokesperson's response to a question on the evolving security situation in South Sudan" 24 December 2013. https://www.mea.gov.in/media-briefings.htm?dtl/22688/Official_Spokespersons_response_to_a_question_on_the_evolving_security_situation_in_South_Sudan accessed 21 August 2018.
84. This view is expressed by India's former Foreign Minister Yashwant Sinha at a keynote address. India, Ministry of External Affairs, "Centre for United Nations Peacekeeping," New Delhi. Keynote Address by Foreign Secretary, August 21, 2003. https://www.mea.gov.in/Speeches-Statements.htm?dtl/4704/Centre_for_United_Nations_Peacekeeping_New_Delhi_Keynote_Address_by_Foreign_Secretary accessed 21 August 2018.
85. Oğultürk, Mehmet Cem (2017) "Russia's Renewed Interests in the Horn of Africa As a Traditional and Rising Power" *Rising Powers Quarterly* 2(1), p. 122.
86. Oliver, Gerrit and Suchkov, Dimtry (2015) "Russia is Back in Africa" *Strategic Review for Southern Africa*, 37(2), p. 159.
87. Data drawn from: https://peacekeeping.un.org/sites/default/files/5_mission_and_country_4.pdf accessed 21 August 2018.
88. UN Security Council, 7396th meeting, 3 March 2015.
89. UN Security Council 8310th meeting 13 July 2018.
90. Brazil, Ministry of Foreign Affairs, "Situation in South Sudan", Nota 436, 21 December 2013. http://www.itamaraty.gov.br/en/press-releases/3626-situation-in-south-sudan accessed 21 August 2019.
91. Brazil, Ministry of Foreign Affairs, "South Sudan Peace Process", Nota 167 27 April 2016. http://www.itamaraty.gov.br/en/press-releases/13943-south-sudan-peace-process accessed 21 August 2018.
92. Data drawn from: https://peacekeeping.un.org/sites/default/files/5_mission_and_country_4.pdf accessed 21 August 2018.

CHAPTER 7

Conclusion: The BRICS Order in the Making

The previous chapters have analyzed the role the BRICS grouping and BRICS countries are playing in large-scale armed conflicts in four case studies in Africa, Asia and Europe. In the ten years of BRICS existence the grouping could gradually establish itself as an influential actor at the world stage. Although BRICS is merely a foreign policy grouping and not a decision-making or implementing agency, key national foreign policy preferences are reinforced through the group, among them the emphasis on a multi-polar world order which is reflecting on how BRICS responds to large-scale armed conflicts. The book only explores how BRICS responds to the four conflict cases; while these are the most important of our time they are also only a selection of behavior. In this regard the study does not provide an all-comprehensive overview of individual foreign policies but closely explores the selected four case studies. It is, however, assumed that these four cases constitute important cases and are constitutive of global order questions.

In the case of Libya BRICS did not shape events decisively but has been the focal institution in which critique was formulated against the combination of R2P action and regime change. The experience of being outpaced by a Western-led coalition was a foundational moment for BRICS and shaped the response to later conflicts and in particular to the events in Syria and to some extent to the Ukraine. In Syria, Russia and China used their veto power frequently and prevented enforcement action by the Security Council on Assad. Russia intervened militarily and saved Assad

© The Author(s) 2019
M. Brosig, *The Role of BRICS in Large-Scale Armed Conflict*, New Security Challenges, https://doi.org/10.1007/978-3-030-18537-4_7

from being toppled by rebel groups and/or Islamist terrorists. During the conflict in the Ukraine the BRICS group was lending Russia critical support by not following Western calls to sanction and isolate Russia after its annexation of Crimea. In the case of South Sudan BRICS countries played a double role as key economic investors (China and India) in the oil sector and conflict mediator (China and South Africa) and peacekeepers (China and India). In three of the four case studies BRICS played an important role (Syria, Ukraine, South Sudan) and could steer events in directions often opposing Western foreign policy priorities. In Syria Assad was kept in power against fierce Western/Arab opposition. In the Ukraine, Russia could operate unabated and steer the conflict from distance. In South Sudan China prevented an arms embargo for a long time and seemed uninterested in how oil wealth is transformed into violence.

If BRICS brings about a post-Western world order it is characterized by a preference for uncompromised sovereignty (Libya, Syria) and respect for national spheres of influence (Ukraine) but also multilateral conflict mediation (South Sudan). In other words, it might not be fundamentally different from instruments Western politics is using. Western states formulate claims in all three categories too but might be less, maybe with the exception of the US, narrow in their interpretation of classical state sovereignty. This is not fully surprising as the BRICS agenda never called for a complete overhaul of exciting concepts but insisted on coherency and criticized hypocrisy in application. The difference between BRICS and Western diplomacy is less about a completely different set of foreign policy tools but more about their application. In Libya, Syria and Ukraine BRICS countries deviated significantly from the preferred Western course of action and managed to obstruct Western calls for the removal of Assad and resisted sanctioning and isolating Russia over the annexation of Crimea. From the perspective of BRICS this serves to prevent Western hegemonic politics but does not change or damage the underlying rules or logics according to which it operates.

The main aim of this study is twofold: First it is empirically exploring how BRICS countries are responding to large-scale armed conflicts, and second it aims at explaining the specific choice of response by using six explanatory variables. Mapping response types is important because the global security order does not exclusively rely on constitutionalized norms such as the UN Charter but is equally built on how pivotal actors such as BRICS respond to immanent situations of crisis. After all, there is still no world government and our ability to predict conflict remains limited. Thus much of what is referred to as order or system is the interplay of meaningful actors, in our case BRICS countries.

No book-length study has so far provided an overview of BRICS countries and armed conflict using cross-case comparative analysis. The empirical mapping of response types is thus an important step to better understand the role regional powers are playing in the global security order. Therefore a detailed typology has been developed based on the literature on regional powers which over the last decade has advanced our conceptual understanding of how regional powers are operating in global affairs. Unfortunately, research on BRICS has largely ignored these conceptual innovations. Therefore this study aims at connecting and further developing these two streams of scholarship. The developed typology of BRICS responses to armed conflict distinguishes between six types of behavior covering a nexus between active cooperative within multilateral structures and reaching neo-imperial and unilateral use of force. The middle-ground position is occupied by hegemonic behavior and mini-lateralism or coalitions of the willing.

Secondly, the study is interested in exploring how states are selecting a particular response type. This fills a gap in the literature on regional powers which has focused more on outcome typologies but is often missing a discussion of input conditions which allows a discussion and explanation for specific forms of behavior. In the end, this study does not only aim at mapping the BRICS response to armed conflict empirically but also provides a discussion of causal pathways leading to specific responses.

In this regard Chap. 2 proposes six trigger conditions: proximity to conflict, capabilities and interest, the type of conflict, economic links to the conflict, resonance with the BRICS normative agenda and humanitarian concerns. The key analytical question is, what combination of conditions is leading to what outcome? Which conditions are causally relevant, which have no or little influence over outcomes? Thus the concluding section will first outline response types and then explore which set of trigger conditions correspond with the selected response. Based on the different causal weight of these six conditions, the chapter formulates a number of hypotheses which reflect upon the empirical case studies and aim at advancing our conceptual thinking about BRICS.

Table 7.1 displays the overall response of the five BRICS countries to the four country case studies covering 20 cases in total. The table maps out individual country responses to specific cases across six response types. Accordingly, BRICS countries respond to armed conflict with a variety of

Table 7.1 Mapping BRICS response to armed conflict

B	L S	SS U				
R		L SS			S	U
I	S	L U SS				
C	SS	L U	S			
S	SS L S	U				
Total:20	7	10	1	0	1	1
Response types	Active	Passive	Leading	Dominant	Temporary	Permanent
	Cooperative		Hegemonic		Neo-imperial	

L=Libya, S = Syria, U=Ukraine, SS=South Sudan

options. Nearly all response types are covered except hegemonic dominance. Despite the variety of responses hegemonic and neo-imperial behavior receives only a low coverage of three cases out of 20. The by far most prominent response is cooperative, 17 out of 20. Within the cooperative mode of response ten cases are categorized as passive cooperative and seven as active cooperative. Thus the preferred way of responding to conflict is passive cooperative followed by active cooperation. Hegemonic and neo-imperial behavior is relatively infrequent.

Interesting to observe is also the split between Russia and China and IBSA (India, Brazil, South Africa) countries. Neo-imperial behavior can be observed only in the case of Russia (Syria, Ukraine) and hegemonic behavior is observable in the case of China (Syria). All IBSA countries remain cooperative in all cases but preferred passive cooperation (seven cases) over active cooperation (five cases). However, within the IBSA group there are also differences. The most passive country is India which in three out of four cases remains relatively inactive. South Africa and Brazil when acting cooperatively select a more active mode of engagement. The greatest disparity within a country can be found in Russia. It is the only country which displays neo-imperial behavior, the most coercive and intrusive form of response, while at the same time also having two cases of passive cooperation (almost showing disinterest).

The BRICS group as such is no implementing agency and thus its actorness rests mainly within individual country foreign policy positions. Generally BRICS summit declarations hardly establish any particular BRICS initiative with regard to the four conflict case studies. There are no BRICS envoys, mediation or deconfliction teams, observers or peacekeepers. If BRICS countries participate in these activities it is in their individual capacity or as members of a regional or global organization such as the UN and BRICS might make reference to them in support of their activities. At the group level BRICS often only either endorse (rhetorically) existing mediation efforts (e.g. Ukraine: Minsk Protocol) or they leave out certain initiatives (Syria: LAS). In cases in which BRICS disagree with the Western course of action criticism is formulated moderately and open confrontation is avoided. This might, however, be different at member state level where a different language and action is sought. In the cases of Libya and Syria individual country criticism against Western policy choices was considerably more pronounced than in BRICS summit declarations. The overall BRICS group response to armed conflict can best be categorized as passive cooperative. In no instance did BRICS start an initiative of its own to get involved in conflict mediation or other forms of engagement. In contrast to economics which has seen a moderate degree of institution-building around the NDB and CRA in the field of security, BRICS often only aims at coordinating policy positions for use in other organizations.[1]

Table 7.2 maps the prevalence and relative strength of conditions with regard to the five response types observed empirically. Analytically the question is if one can attribute a certain combination of conditions to a particular response type. The logic of analysis is akin to that of Qualitative Comparative Analysis (QCA). Table 7.2 resembles a so-called truth table used in QCA to attribute causal pathways to empirical cases. In principle, QCA is case-oriented in contrast to variable-oriented research design and inquires into the combinational effect of various causes instead of isolating a single cause for a particular outcome which traditional methods of comparative analysis (Mill) would do.[2]

This is warranted because the complexities of foreign policy decision-making hardly allow the search for single master variables. Simply said, the assumption of deterministic causality does not make much sense in our context. More important is a discussion of the relative and combinational weight of certain conditions vis-à-vis particular outcomes. Causes for a particular outcome can be several but this does not undercut the relevance

Table 7.2 Trigger variables and responses

Proximity	4×---- 2×+	6×---- 3×+ 2×–	1×+	1×++	1×+++
Capability Interests	2×---- 2×– 2×++	5×---- 1×-- 3×– 1×+ 1×++	1×+	1×++	1×+++
Type of Conflict	1×++ 3×+++ 1×+ 1×--	4×++ 4×– 2×-- 1×---	1×+++	1×+++	1×–
Economics	3×---- 2×+ 1×++	3×---- 2×-- 1×– 2×++ 3×+	1×++	1×+	1×++
BRICS agenda	2×+++ 1×++ 3×+	4×+++ 5×++ 2×++	1×++	1×++	1×++
Humanitarian Concerns	3×+ 2×++ 1×--	1×++ 6×+ 4×--	1×--	1×--	1×--
Response types	Active	Passive	Leading	Temporary	Permanent
	Cooperative		Hegemonic	Neo-imperial	

of individual conditions per se in situations in which there is no single golden variable which permanently causes an outcome. In such a setting causality is understood as complex taking account of equifinality.[3] Equifinality is usually framed in terms of looking for necessary and sufficient conditions for an outcome. Necessary and sufficient conditions for particular outcomes have the advantage that we can attribute causal relevance even in conditions of combinational effects of variables and in cases of interrupted causal effects.[4] For example, if we argue that the absence of economic interests makes BRICS countries more likely to respond cooperatively to a conflict but actors also cooperate while economic interests

7 CONCLUSION: THE BRICS ORDER IN THE MAKING

can be identified, we would still argue for the causal relevance of the condition (its absence) if countries always act cooperatively when economic interests are absent. In cases in which they are not but countries cooperate one would need to look for additional conditions to explain the outcome. QCA is not applied in this study but its underlying logic is helpful in identifying and discussing the causal relevance of our six input variables.

Now which combination of conditions is leading to neo-imperial behavior? Empirically we have only two cases, both relating to Russian foreign policy action in Syria (temporary) and the Ukraine (permanent). What can be seen here is the rather strong influence of two conditions: proximity to war as well as capabilities to project power and willingness (interests) to use them. In no other BRICS country and conflict case study can we observe a correlation of proximity to war, the availability of military resources and the unilateral use of force. The type of conflict (localized vs. regional/global) does not seem to play a greater role as Russia's response was almost equally strong to the regional/global conflict in Syria as it was in the localized conflict in the Ukraine. Economic benefits are also not the sole or key driver for neo-imperial behavior. While they played a certain role for Russia in the case of the Ukraine they played a far less prominent role in Syria and other BRICS countries displaying an equally strong or even stronger economic links to conflict-affected countries did not opt for a coercive response. It is also difficult to argue for the BRICS normative agenda to be a key trigger for neo-imperial behavior. There is simply not much variation between cases which would allow us to assume that this variable is individually causing a specific response. Lastly, humanitarian concerns are also difficult to attribute to a particular set of responses. While they are prominently missing in cases in which hegemonic and neo-imperial behavior can be observed we also find five cases with the same negative value (− −) out of a total of eight in situations of cooperative behavior. In such situations the impact of humanitarian norms is rather inconclusive.

Which conditions are leading to cooperative behavior? From the empirical observation we can see that cooperative responses are occurring when countries are at distance to the conflict. In 10 out of 17 cases BRICS countries are strictly not affected or linked to the armed conflict, coded as (10×−−−) and in 5 cases there is a slight connection (5×+); in further two cases there is a slight disconnection. A cooperative mode of interaction also seems to be linked to relatively weakly developed capabilities to project power and missing interests to use power resources. For cooperative behavior we can observe seven incidents in which practically no power resources are available (7x−−−), five with rather little (5x−) and few situations in which some resources are available (3x++, 1x+). The role of economic interests in relation to the conflict also seems to play a certain, although only moderate, role for cooperative behavior. In 9 of 17 cases countries responding cooperatively have no significant economic interests (6x−−−, 2x−−, 1x−) while there are 8 cases in which countries have economic interests (3x++, 5x+).

In comparison to those countries which respond more coercively (hegemonic, neo-imperial) only countries which act cooperatively demonstrate the greatest detachment from economic incentives. Here the absence of economic interests is the causally more relevant condition predicting behavior while the presence leads to both cooperative and more coercive forms of response. Drawing conclusions from the type of conflict to the response of BRICS countries is more problematic, localized as well as regional/global conflict lets countries respond in many different ways. Resonance with the BRICS agenda is also not leading to a clear outcome. In most conflict cases there is a fair degree of resonance with the BRICS agenda but countries respond differently. Regarding humanitarian norms we can observe that they are playing a relatively greater role in situations in which states respond cooperatively than in other occasions. However, the absence of humanitarian concerns leads to cooperative as well as more coercive responses.

What makes states respond active or passive cooperatively to armed conflict? When looking at the two most relevant conditions—proximity to conflict and capabilities and will to project power—there are no major differences in the relative weight of the trigger variables. The same is true with regard to economics, resonance with the BRICS agenda and humanitarian concerns. There is not enough variation which would allow drawing causal conclusions. Only one condition, the type of conflict, displays some variance. With regard to the type of conflict we can observe that countries respond more pro-actively if the conflict is regionalized in opposition to a more localized conflict. It remains doubtful if this condition can explain the response choice satisfactorily because we also have cases in which BRICS countries responded more coercively in regionalized conflict (Russia, China in Syria).

Based on the above observations what conditions are the most relevant and what hypotheses can be formulated to accurately predict behavior?

7 CONCLUSION: THE BRICS ORDER IN THE MAKING

The most relevant conditions are proximity to the conflict and available power capabilities and will to act. Conditions with inconclusive results are the type of conflict and resonance with the BRICS normative agenda. A middle-ground position of moderate influence is occupied by the absence of economic conditions and humanitarian concerns. Accordingly we can formulate the following hypotheses:

H1: The greater the proximity to conflict and the greater the capacity to project power, the stronger, more coercive, the response.
H2: The larger the distance to the conflict and the more limited the capabilities to project power, the more cooperative the behavior.

The combination of these two variables leads with relative certainty to the predicted outcome. Beyond these two conditions we can also formulate hypotheses for the impact of economic interests and the role humanitarian norms are playing. With regard to economic interests it is the absence of them which correlates with cooperative behavior. In all cases in which economic interests are minimal or fully absent countries respond cooperatively. Thus:

H3: Cooperative behavior increases with the absence of economic interests.

More complicated is the presence of economic interests. On its own it is leading to various outcomes. Only in combination with other conditions such as proximity to conflict or capabilities to project power is the presence of economic interests becoming more relevant.

H4: The larger economic interests but smaller capacity to project power, the more cooperative the response to armed conflict.

Or

H5: The larger economic interests and the greater the distance to the conflict, the more cooperative the response.

While H4 and H5 are generally true, there is not much empirical coverage, meaning we do not observe many cases in which countries have vested economic interests but few capabilities and are far from conflict. There H3 is the more relevant hypothesis.

With regard to the role humanitarian norms are playing we can observe that their absence leads to different outcomes but their presence is positively associated with cooperative behavior. Here we can conclude that when humanitarian norms are considered by BRICS countries they play a somehow relevant role; they do act cooperatively.

H6: The more relevant humanitarian norms are for BRICS countries, the more likely they are to respond cooperatively to armed conflict.
H7: The less relevant humanitarian norms but shorter the distance to the conflict and the more power capabilities are available, the more likely are hegemonic or neo-imperial responses.

In order to map the relationship between country responses and the four most important trigger variables in combination with the hypotheses formulated above, Table 7.3 provides a complete overview. What is interesting in this table are the different degrees of congruence between BRICS countries and the stated hypotheses.

Brazil is the almost perfect example for the application of hypothesis two. Distance from the conflict area and the absence of power capabilities and interests to get involved are stringently correlating with the country's choice for cooperative behavior within multilateral structures. We can also confirm hypothesis three which links the absence of economic incentives to cooperation and hypothesis six which links humanitarian norms to cooperation. Brazilian foreign policy positioning strongly confirms these hypotheses without exceptions.

Similar to Brazil, South Africa also displays a large congruence with these three hypotheses. In all cases in which the country responds cooperatively, South Africa is at distance to the conflict, commands over moderate power capabilities and has little economic interests but attaches some value to humanitarian norms. Only the case of South Sudan would indicate a slightly stronger role than cooperation and in fact South Africa keeping the rebel leader Riek Machar under house arrest may be counted as exceeding the cooperative type of response.

India completes the picture of the IBSA group in which all members only display cooperative behavior. Hypotheses two, three and six are strongly confirmed with regard to India's response to the crises in Libya, Syria and Ukraine. In the case of South Sudan India does not fully conform to the

Table 7.3 Country, trigger variables and responses

Country	Response types	Trigger variables/conflict cases					Equivalent to hypothesis
			LI	SY	UKR	SS	
Brazil	Cooperative active and passive	Proximity	---	---	---	---	H2
		Capability	---	---	---	---	H3
		Economy	---	---	---	---	H6
		Norms	++	++	+	+	
Russia	Neo-imperial temporary and permanent	Proximity		++	+++		H1
		Capability		++	+++		H7
		Economy		+	++		
		Norms		--	--		
	Cooperative passive	Proximity	+			---	H2
		Capability	−			−	
		Economy	+			--	
		Norms	--			--	
India	Cooperative active and passive	Proximity	−	+	---	+	H2
		Capability	--	−	---	++	H3
		Economy	---	---	--	+	H6
		Norms	++	++	+	+	
China	Cooperative active and passive	Proximity	−		+	+	None
		Capability	+		−	++	
		Economy	++		+	+	
		Norms	--		--	--	
	Hegemonic leadership	Proximity		+			None
		Capability		+			
		Economy		---			
		Norms		+			
South Africa	Cooperative active and passive	Proximity	---	---	---	---	H2
		Capability	−	---	---	++	H3
		Economy	---	---	−	+	H6
		Norms	+	+	+	++	

+ and − indicate various degrees of relevance of the respective variable

expected way of action. Despite India having power capabilities available, being moderately affected by the war and invocating humanitarian concerns India remains fairly passive over its response to the crisis.

Russian cooperative behavior in the cases of Libya and South Sudan is congruent with hypothesis two. In these cases Russia is at distance to the conflict area and does not command over significant power resources to dominate the international course of action. What is interesting in the Russian case is that humanitarian concerns do not play a role in contrast to the IBSA countries. Chinese cooperative behavior does not neatly fit into the formulated hypotheses. China acts cooperative even if it holds vested economic interests, commands over some power resources and is in relative proximity to the conflict. In other words, China could afford hegemonic behavior but in most cases opts not to leave the cooperative field of action.

With regard to Russian neo-imperial behavior in the case of Syria and the Ukraine we see a correlation with hypotheses one and seven. The close proximity to conflicts in Syria and Ukraine in combination with readily available power resources and the political will to use them can be identified as most relevant trigger condition. The absence of humanitarian concerns completes the picture.

Chinese hegemonic behavior over its reaction to the Syrian conflict does not fully fit into the picture. Chinese economic expansion and thereby increased exposure to armed conflicts have not triggered the country to respond more coercively. The case in which China displayed hegemonic behavior was Syria in which it was not holding significant investments. Proximity to the conflict as well as power capabilities is moderately developed and may be congruent with a hegemonic but not neo-imperial response to the conflict. However, in the case of South Sudan the trigger variables are even more clearly speaking in favor of a stronger response but China opts for a cooperative engagement.

What Value for the Study of BRICS and Regional Powers?

Until today research on traditional centers of power in the Global North is still predominant in the discipline of international relations. In fact, at times world politics seem to faster globalize than the discipline of IR. While the world is becoming multi-polar, multiplex or even non-polar or multi-order in design, knowledge production in the field of IR remains concentrated on traditional centers.[5] This leaves gaps in the literature which this study aims at addressing.

One of the aims of this book is to provide a more nuanced account of regional powers which does not only understand them as either followers of existing pathways or obstructers of the global order. This somehow simple view which is cross-cutting the literature is rather an observation from a Western-centric perspective than an accurate description of empirical realities. This study has shown that a wide repertoire of responses is available and BRICS countries have used five of the six response types although in most cases they opted for a cooperative response including active engagement and passive acceptance of existing initiatives.

What Consequences for World Order?

The analysis of BRICS countries' responses to large-scale armed conflict provides us with some valuable information of how BRICS are influencing the global security architecture. It is of course not to argue that the analysis of BRICS is sufficient in understanding how global order works and what it entails. BRICS only constitute one part of it but an increasingly important one. For sure global order also comes in different forms and shapes. This book was placing the focus not on formal legal (treaty) reforms but on creating order through responding to armed conflict. While the former entails a top-down element, acting out or complying with regulatory norms, the emphasis of this book is much more on bottom-up processes of creating order through responding to major security crises. The advantage of the former is relative stability and security about the established order, while the latter depends much more on case-specific circumstances and is evolving but not stagnant. However, for BRICS the first option turned out to be the part of global order in which it achieved relatively little changes. It is at the ground level of creating order through action in which there are more opportunities to induce gradual changes. Though these changes are not as easily detectable as, for example, a change in treaty obligations of global governance institutions. For this reason, Chap. 2 developed a detailed typology measuring BRICS responses to armed conflict.

Closeness to the conflict and power capabilities are the main trigger variables for deciding to act either cooperatively or more coercively. Where does this leave BRICS and its members in questions of global order? Countries like Russia, China and India are the most exposed to violent conflicts and contestation of their power within their regional neighborhood. Examples are the nuclear crisis on the Korean peninsula, the Kashmir conflict or the ongoing war in the Donbas. They are also the largest military powers within BRICS as well as globally and have shown determination to modernize their armed forces and increase defense budgets and are among the most active buyers and sellers of weapons and ammunition worldwide.[6] Their military capabilities outstretch those of most of their regional neighbors and in particular smaller nations. Based on the findings of this study, this bears considerable risks for armed conflict as the willingness to use force outside multilateral frameworks increases with rising power capabilities and proximity to conflict. For Russia, India and China conflict is close and military capabilities are expanding.

Despite this trend BRICS have not developed a mechanism which could mediate these risks. In fact, its internal organizational culture avoids the discussion of contentious issues among BRICS countries. The emphasis on uncompromised sovereignty in combination with multi-polarity and an organizational culture of keeping quiet about all issues which are seen as national (domestic) prerogatives blocks BRICS from becoming an effective conflict prevention or conflict managing grouping. As a group BRICS have only acquired the position of passive cooperation but not actively initiated BRICS-specific conflict mediation/management instruments. At maximum BRICS rhetorically support existing conflict mediation initiatives of other actors such as the UN or other regional organizations.

When BRICS summit declarations make reference to issues of peace and security it is usually not touching upon conflicts which have an intra-BRICS perspective. Thus BRICS tend to take position on conflicts which are mostly external to them. The reason for this is to avoid inner-group frictions and upholding the principle of uncompromised sovereignty which can be seen as acknowledging national spheres of interest in which external interference is not welcome. In this context the emphasis on multi-polarity is self-serving, reinforcing state sovereignty and a free hand on vital foreign policy interests. However, in the long run the absence of inner-BRICS conflict resolution mechanisms but the constant reference to external security issues might prevent the group from becoming a credible and functioning security actor if the group aspires to become one.

The study also reveals gaps and asymmetries within the BRICS group. BRICS is divided between larger military powers such as Russia, China and India on the one side and Brazil and South Africa on the other side. As India often appears to be a reluctant power which under-utilizes its power capabilities the division within BRICS is between IBSA countries and China and Russia. We could observe that IBSA countries only respond cooperatively, while China and Russia are also willing to use more coercive means of foreign policy. Assuming that China's ascendency in global politics has not peaked yet and assuming that Russia will not compromise on the use of military force (as this is its most credible instrument to claim great power status) if it deems it necessary to defend its core interests, the power gap between IBSA countries and China and Russia is likely to widen and less likely to close.

A further challenge for the BRICS grouping is its normative discourse emphasizing non-coercive diplomacy, sovereign equality and a more democratic world order but the use or acceptance of power politics as a means to foster national security interests. While BRICS countries are quick in pointing out the hypocritical use of norms and values versus power politics by the West, neo-imperial and hegemonic behavior of Russia and China and the tacit acceptance of these instruments by the BRICS group undermine the credibility of the BRICS normative ambition and claim to reforming global order to the better. Given the size of BRICS countries and economies their existing leverage in global affairs, as shown in this book, they are hardly marginalized powers anymore. This might turn out to be a real problem because BRICS is only a grouping with little to no actorness of itself. The reformist rhetoric plays an important role in bringing the group together in the absence of a joint strategic vision or permanently institutionalized structures. If the rhetoric loses credibility it will be difficult to take substantial positions and maintain them.

Notes

1. Abdenur A.E. (2017). "Can the BRICS Cooperate in International Security?" *International Organisations Research Journal*, 12(3) 73–93.
2. Wagemann, Claudius and Schneider, Carsten (2010) "Qualitative Comparative Analysis (QCA) and Fuzzy-Sets: Agenda for a Research Approach and a Data Analysis Technique," *Comparative Sociology*, 9376–9396.
3. George, Alexander and Bennett, Andrew (2005) *Case Studies and Theory Development in the Social Sciences*. Chapter 8 "Comparative Methods: Controlled Comparison and Within-Case Analysis" Cambridge, MA: MIT Press, 152–179.
4. Schneider, Carsten and Wagemann, Claudius (2007) *Qualitative Comparative Analysis (QCA) und Fuzzy Sets*. Opladen, Farmington Hills: Verlag Barbara Budrich, pp. 31–42.
5. Tickner, Arlene (2013). "Core, periphery and (neo)imperialist International Relations." *European Journal of International Relations*, 19(3), 627–646.
6. Wezeman, Pieter, et al. (2018) "Trends in International Arms Transfers 2017" *SIPRI Factsheet*, March 2018.

Index[1]

A

African National Congress (ANC), 78, 157, 158, 172
African Union (AU), 13, 14, 34, 65, 66, 68, 74, 79–81, 84, 158, 162, 165, 171–173, 175, 177
Assad, Bashar Al, 12, 64, 93–117, 122n59, 125, 187, 188
AU, *see* African Union

B

Belt and Road Initiative (BRI), 25, 26, 31, 114, 142
Brazil, 2, 13, 15, 18–23, 30, 34, 36, 53, 54, 65–72, 75, 77, 84, 96, 99, 101, 102, 104, 108, 114–117, 119, 134, 141, 148–149, 158, 166, 177, 179, 190, 196, 200

C

Chemical weapons, 14, 93, 102, 104, 105, 107, 108, 115, 121n32
China, vii, 6, 15–20, 23–32, 34, 35, 39n72, 50, 51, 53, 55, 65, 66, 68, 71–78, 83, 84, 89n43, 89n45, 96, 97, 99–103, 105, 106, 108, 109, 112–115, 117, 134, 139, 140, 142–146, 155n62, 156n69, 158, 161, 162, 164, 166–175, 178, 179, 187, 188, 190, 194, 198–201
China National Petroleum Company (CNPC), 168, 169
Churkin, Vitaly, 77, 99, 105
CNPC, *see* China National Petroleum Company
Comprehensive peace agreement (CPA), 160, 161, 173
CPA, *see* Comprehensive peace agreement

---

[1] Note: Page numbers followed by 'n' refer to notes.

D
Delhi summit, 12
Donbas, 133, 136, 138, 139, 141, 144, 149, 151, 199

F
Fortaleza summit, 13, 134

G
Gaddafi, Muammar, 8, 22, 61, 63–71, 73, 75–80, 82–84, 89n44
Goa summit, 12, 15
G20, 6, 11, 21, 28, 134, 150

H
Haftar, Khalifa, 67, 76
Hegemony, 28, 46, 48, 104
Humanitarian norms, 7, 55, 193–196

I
IBSA, *see* India, Brazil, South Africa
ICC, *see* International Criminal Court
IGAD, *see* Intergovernmental Authority on Development
India, 6, 15, 17–20, 23, 26–30, 32, 34, 36, 53, 65, 66, 68, 70–73, 75, 77, 78, 83, 84, 96, 99–104, 108, 114, 116, 117, 119, 145–147, 156n69, 158, 166, 174–176, 179, 185n83, 185n84, 188, 190, 196, 197, 199, 200
India, Brazil, South Africa (IBSA), 6, 9, 28, 69, 86, 98, 100–104, 109, 114–117, 119, 121n31, 190, 196, 198, 200, 201
Intergovernmental Authority on Development (IGAD), 162–165, 169, 171–173, 177
International Criminal Court (ICC), 65, 67, 68, 70, 71, 74, 77, 78, 84, 105, 112

J
Johannesburg summit, 7, 11, 33

L
LAS, *see* League of Arab States
League of Arab States (LAS), 64, 65, 68, 98, 100–104, 111, 112, 191
Li Baodong, 74

M
Machar, Riek, 161–164, 166, 171–173, 181n25, 196
Mbeki, Thabo, 33, 78, 172, 173, 175
Medvedev, Dimitri, 31, 77, 78, 128
Mini-lateralism, 49, 82, 106, 189
Minsk Protocol, 131–133, 140, 143, 146, 191
Modi, Narendra, 156n67
Multilateralism, v, 8, 10, 12, 13, 15, 16, 21, 33, 46, 48, 49, 81, 83, 97, 103, 117

N
NATO, *see* North Atlantic Treaty Association
Neo-imperialism, 46, 49
North Atlantic Treaty Association (NATO), 17–19, 30, 69, 72, 83, 126–128, 137

P

Putin, Vladimir, 30–32, 66, 77, 78, 128, 136–141, 146, 155n65, 156n67

R

Ramaphosa, Cyril, 35, 172, 173, 183n61
Regional powers, v, vi, 6, 21, 22, 36, 46–50, 145, 173, 189, 198–199
Responsibility to protect (R2P), 10, 24, 26, 61–86, 187
Responsibility while protecting (RwP), 22, 35, 69
Rousseff, Dilma, 21, 22, 69, 148, 149, 156n75
R2P, *see* Responsibility to protect
Russia, vii, 6, 14, 17–19, 24, 29–32, 34, 35, 53, 54, 64–66, 68, 71, 75–78, 84, 94, 96, 97, 99–115, 117, 125–129, 131–151, 158, 164, 166, 173, 176–179, 187, 188, 190, 193, 194, 197, 199–201
RwP, *see* Responsibility while protecting

S

Sanya summit, 12
South Africa, vi, 2, 13, 14, 16, 18, 19, 32–36, 41n98, 41n109, 53, 54, 65–69, 75, 78–81, 84, 96, 99–104, 108, 114–117, 119, 147–148, 156n69, 157, 158, 162, 163, 166, 171–173, 175, 179, 180, 188, 190, 196, 200
SPLM, *see* Sudan's People Liberation Movement
Sudan's People Liberation Movement (SPLM), 157, 158, 160–162, 164, 168, 169, 172, 173, 178

T

Temer, Michel, 21, 22

U

Ufa summit, 108, 135
Ukraine, v, 6, 14, 16, 18, 30, 31, 54, 76–78, 125–151, 157, 166, 176, 177, 179, 187, 188, 190, 191, 193, 196, 198
UN General Assembly, 72, 88n28, 90n72, 91n80, 101, 120n22, 135, 140, 141, 143, 146, 148
United Nations Mission in South Sudan (UNMISS), 158, 162, 164, 167, 169, 170, 173–177
UNMISS, *see* United Nations Mission in South Sudan
UN Security Council, 9, 11, 13, 18, 22, 24, 26, 31, 34, 48, 54, 63, 64, 80, 96, 97, 101, 103, 115, 116, 135, 155n61, 164, 165, 176, 181n22, 181n23

W

World order, vii, 9, 15, 17, 18, 35, 85, 93–119, 133, 137, 146, 151, 175, 187, 188, 199–201

X

Xi, Jinping, 26, 122n63
Xiamen summit, 29

Y

Yanukovych, Viktor, 128, 129, 132, 139, 145, 148, 151
Yushchenko, Viktor, 127

Z

Zuma, Jacob, 32, 33, 35, 41n109, 66, 79, 80, 87n14, 90n72, 172, 173

Printed in the United States
By Bookmasters